The Worldview of Modern
American Proverbs

Alan Dundes
Founding Editor

Wolfgang Mieder
General Editor

Vol. 15

The International Folkloristics series is part of the Peter Lang Humanities list.
Every volume is peer reviewed and meets
the highest quality standards for content and production.

PETER LANG
New York • Bern • Berlin
Brussels • Vienna • Oxford • Warsaw

Wolfgang Mieder

The Worldview of Modern American Proverbs

PETER LANG

New York • Bern • Berlin
Brussels • Vienna • Oxford • Warsaw

Library of Congress Cataloging-in-Publication Control Number: 2020026085

Bibliographic information published by **Die Deutsche Nationalbibliothek**.
Die Deutsche Nationalbibliothek lists this publication in the "Deutsche
Nationalbibliografie"; detailed bibliographic data are available
on the Internet at http://dnb.d-nb.de/.

ISSN 1528-6533
ISBN 978-1-4331-8193-1 (hardcover)
ISBN 978-1-4331-8194-8 (ebook pdf)
ISBN 978-1-4331-8195-5 (epub)
ISBN 978-1-4331-8196-2 (mobi)
DOI 10.3726/b17542

Cover image: W. Scott McGill © 123RF.COM

© 2020 Peter Lang Publishing, Inc., New York
80 Broad Street, 5th floor, New York, NY 10004
www.peterlang.com

Contents

Preface

There was a time when the word "modern" would not have appeared in folklore scholarship. After all, folklorists and cultural historians were primarily interested in traditional materials with some consideration also being given to their innovative adaptations. While this interplay of tradition and innovation informed many studies that exemplified a certain constancy in change, little attention was paid to new or modern folklore items. But there has been a revolutionary change during the past few decades in that scholars have looked at the creation of new folklore that has become generally known during the past hundred years. This change in emphasis has also influenced paremiographers (proverb collectors) and paremiologists (proverb scholars) who after paying little attention to the origin of new proverbs have slowly but surely realized that not all proverbs were coined centuries ago. The idea that proverbs contain wisdom handed down from one generation to the next had led to such designations as "the old proverb" or "the ancient saw" leaving little room for the intriguing question whether people today couch their experiences and observations into general-ized proverbs. In fact, a statement like "as the modern proverb says" would have been considered an oxymoron by most folklorists and paremiologists through the mid-twentieth century. Starting with the 1970s, this regrettable stagnation of proverb scholarship changed with American proverb scholars taking the lead in registering and studying hitherto not recorded Anglo-American proverbs that were coined after the year 1900—a somewhat arbitrarily chosen year to qualify as a modern proverb. Following some smaller studies of individual proverbs, Charles Clay Doyle (University of Georgia), Fred R. Shapiro (Yale University), and I from the University of Vermont took the lead and edited *The Dictionary of Modern Proverbs* (2012) after several years of concentrated work.

Of course, the work goes on, with Charles Doyle and I by now having published three supplements in *Proverbium: Yearbook of International Proverb Scholarship* (2016, 2018, and 2020). The dictionary contains 1422 individual proverbs to which the supplements add 195 texts for a total of 1617 modern proverbs each with its earliest recorded reference and additional contextualized sources and explanatory comments. While there are some proverbs of British, Australian, and Canadian origin, the vast majority of them had their start in the United States. This fact makes these proverbs a cohesive data base of American proverbs to attempt some conclusions about the mentality, worldview, or folk ideas expressed in them. Using proverbs to extrapolate such information has its problems if not pitfalls, as can be seen from studies that have employed proverbs to describe national characters or stereotypes about ethnic groups, women, and others. Such investigations have often been based on a mixed bag of proverbs without any historical or contextual considerations, ignoring also frequency of their use today. American proverbs present a special problem in this regard, as a glance into the massive *Dictionary of American Proverbs* (1992) reveals that Stewart A. Kingsbury, Kelsie B. Harder, and I edited some years ago. While there are first recorded British and American dates for the more than 15,000 proverbs, it is clear that many of them are in fact translations of classical, Biblical, and medieval proverbs that became current in the English language. Immigrants also brought their proverbs to North America that have been accepted as loan translations. And, to be sure, there are hundreds of proverbs that had their start in Great

Britain. Only painstaking labor could ascertain which proverbs were in fact coined in the United States. I have attempted this for at least some proverbs in my German book *"Different Strokes for Different Folks"*. *1250 authentisch amerikanische Sprichwörter* (2015). Be that as it may, world-view studies based on proverbs should definitely pay attention to the actual origin and frequent use of these texts in society.

The good fortune is that the proverbs listed in *The Dictionary of Modern Proverbs* and its supplements represent a controlled albeit small data base of 1617 proverbs. Most of them are of proven American origin and were all coined in the twentieth century (a few in the twenty-first). Using the Internet and various other electronic and printed sources they have been shown to have a wide currency and frequency through-out the United States, usually in the larger society but at times also somewhat more restricted among certain folk groups such as African-Americans, professionals, students, and others. Some careful conclusions can be drawn from this rich corpus of modern American proverbs, but only by stressing that proverbs play only a small but not insignificant part in gaining an understanding of the multifaceted worldview of Americans. Included therein are aspects like being forward looking, regarding life as a journey, being competitive and successful, stressing good use of time, staying young and attractive, making money, and so on. These are generalizations, and not every American from this complex society will fit neatly into these concepts. Anthropologists, cultural historians, folklorists, linguists, psychologists, sociologists, and others can add to this composite picture of the American mentality, worldview, or folk ideas.

As the table of contents reveals, the book *"Different Strokes for Different Folks": The Worldview of Modern American Proverbs* is comprised of nine independently written chapters of which five were previously published in Portugal, Russia, Spain, and the United States. They are units to themselves with their own bibliographies, making it possible to provide students with individual chapters that might be of particular interest to class. Since their places of publication are in journals and proceedings not easily accessible, they appear here together as a cohesive whole. Naturally a few repetitions do appear that will not lessen the value of the individually conceived chapters. It is with much gratitude that I acknowledge the permission of presenting these studies in the present unified compilation.

The first chapter on "'Think Outside the Box': Origin, Nature, and Meaning of Modern American Proverbs" was written in 2012 at the time we published our *Dictionary of Modern Proverbs*. Its proverbial title summarizes the idea that proverb scholars have to make the leap into the modern age while at the same time presenting a detailed overview of the character, content, form, language, and structure of modern American proverbs. This is followed by the second chapter on "'The Journey Is the Reward': Worldview of Modern American Proverbs" that I finished as a general overview of their forward-looking message while working on this book. The proverbs discussed here show the American spirit of mobility with its emphasis toward a successful and exciting future.

Americans in general are an active and engaged lot. No wonder they came up with the new proverb that is included in the title of the third chapter on "'Life is not a Spectator Sport': Proverbial Emotions about Modern Life." Sure, life has its challenges, but it is certainly worthwhile to face them. To do so, it is important to stay physically fit and young in spirit, pushing old age and aging aside as best as possible, as indicated in the fourth chapter on "'Age Is Just a Number': American Proverbial Wisdom about Age and Aging." Staying young, beautiful, and in good shape has led to many proverbs dealing with physical appearance. And yet, "No Body Is Perfect': Somatic Aspects of Modern American Proverbs," as a new proverb states. There is pain in staying fit and being beautiful, as proverbs dealing with the body make perfectly clear.

The next two chapters deal with two preoccupations of most Americans, namely time and money. No wonder that the proverb "Time is money" is so popular! But it originated in Great Britain in 1719 and was subsequently popularized by Benjamin Franklin to such a degree that it has remained a favorite proverb ever since. Time is indeed of the essence in America, as the proverbs of the sixth chapter on "'Time Spent Wishing Is Time Wasted': Temporal Worldview in

Modern American Proverbs" explain in ever new proverbs. And there is the seventh chapter on " 'Money Makes the World Go 'Round': The Pecuniary Worldview of Modern American Proverbs" that is ample proof that Americans are members of a capitalistic society. Quite a few of these proverbs were coined on Wall Street and emphasize that America means business in all senses of that word.

The eighth chapter on " 'Dogs Don't Bark at Parked Cars': Zoological Messages in Modern American Proverbs" takes a look at whether new proverbs still base their metaphors on the rich world of animals as they have done for centuries. The answer is an emphatic yes, with domestic and wild animals serving as representatives of human behavior. In fact, surprising as it might seem, animal metaphors appear with much more frequency than references to technology. The computer and the internet don't seem to be particularly productive in the creation of proverbs. But finally, then, there is the ninth chapter on "Love Is Just a Four-Letter Word': Sexuality and Scatology in Modern American Proverbs." There are plenty of old proverbs that deal with these matters, but they were often not included in proverb collections because of their risqué or obscene language. With the much greater openness about love, sex, and various other taboos, proverbs have also become much more open literally or figuratively about these matters that are an obsession of sorts throughout the society. It will be interesting to find out how pervasive sexuality and scatology appear in modern proverbs of other cultures. While these nine chapters deal with the worldview expressed in modern American proverbs, it makes sense to assume that similar proverbs might circulate elsewhere as well. There is much more work to be done by proverb scholars worldwide and care must be taken not to fall into the trap of American exceptionalism. As already stated, the idea of a general American worldview can only be an approximation at best, with proverbs being part of a larger mosaic of folk ideas.

There is no doubt that the work contained in this book was only possible because of my long collaboration and deep friendship with Charles Clay Doyle. We have tilled the rich field of proverbs together for many years as untiring but joyful yokefellows in the service of

American and international paremiology. It is therefore with heartfelt gratitude for his help and support and in recognition of his own accomplishments that I dedicate these ruminations on the worldview of modern American proverbs to my special friend.

Wolfgang Mieder
Spring 2020

Chapter One

"Think Outside the Box"

Origin, Nature, and Meaning of Modern American Proverbs

Among modern proverb scholars it has become almost proverbial to call for the collection and study of proverbs that have been coined in more recent times. Far too long have paremiologists and paremiographers looked backwards at traditional proverbs without paying much attention to what modernity has contributed to the treasure trove of proverbial wisdom. Archer Taylor, the doyen of twentieth-century paremiology, lamented this unfortunate situation in an invaluable article on "The Study of Proverbs" (1939), calling for new collections that would be "made as complete as humanly possible, showing not only old proverbs and variations of old ones that are still current, but also new ones that have come into use, thus giving a complete cross-section of the proverbs of our time" (1939 [1975]: 62–63 [46], see also Taylor 1969). Following my revered mentor in this plea, I observed some fifty years later in my "Prolegomena to Prospective Paremiography" (1990b) that "paremiography cannot remain a science that looks primarily backwards and works only with texts of times gone by. Modern paremiographers can and should also assemble proverb collections that include the texts of the twentieth century [and beyond]" (1990b: 142, see also

2000: 16). Such calls have not remained unheeded for English language proverbs, as my survey "'New Proverbs Run Deep': Prolegomena to a Dictionary of Modern Anglo-American Proverbs" (2009a, see also Sevilla Muñoz 2009) has shown.

This overview was a direct result of a contract for a new *Dictionary of Modern Proverbs* Published 2012) that my friends Charles Clay Doyle, Fred R. Shapiro, and I signed on September 21, 2007, with the prestigious Yale University Press of New Haven, Connecticut. Even before signing the contract, we had already more or less independently begun to assemble modern Anglo-American proverbs, that is, proverbs for which no references before the year 1900 can be found. Doyle had published about 200 such texts in his invaluable compilation "On 'New' Proverbs and the Conservativeness of Proverb Dictionaries" (1996 [2003], see also Doyle 2001 and 2007b), Shapiro had included a list of 104 "Modern Proverbs" in his invaluable *The Yale Book of Quotations* (2006: 526–530), and I had amassed about 300 texts that qualified as modern proverbs during the four decades of establishing my International Proverb Archives. After combining these three sets of modern proverbs, of which many quite expectedly proved to be duplicates, we examined six major and eighteen minor proverb collections published during the past few decades for possible modern proverbs, among them Nigel Rees, *Sayings of the Century. The Stories Behind the Twentieth Century's Quotable Sayings* (1984), Bartlett Jere Whiting, *Modern Proverbs and Proverbial Sayings* (1989), Nigel Rees, *Bloomsbury Dictionary of Phrase & Allusion* (1991), Wolfgang Mieder, Stewart A. Kingsbury, and Kelsie B. Harder, *A Dictionary of American Proverbs* (1992), David Pickering, Alan Isaacs, and Elizabeth Martin, *Brewer's Dictionary of 20th-Century Phrase and Fable* (1992), Anne Bertram and Richard Spears, *NTC's Dictionary of Proverbs and Clichés* (1993), Linda and Roger Flavell, *Dictionary of Proverbs and Their Origins* (1993), Nigel Rees, *Phrases & Sayings* (1995), Anna T. Litovkina, *A Proverb a Day Keeps Boredom Away* (2000), Adrian Room, *Brewer's Dictionary of Modern Phrase & Fable* (2000), David Pickering, *Cassell's Dictionary of Proverbs* (2001), Gregory Titelman, *Random House Dictionary of Popular Proverbs and Sayings* (2000), Martin H. Manser, *Facts on File Dictionary of Proverbs* (2002), Wolfgang Mieder, *English Proverbs* (2003b), George B. Bryan and

Wolfgang Mieder, *A Dictionary of Anglo-American Proverbs & Proverbial Phrases Found in Literary Sources of the Nineteenth and Twentieth Centuries* (2005), Stan Nussbaum, *American Cultural Baggage[i.e., Proverbs]. How to Recognize and Deal with It* (2005), Susan Ratcliffe, *Oxford Dictionary of Phrase, Saying, and Quotation* (2006), Nigel Rees, *A Word in Your Shell-Like: 6,000 Curious and Everyday Phrases Explained* (2006), and Jennifer Speake, *The Oxford Dictionary of Proverbs* (2008). In addition, we looked through about seventy publications that in one way or another also cite some modern proverbs, as for example Richard Jente, "The American Proverb" (1931–1932), Frances M. Barbour, "Some Uncommon Sources of Proverbs" (1963), Kenneth L. Higbee and Richard J. Millard, "Visual Imagery and Familiarity Ratings for 203 Sayings" (1983), Jess Nierenberg, "Proverbs in Graffiti: Taunting Traditional Wisdom" (1983 [1994]), Robert R. Hoffman and Richard P. Honeck, "Proverbs, Pragmatics, and the Ecology of Abstract Categories" (1987), Wolfgang Mieder, *American Proverbs: A Study of Texts and Contexts* (1989a), Wolfgang Mieder, *Proverbs Are Never Out of Season: Popular Wisdom in the Modern Ages* (1993a), Christoph Chlosta and Peter Grzybek, "Empirical and Folkloristic Paremiology: Two to Quarrel or to Tango?" (1995), Kimberly Lau, "'It's about Time': The Ten Proverbs Most Frequently Used in Newspapers and Their Relation to American Values" (1996 [2003]), Roumyana Petrova, "Language and Culture: One Step Further in the Search for Common Ground (A Study of Modern English Proverbs)" (1996), Sw. Anand Prahlad, *African-American Proverbs in Context* (1996), Stephen D. Winick, *The Proverb Process: Intertextuality and Proverbial Innovation in Popular Culture* (1998), Anna Tóthné Litovkina, "An Analysis of Popular American Proverbs [found in the Folklore Archive at UC Berkeley] and Their Use in Language Teaching" (1998), Paul Hernadi and Francis Steen, "The Tropical Landscape of Proverbia: A Crossdisciplinary Travelogue" (1999 [2003]), George B. Bryan, "An Unfinished List of Anglo-American Proverb Songs" (2001), Charles Clay Doyle, "Collections of Proverbs and Proverb Dictionaries: Some Historical Observations on What's in Them and What's not" (2007b). After pooling all of these references we eventually had the impressive database of not quite 700 modern Anglo-American proverbs (for more details see Mieder 2009a).

For all these texts we undertook the laborious task to prove that they in fact were not older than the 1900 cut-off year. Many of our sources did not provide any dates of occurrences, and we consequently had to use various databases (Google, Google Books, Google News, ProQuest Historical Newspapers, Newspaperarchive, America's Historical Newspapers, 19th Century U.S. Newspapers, LexisNexis Academic, JSTOR, etc.) to find the earliest citation possible (Chlosta and Ostermann 2002, Colson 2007, Kleinberger Günther 2006, Lauhakangas 2001, Rittersbacher and Mösch 2005, Umorova 2005, and Winick 2001). But not just that, for as I have said in my earlier description of this vexing and time-consuming task: "Texts alone no proverbs make, and as with all folklore genres, it takes currency and traditionality, usually also variants, […] to decide whether a text is in fact in more or less general use beyond being a mere one-day wonder!" (2009a: 257). In other words, we felt compelled to establish the proverbiality of each and every text, thus going far beyond all previous background material accumulated on these proverbs. But our work did not stop there, for we clearly were not satisfied with just about 700 modern proverbs! Many contenders to be included eventually had to be dropped because we were able to establish that they were already in use before 1900 (Mieder, Kingsbury, Harder 1992, Stevenson 1948, Wilson 1970), among them such surprises as the following (our dictionary includes a much longer appendix with additional texts):

Business before pleasure.
Buy low, sell high.
The camera cannot lie.
You are what you eat.
An elephant never forgets.
The future is already here.
Behind every great man there's a great woman.
The second million (dollars) is always easier (than the first).
Money isn't everything.
There is nothing to fear but fear itself.
It pays to advertise.
Records are set to be broken.
Safety first.
You can prove anything with statistics.

First things first.
The best things (in life) are free.
No tickee, no washee (shirtee). (Arora 1988, Mieder 1996 [1997])
Use it or lose it. (Doyle 2009)

But the sixty-four thousand dollar question was and remains: How do we find ever more modern proverbs? Our own reading, relatives, friends, colleagues, and above all our students were of great help. We also continued gathering possible proverbs from literature, the mass media, films, songs, advertisements, speeches, and oral communications of all types (Mieder and Sobieski 2006), and finally we were able to publish our *Dictionary of Modern Proverbs* in May 2012 with 1422 modern proverbs, of which 731 had not been registered before! The voluminous e-mail correspondence among the three of us living relatively far apart in Athens, Georgia (Charles Doyle), New Haven, Connecticut (Fred Shapiro), and my Burlington, Vermont, is a telling testimony for the wondrous excitement in discovering one proverb after another during about four years of enthusiastic and rewarding work on this fascinating project. We did our very best throughout to establish the earliest possible reference for each proverb, citing this reference in its context with precise bibliographical information. We also included variants and, where necessary, some explanatory comments regarding linguistic, cultural, and semantic matters. We checked every proverb for its currency and frequency, with most proverbs garnering some tens of thousands of raw Google hits (we are obviously aware of duplications and errors in these electronic searches). The hits in Google Books and Google News are significantly less "raw", but even there the results are not always reliable. Of course, Google also shows deceptively low numbers for proverbs that became obsolete by mid-century, or that are extremely recent in their coinage.

Did we find and include all possible modern Anglo-American proverbs in our *Dictionary of Modern Proverbs*? Of course not! We will have missed plenty new proverbs and also those that are presently being created (Honeck and Welge 1997 [2003]), and it is for this reason that we have included the address of a website so that readers can hopefully draw our attention to numerous additional texts. Obviously this project will be on-going, and we hope in due time to bring out updated and expanded versions of our proverb dictionary (see now the three supplements by Doyle. But we do want to stress once again that the identification of modern proverbs is extremely difficult and is in need of as much help as possible from people interested in the proverbial wisdom of the modern age. But by now we can certainly draw some conclusions about the nature, origin, and meaning of these modern Anglo-American proverbs. What follows is my attempt to draw some general conclusions from our 1422 truly modern proverbs regarding such matters as variants, form, syntax, structure, length, poetics, metaphor, origin (authorship, attribution, anonymity), semantics, etc. I will also comment on how these proverbs reflect on modern social, political, economic, psychological, and sexual matters, showing that some of the major sources of the proverbs are advertising slogans, so-called "laws" of modernity, songs, motion pictures, the world of business, sports, technology, and sexuality (also obscenity and scatology). It will also be shown that animal and somatic metaphors are quite prevalent, but clearly there are also numerous proverbs concerned with religion (God), beauty, love, success, and other matters. As has always been the case with traditional wisdom, modern proverbs also show themselves to be observations and generalizations about basic human behavior and the trials and trepidations of human life (Mieder 1987 [1993] and 2004).

Regarding the numerous examples of modern proverbs, it should be noted that I have chosen only texts that we have listed with an American reference as their earliest registered source. Most of the proverbs are in any case of American origins, but as one would expect, there are also some proverbs that had their start in Great Britain, Australia, and Canada. With further historical research it might well be possible that for some of the American proverbs mentioned in the following pages an origin outside of the United States might be located. For now, all the proverbs mentioned here have been coined in the United States sometime after the beginning of the twentieth century. They thus to a certain degree at least reflect the beliefs, convictions, generalizations, ideas, observations, and thoughts of Americans, amounting at least in a small way to a part of a general composite worldview.

Following the lead of some of the major proverb collections already mentioned, we have alphabetized the proverb entries according to the first noun in each proverb. If the text has no noun, then the first finite verb serves as the keyword, using bold face print in both cases to mark the keywords. For cases in which variants of a given proverb have differing keywords, cross-references are included with a "See" indicator followed by the standard variant of the proverb showing the user where to find more information about it. Each entry begins with the proverb itself with some principal variants shown in parentheses. Then, introduced by its date, follows the earliest contextualized reference with precise bibliographical information. Usually further dated examples of the text in context follow, especially if the earliest reference cited leaves some doubt as to its proverbiality, if the proverb is not well known or has not been recorded in any proverb collection before, if important variants need to be illustrated in actual use, or if additional textual references shed further light on the origin, attribution, evolution, or meaning of the proverb. Where it seemed necessary to us, we have also added further brief comments. Finally, all of this is augmented by precise references to those proverb collections and other sources in which 691 of the 1422 proverbs have been registered before.

As all paremiographers know, it is at times quite difficult to decide on the precise wording of the lemma for a particular proverb, especially since many proverbs are current in various degrees of variation. It is for this reason that quite a large number of lemmas contain principal variants in parentheses, as for example (every American proverb cited throughout is followed by the date of its earliest registered source and the page number in the *Dictionary of Modern Proverbs*):

Free advice is worth (exactly) what you pay for it. (1913, 3)
No matter how (thin) you slice (cut) it, it's still baloney. (1924, 13)
Don't take (tear) down a fence (wall) unless you are sure why it was put up. (1964, 75–76)
Flattery will get you everywhere (anywhere). (1938, 82)
If life hands (gives, throws) you scraps, make a quilt. (1992, 140)
It is (is always, must be) five (six) o'clock somewhere (in the world). (1964, 183)
There are no problems, only opportunities (challenges). (1948, 207)
Tragedy (Every tragedy) is an opportunity. (1978, 262)
Trust is (must be) earned. (1947, 264)

In those cases where the variants are more substantial (i.e., having a different keyword), we do list the variant as a separate entry followed with a "See" and the standard proverb lemma where the variant is to be found. Scholarly proverb dictionaries need to include such cross references so that their users do not miss those proverbs that, as all verbal folklore, exist in considerable variants.

> Almost doesn't count. See "CLOSE doesn't count." (1921, 5)
> Never trust a skinny cook. See "Never trust a skinny CHEF." (1976, 37)
> Grow where you are planted. See "BLOOM where you are planted." (1971, 23)
> Nearly is not good enough. See "ALMOST is not good enough." (1921, 3)
> There will always be another streetcar. See "There will always be another BUS." (1925, 30)
> Think big thoughts. See "THINK big." (1907, 255)
> The older the violin, the sweeter the tune. See "The older the fiddle, the sweeter the tune." (1909, 76–77)

Turning to syntactical matters it can be stated that most modern proverbs are straight-forward indicative sentences, with 61 of 1422 or 4.4% following the pattern "A(n) / noun / verb / ...", as for example:

> A boy cannot do a man's work. (1904, 25)
> A candle loses nothing by lighting another candle. (1918, 32)
> A chip on the shoulder is a good indication of wood higher up. (1926, 39)
> A crisis is an opportunity. (1900, 47)
> A diamond is (Diamonds are) forever. (1948, 55)
> An expert is only a fool a long way from home. (1926, 70)
> A handicap is what you make it. (1946, 116)

Another 33 proverbs or 2.3% expand the pattern by a descriptive adjective, that is, "A(n) / adjective / noun / verb ... ", as can be seen from the following examples:

> A clear conscience is (usually) a sign of (usually comes from) a bad memory. (1953, 42)
> A boiled (fried, cooked) egg won't hatch. (1901, 67)
> A good start often means a bad finish. (1905, 240)
> A kind thought is never lost. (1914, 257)
> A rising tide lifts all boats (ships). (1915, 258)

As one would expect, quite a few proverbs (namely 67 or 4.7%) follow the indicative pattern "The / noun / verb ...":

> The future is not (is no longer) what it used to be. (1948, 90)
> The joy is in the journey. (1915, 130)
> The mountains are calm even in a tempest. (1912, 173)
> The nail that sticks out gets pounded (hammered down). (1969, 177)
> The sun will come out tomorrow. (1938, 246)

The same pattern expanded by a modifying adjective is not quite as prevalent, but the collection does contain 39 (2.7%) texts based on "The / adjective / noun / verb ...":

> The unaimed arrow never misses. (2001, 8)
> The longest mile is the last mile home. (1949, 166)
> The best (easiest, safest) place to hide is in plain sight. (1920, 199)
> The best way to kill time is to work it to death. (1914, 271)
> The first hundred years are the hardest. (1918, 284)

In addition to these quite similar syntactical patterns totaling 200 (14.1%) texts, a considerable number of proverbs, 57 or 4.0% to be precise, follow the pattern "You can't (cannot) verb ...", thereby continuing an established proverbial way of expressing the impossibility of a situation or action:

> You cannot tell the depth of the well by the length of the handle on the pump. (1915, 53)
> You can't unscramble eggs. (1911, 67)
> You can't go home again. (1940, 123)
> You can't be (There is no such thing as) a little (bit) pregnant. (1942, 206)
> You can't fix stupid. (1995, 243)
> You can't put toothpaste back in the tube. (1936, 261)

Somewhat related to the sentiment expressed by way of the "You can't" impossibility marker are the messages contained in those proverbs (68 or 4.8%) that state their messages by way of the "Don't (Do not) / verb ..." imperative, which certainly is a well-established proverbial formula:

> Do not (You cannot) compare apples and oranges. (1949, 6)
> Don't draw a gun unless you're going to use it. (1905, 112)
> Don't judge yourself by others. (1909, 130)
> Don't knock it till you've tried it. (1960, 133)
> Don't try to be someone you are not. (1956, 265)

Another 30 (2.1%) proverbs follow the formula "Never / verb …", once again expressing their advice in the form of an imperative:

> Never miss a chance to sit down and rest your feet. (1951, 36)
> Never (You don't) bring (take) a knife to a gunfight. (1988, 133)
> Never play leapfrog with a unicorn. (1977, 137–138)
> Never (Don't) let them see you sweat. (1970, 138)
> Never try to teach a pig to sing; it wastes your time, and it annoys the pig.
> (1973, 197)

Altogether then there are 98 (6.9%) proverbs that state their message in the form of an imperative, not a particularly high number to be sure. Perhaps this is due the fact that people today are less willing to be told directly what to do or not to do. In other words, the obvious didactic nature of many traditional proverbs appears to be on the decline.

Proverbs in the form of humorous, ironic, or sarcastic interrogatives have never been especially numerous, and this is also true for modern proverbs. In fact, in some of the 14 (1%) texts the interrogative is merely a variant of the standard proverb. Nevertheless, these proverbs in the form of a question add some rhetorical spice to the intended message:

> A bird may love a fish, but where would they live (build a home, build a nest)?
> (1964, 21)
> Birds sing after a storm, so why shouldn't we? (1974, 21)
> Who cares if a cat is black or white as long as it catches mice? (1968, 35)
> Where does a 500-pound (800-pound, etc.) gorilla sit? (1976, 109)
> Why go out for hamburger when you can get steak at home? (1971, 114)
> Who ever said life is fair? (1929, 146)

Concerning prevalent structures, it certainly comes as a surprise that the well-established pattern of "Where there is X, there is Y" does not at all appear among these modern proverbs. This can perhaps be taken as a sign that some of the traditional structures are not necessarily of great importance in the formulation of new proverbs any longer. The most dominant structure in our corpus is "If you X, (you) Y" with 62 (4.4%) proverbs, as for example:

> If you don't believe in cooperation, watch what happens to a wagon (car) when one wheel comes off. (1921, 43)
> If you can dream it, you can do it (be it, have it). (1970, 62)
> If you can't be good, be careful. (1902, 108)
> If you can't stand (don't like) the heat, get out of the kitchen. (1931, 119; Mieder and Bryan 1997: 59–61)
> If you (can) make it here, you can make it anywhere. (1959, 155)
> If you keep your mouth shut, you won't put your foot in it. (1915, 174)
> If you want something done, ask a busy person. (1905,195)

But this is really the only structure that has at least somewhat of a claim for being of considerable frequency. The number of texts based on other structures falls off rather drastically, showing once again that by far the majority of modern proverbs are rather straight-forward indicative sentences with little formulaic or poetic characteristics. Here then are the examples for eleven structures, with nine groups of texts not even reaching 1% of the corpus:

> "X is Y" (24, 1.7%; definitional proverbs)
>> Age is just a number. (1957, 4)
>> Beauty is only skin. (1963, 17)
>> Black is beautiful. (1927, 22)
>> History is bunk. (1916, 121)
>> Life is a funny (strange) old dog. (1976, 142)
>> The sky is the limit. (1909, 233)
>> The world is a place. (1976, 282; Mieder 2009b: 56–57, 2010c, 2011: 24–26)

> "X is (are) better than Y" (16, 1.1%)
>> Old age is better than the alternative. (1960, 4)
>> The chase (hunt) is better than the kill. (1904, 36)
>> Each generation is better than the last. (1954, 95)
>> New goods are better than bargains. (1919, 109)
>> A long short is better than no shot. (1947, 229)
>> Once seen is better than a hundred times heard. (1947, 258–259)

"It's not X, it's (but) Y" (9, .63%)

It's not the crime but the cover-up. (1973, 47)

It's not the years, it's the mileage (miles). (1957, 284)

"When you X, (you) X(Y)" (9, .63%)

When you pray, move your feet. (1936, 84–85)

When you're good, you're good. (1967, 108–109)

When you are in a hole, stop digging. (1911, 122–123)

When you have nothing, you have nothing to lose. (1965, 182)

"Better X than Y" (8, .56%)

Better to cheat than repeat. (1966, 36–37)

Better a big fish in a little pond (puddle, pool) than a little fish in a big pond (mighty ocean). (1903, 78)

Better Red than dead. (1958, 215; Barrick 1979)

"No X, no Y" (8, .56%)

No guts, no glory. (1945, 112–113; Prahlad 1994 [2003])

No harm, no foul. (1956, 117)

No pass, no play. (1984, 191)

No victim, no crime. (1971, 268)

"X is (are) X" (7, .49%, tautologies)

Bosses are (will be) bosses. (1907, 24)

A deadline is a deadline. (1933, 51)

Good enough is good enough. (1910, 107–108)

"There is no such thing as X" (7, .49%)

There is no such thing as a definitive study (text, edition, etc.). (1936. 252–253)

There is no such thing as a free lunch (There is no free lunch). (1917, 253)

There is no such thing as bad publicity (press, P.R., ink). (1941, 253)

There is no such thing as bad weather, only the wrong clothes. (1979, 254)

"He who Xs, Ys" (6, .42%)

He who slings dirt loses ground. (1923, 56)

He who has the gold makes the rules. (1967, 106)

He who dies with the most toys still dies. (1983, 262)

"There are no X, only (just) Y" (6, .42%)

There are no bad children, only bad parents. (1910, 38)

There are no bad dogs, only bad owners. (1949, 59)

There are no problems, only opportunities (challenges). (1948, 207)
There are no bad students, just bad teachers. (1958, 242)

"One man's X, is another man's Y" (4, .28%)
   One man's floor is another man's ceiling. (1929, 161)
   One man's terrorist is another man's freedom fighter. (1970, 162)
   One man's trash is another man's treasure. (1924, 162)

From this dearth of proverbs based on repeated structures we can move on to an analysis of the length of proverbs. Taking all 1422 proverbs without variants, the total word count is 10,225 words, resulting in an average length of 7.2 words per proverb. This corresponds very much to the length of traditional Anglo-American proverbs in general (Grzybek 2000). As one would expect, our corpus includes texts that consist of the minimum of two words required for a *bona fide* proverb (Dundes 1975 [1981]). Old proverbs like "Time flies" and "Money talks" (Kirshenblatt-Gimblett 1973 [1981]) easily come to mind, but considering the predisposition of modern speakers for short sound bites, it is surprising that our collection contains but 11 (.77%) two-word proverbs. The range of messages clearly goes from the didactic boy-scout motto "Be prepared" via the slang proverb "Life sucks" all the way to proverbs based on scatological and sexual images:

Question authority. (1958, 10)
Life sucks. (1979, 145)
Manners matter (much). (1909, 163)
Sex sells. (1926, 226)
Shit (Stuff) happens.(1944, 228)
Speed kills. (1939, 238)

The group of proverbs consisting of three words comprises 39 (2.7%) texts, of which about a fifth are definitional proverbs of the structure "X is Y" already listed above. Some texts are simple imperatives like "Just do it" or "Just say no", while others are very short statements expressing some basic generalizations about modern life and behavior:

Everyone finds someone. (1943, 77)
Gentlemen prefer blondes. (1925, 95)

Money never sleeps. (1907, 169)
Just say *no*. (1983, 178)
Nothing grows forever. (1978, 180)
Publish or perish. (1927, 209)
Signs don't vote. (1981, 231)

The group of proverbs consisting of four words is expectedly much larger with its 150 (10.5%) texts. There is a predominance of mono-syllabic words in these texts, making them very short pieces of rather directly expressed insights that often lack any metaphorical element. However, many of them follow a parallel structure with or without rhyme. Regarding rhyme, it should however be noted that this prover-bial marker does not play a major role in modern proverbs (about 51 texts or 3.6%), among them "Your ego is not your amigo" (1979, 67), "Move your feet, lose your seat" (1987, 84), "Drive for show, put for dough" (1942, 230), and "Different ways for (on) different days" (1971, 272). A few more rhymed proverbs are included in this list of four-word proverbs:

Get your act together. (1972, 2)
No beauty without pain. (1987, 17)
Think outside the box. 1971, 25)
The buck stops here. (1942, 28; Mieder and Bryan 1997: 62–65)
Everyone can't be first. (1955, 78)
Go with the flow. (1962, 82)
Garbage in, garbage out. (1957, 94; Winick 2001)
Last hired, first fired. (1918, 121)
You can't fix stupid. (1995, 243)

Of course, there are also proverbs of a much greater length, reaching as many as 23 words. Some of them have parallel structures, others begin with a statements that is elaborated in the second part (often beginning with the conjunction "but"), and there are also those texts that
simply state a truism in a somewhat wordy way. Owing to their length and perhaps to the problem of memorability, these texts do not belong to those of frequent use. If they are used, they are most likely only cited partially, assuming that people will be able to complete them in their own minds:

16 words:
Be nice to people on your way up because you'll meet them on your way down. (1932, 193)

17 words:
The toes you step on today may be attached (connected) to the ass you have to kiss tomorrow. (1999, 261)
Worry is like a rocking chair: it gives you something to do but doesn't get you anywhere. (1916, 283)

18 words:
When you're up to your ass in alligators, it's hard to remember you're there to drain the swamp (it's too late to start figuring out how to drain the swamp). (1971, 8–9; Dundes and Pagter 1987)
A government big enough to give you everything you want is big enough to take everything you have. (1952, 110)

19 words:
You can take a boy (man, girl, etc.) out of the country, but you can't take the country out of a boy (man, girl). (1916, 26)
It is better to be thought a fool than to open your mouth and let the world know it. (1907, 83)

20 words:
It is better to be a big duck in a little puddle (pond) than a little duck in a big puddle (pond). (1934, 64)

21 words:
It's not the size of the dog in the fight that matters; it's the size of the fight in the dog. (1911, 232)

23 words:
The caribou and the wolf are one; for the caribou feeds the wolf, but it is the wolf who keeps the caribou strong. (1963, 34)

As has been shown, a considerable number of modern proverbs are based on traditional structures, giving them a familiar appearance albeit with new contents. This is also the case with two special types of new proverbs, namely so-called counter-proverbs and anti-proverbs. According to Charles Doyle, who coined the term *counter-proverb* in

1972, "a *counter-proverb* is simply an overt negation or sententious-sounding rebuttal of a proverb, an explicit denial of the proverb's asserted truth. A counter-proverb does not typically aim for any ironic effect, other than calling into doubt whatever wisdom it is that proverbs are supposed to encapsulate. For example, in the twentieth century we find, with some frequency, 'One rotten apple does not spoil the whole barrel,' rebutting the very old proverb 'One rotten apple will spoil the whole barrel.' Sometimes [especially when both texts are modern] it is impossible to determine which is the original proverb and which the counter-proverb: 'Good enough is not good enough' seems to be about the same age as 'Good enough is good enough'; the sayings 'Life is just a bowl of cherries' and 'Life is not a bowl of cherries' are contemporaneous" (Doyle, Mieder, Shapiro 2012: xi-xii). Just as such traditional contrasting proverb pairs as "Absence makes the heart grow fonder" and "Out of sight, out of mind", these counter-proverb pairs mirror the contradictions of life itself. Since proverbs are not a logical system, such opposing bits of wisdom are perfectly legitimate. But be that as it may, our collection only includes 11 (.77%) counter-proverbs. In the following list the counter-proverb is cited with the date of its earliest recording but without contextualized references. After that I cite the original proverb on which the new counter-proverb is based:

> Bigger is not always (necessarily) better. (1928, 20). [...] The proverb perhaps originated as counter-proverb responding to "The bigger the better."

> You cannot fight fire with fire. (1917, 77). [...] The proverb perhaps originated as a counter-proverb rebutting the very old "Fight fire with fire" or "You've got to fight fire with fire."

> Flattery will get you everywhere (anywhere). (1926. 81–82). [...] The proverb probably originated as a counter-proverb rebutting "FLATTERY will get you nowhere"—or else "FLATTERY will get you nowhere" rebuts "FLATTERY will get you everywhere."

> Life is not a bowl of cherries. (1931, 143). [...] Presumably the proverb originated as a counter-proverb rebutting "LIFE is a bowl of cherries."—or vice versa.

The plural of *anecdote* is not *data* (*evidence*). (1980, 202). [...] Presumably the proverb originated as a counter-proverb responding to the waggish "The plural of *anecdote* is *data*"—or vice versa.

Not all publicity (press) is good (publicity). (1915, 208–209). [...] The proverb perhaps originated as a counter-proverb rebutting "Any PUBLICITY is good publicity"—or vice versa.

Our collection also includes a considerably larger number of anti-proverbs (Litovkina and Lindahl 2007, Litovkina and Mieder 2006), namely 118 (8.3%). I had coined the term *anti-proverb* in 1982, with an anti-proverb being "an allusive distortion, parody, misapplication, or unexpected contextualization of a recognized proverb, usually for comic or satiric effect. Anti-proverbs occur frequently in commercial advertising, on greeting cards, in the captions of cartoons, and as the punch lines of 'shaggy dog' jokes. Sometimes they pass into oral tradition as proverbs in their own right (Valdaeva 2003): for example, 'Absence makes the heart go wander'; 'Beauty is only skin'; 'No body is perfect'; 'Do unto other before they can do unto you'; 'Dynamite comes in small packages'" (Doyle, Mieder, Shapiro 2012: xi). In the following selection of examples, I cite first the anti-proverb with the date of its earliest recording, once again leaving our all contextualized references. This is followed by the traditional proverb upon which the anti-proverb was formulated:

Don't believe everything you think. (1948, 19). [...] The proverb originated as an anti-proverb based on "Don't believe everything you hear (read, see)."

You booze, you lose. (1986, 24). [...] The rhyming proverb may have originated as an anti-proverb based on "You SNOOZE, you lose."

Do unto others before they (can) do unto you (before they do you). (1915, 57). [...] The proverb originated as an anti-proverb based on the golden rule (Matt. 7:12) "Do unto others as you would have them do unto you." (Mieder 2010b). Expedience is the best teacher. (1966, 70). [...] The proverb originated as an anti-proverb based on "Experience is the best teacher."

A ms. (miss) is as good as a male. (1942, 175). [...] The proverb originated as an anti-proverb based on "A miss is as good as a mile."

Love thy neighbor, but don't get caught. (1967, 177). [...] The proverb is an anti-proverb based on the Jesus's advice to "love thy neighbor as thyself."

People who live in glass houses should (always) wear clothes. (1904, 194). [...] The proverb originated as an anti-proverb based on "People who live in glass houses shouldn't throw stones."

Somewhat related to counter-proverbs and anti-proverbs are what we have called reincarnations of older proverbs, that is, modern proverbs based on the general wording, metaphor (if there is one), and meaning of an older proverb. Such pairs of texts may coexist, of course, but usually the more modern one will win out in the struggle for dominance. A few truncated examples will illustrate this phenomenon:

You break it, you buy (bought, own) it (If you break it, it's yours). (1952 27). [...] Sometimes, in recent years, the proverb is called "the Pottery Barn rule." Cf. the older proverb (and legal maxim) "He who breaks pays."

You never get a second chance to make a first impression. (1952, 36). [...] Cf. the older proverb "First impressions are lasting."

The older the fiddle (violin), the sweeter (finer) the tune (melody, sound). (1909, 76–77). [...] Cf. the older proverb "There's many a good tune played on an old fiddle."

Only dead fish go with the flow. (1989, 79). [...] Cf. the older proverb "A dead fish can float downstream, but it takes a live one to swim upstream." The modern variant (among other implications) satirizes—and sometimes retorts to—the proverbial advice "Go with the FLOW."

Nobody ever said life is easy (Who ever said life is easy?). (1965, 146). [...] Cf. the older proverb—from which this one perhaps evolved—"Life is not meant to be easy."

A good man is hard to find. (1918, 157). [...] The proverb is the twentieth-century incarnation (or equivalent) of the older proverb "Good men are scarce." (Doyle 2007a)

Modern proverbs also are consciously created by individuals as so-called "laws" summarizing life's trials and tribulations that appear to

repeat themselves. Usually these insights have the name of their originator attached to them, and there are entire books on such (in)famous
laws. Some of them have clearly become proverbial, and our collection
includes 15 (1.1%) of them (Bloch 1979, 1982a, 1982b). A few are listed
here with their date and the name of the person who (supposedly)
coined them. Our actual entries provide much more material, as can be
seen from this one complete text for perhaps the most famous of these
laws which might be of British origin:

> If anything can **go wrong**, it will (Anything that can go wrong, will go wrong.,
> Anything that can possibly go wrong usually does). (1908, 101–102). Nevil
> Maskelyne, "The Art in Magic," *The Magic Circular* (June) 25: "It is an expe-
> rience common to all men to find that, on any special occasion, such as the
> production of a magical effect for the first time in public, everything that *can*
> go wrong *will* go wrong. Whether we must attribute this to the malignity
> of matter or to the total depravity of inanimate things, whether the exciting
> cause is hurry, worry, or what not, the fact remains" (italics as shown). 1951
> Anne Roe, "Child Behavior, Animal Behavior, and Comparative Psychology,"
> *Genetic Psychology Monographs* 43 (May) 204: "As for himself he realized that
> this was the inexorable working of the second law of the thermodynamics
> which stated Murphy's law 'If anything can go wrong it will.' I always liked
> Murphy's law." 1955 Lee Corey, "Design Flaw," *Astounding Science Fiction* 54
> (Feb.) 54: " 'Reilly's Law,' Guy Barclay said cryptically. 'Huh?' 'Reilly's Law,'
> Guy repeated. 'It states that in any scientific or engineering endeavor, any-
> thing that can go wrong *will* go wrong" (italics as shown). [references to col-
> lections are deleted here and elsewhere]. In popular legend, Murphy's Law
> originated in 1949 at Edwards Air Force Base in California, coined by project
> manager George E. Nichols after hearing Edward A. Murphy, Jr., complain
> about a wrongly-wired rocket-sled experiment. However, there is no docu-
> mentation of that connection until 1955. The idea embodied in Murphy's Law
> (less often, "Reilly's Law" or "O'Reilly's Law") has appeared in numerous
> forms, in reference to a variety of activities, from antiquity forward (see the
> cross-references at the *YBQ* entry). For example: 1878 Alfred Holt, "Review
> of the Progress of Steam Shipping during the Last Quarter of a Century,"
> *Minutes of Proceedings of the Institution of Civil Engineers*, 51: 8: "It is found that
> anything that can go wrong at sea generally does go wrong sooner or later."
> 1941 George Orwell, "War-Time Diaries," in *Collected Essays, Journalism and
> Letters*, edited by Sonia Orwell and Ian Angus (New York: Harcourt, Brace &
> World, 1968) 2: 400–01: "Iraq, Syria, Morocco, Spain, Darlan, Stalin, Raschid
> Ali, Franco—sensation of utter helplessness. If there is a wrong thing to do,

it will be done, infallibly. One has come to believe in that as if it were a law of nature." The term "Murphy's law" has come to designate a range of seemingly reasonable but often paradoxical or absurd-sounding propositions.

But here then are a few more laws in much truncated form to save space. They make clear that at times they are simply attributed to a person, with Edward A. Murphy winning the prize as the supposed coiner of such laws of which but a few have become proverbial:

> When you are in a hole, stop digging. (1911, 122–123). *Washington Post* 25 Oct.: "Nor would a wise man, seeing that he was in a hole, go to work and blindly dig it deeper, as [William Jennings] Bryan did when he shifted ground and assailed the integrity of the President and the Judges." [...] 1984 *New York Times* 11 Sep.: "There is a Law of Holes that says, when you are in one, stop digging. That is a law Congress finds it almost impossible to observe." [...] In British publications, the "Law of Holes" is often referred to as "Healey's Law," after the statesman Denis Healey, a popularizer of the expression in the later 1980s.

> Everything (always) takes longer than it should (it does, it takes, you expect). (1900, 248–249). Florence Converse, *The Burden of Christopher* (Boston: Houghton, Mifflin) 139: "To be sure, we're still profit sharing, we have n't gone into real coöperation yet; but then, things always take longer than you think they will ..." [...] Especially in absurdly-worded forms like "Everything takes longer than it takes," the proverb is often given as one of "Murphy's Laws."

> Work expands to fill the available (allotted) time. (1955, 281). "Parkinson's Law," *The Economist* 177: 633 (the reference is to C. Northcote Parkinson): "It is a commonplace observation that work expands so as to fill the time available for its completion ... Before the discovery of a new scientific law—herewith presented to the public for the first time, and to be called Parkinson's Law—there has, however, been insufficient recognition of the implications of this fact in the field of public administration."

These examples show that the actual authorship of some of these proverbial laws is not at all certain. This is quite naturally also the case with the other proverbs in our corpus. To be sure, some modern proverbs have simply been attributed to certain well-known persons, just as this has been done in previous times (Taylor 1931: 34–43). Detailed research on our part has shown that such attributions can usually not be proven, even though people will cling to these claims when citing such proverbs. What it takes to come to terms with such attributions can best be seen from our discussion of the internationally disseminated modern proverb "A woman without a man is like a fish without a bicycle" (Mieder 1982):

A woman without a man is like a fish without a bicycle (A woman needs a man like a fish needs a bicycle). (1976, 279–280). *Corpus Christi [TX] Times* 5 May (quoting Barbara Hower): "... [A] feminist said recently an independent woman needs a man like a fish needs a bicycle. That's horse feathers, at least for me. I like what I'm doing but I'd like someone to scratch and giggle with" (credited to *Chicago Daily News*). 1976 *Seattle Times* 5 Jun.: "Sign in a (feminist?) dress shop in Seattle, Wash.: 'A woman without a man is like a fish without a bicycle.'" 1976 *People* 6, no. 4 (26 Jul.) 20 (photo caption): "Gloria Steinem (left) planned to wear a shirt that said, 'A woman without a man is like a fish without a bicycle,' but, like Candy Bergen, arrived unlettered at a [Democratic Party] women's fund raiser." 1976 Mary Murphy, "Superstar Women and Their Marriages," *New York Magazine* 9, no. 32 (9 Aug.) 26: "[Gloria] Steinem sums it up: 'Today a woman without a man is like a fish without a bicycle." 1979 Deborah Goleman Wolf, *The Lesbian Community* (Berkeley: U of California P) [vi] (epigraph): "'A woman without a man is like a fish without a bicycle.' (Graffito in the women's lavatory, Student Union, University of California Berkeley, 1975, attributed to Flo Kennedy)" (italics as shown). 1976 *Seattle Times* 5 Jun. "Sign seen in a (feminist?) dress shop in Seattle, Wash.: 'A woman without a man is like a fish without a bicycle.'" [...] The proverb perhaps originated as an anti-proverb patterned after "A woman without a man is like a handle without a pan" (or other old similes suggesting uselessness or absurdity). Steinem, in *Time* 156, no. 15 (9 Oct. 2000) 20, disclaimed credit for originating the feminist expression: "Irina Dunn, a distinguished Australian educator, journalist and politician, coined the phrase back in 1970 ..." The image of a fish without (or not needing) a bicycle has had a life of its own. Cf. "A MAN without faith is like a fish without a bicycle" and "A MAN without a woman is like a fish without a bicycle" and "A WOMAN without a man is like a fish without a net."

Here are but a few more examples of this phenomenon, once again stripped of many additional contextualized references:

Old age is not for sissies. (1969, 4). Eugene P. Bertin, "Ravelin's: Threads Detached from Texture," *Pennsylvania School Journal* 17: 546 (in a series of witty sayings commemorating Senior Citizen Month, May): "Old age is not for sissies." [...] The proverb's origin is often attributed to the actress Bette Davis.

Float like a butterfly, sting like a bee. (1964, 31). *New York Times* 19 Feb.: "'Put the poison on him,' yelled Drew (Budini) Brown, Clay's spiritual adviser and assistant trainer. 'Float like a butterfly, sting like a bee. Oh, beautiful, Cassius, you should see yourself.'" [...] The saying has generally been attributed to Mohammed Ali (*né* Cassius Clay) himself.

It's (The game is) not over till it's over. (1921, 186). Roy Sahm, "It Is Believed Rotarians Won," *The Delta of Sigma Nu Fraternity* 38: 667: "It is said the score was 23 to 21 in favor of Rotary, they having tied the score in the seventh. They passed Kiwanis in the eighth and held Kiwanis in the ninth. all of which goes to prove that a ball game's never over until it's over" (credited to the *Indianapolis News*). [...] Often, the saying is apocryphally attributed to Yogi Berra. Cf. the older expression "When it's over, it's over," which has a different meaning.

A week is a long time in politics. (1961, 274). Richard Cox, "Nyerere Sees a Middle Way for Africa," *New York Times Magazine* (3 Dec.) 121: "He [Prime Minister Julius Nyerere] will undoubtedly find it difficult to negotiate federation when it comes to the details, but as the weeks pass—and a week is a long time in African politics—it seems more and more likely that he will succeed." [...] The proverb is commonly attributed to Prime Minister Harold Wilson; however, no record of his using it can be found from earlier than 1968, and Wilson himself is on record saying he cannot remember when he first uttered it.

All of this is not to say that our collection does not contain modern proverbs for which we know precisely who originated it when and where. Such original citations by known persons begin basically as statements in books, articles, speeches, motion pictures, songs, etc. As they are repeated, they become quotations and with ever more frequent use, eventually often without any awareness of the originator, these memorable texts can become proverbs. Sometimes quite similar statements precede such a quotation that for various reasons caught on and thus became proverbial. This is well illustrated by one of John F. Kennedy's most famous statements:

Ask not what your country can do for you—ask what you can do for your country. (1960, 45–46). The saying (often slightly misquoted) entered oral tradition as a proverb from President John F. Kennedy's inaugural address, 20 Jan. 1960. An 1884 speech by Oliver Wendell Holmes, Jr., is sometimes cited as a prototype of Kennedy's wording, since it anticipates the (commonplace) idea and the parallel phrasing, the chiasmus: "… [W]e pause … to recall what our country has done for each of us, and to ask ourselves what we can do for our country in return." A closer prior analog: 1922 Isaac Doughton, *Preparing for the World's Work* (New York: Charles Scribner's Sons) 4: "But as good citizens you are not so anxious to know what your country does for you as you are to know what you can do for your country." The eeriest anticipator of both Holmes's and Kennedy's wording occurred in 1858—except that the writer, one Rev. M. Thomson, was engaging in satire, proffering ironic advice—and thus inverting the clauses—in "Our Youth: Their Principles and Prospects," *Ladies' Repository* 18: 285: "Fetter the noblest powers and impulses of the soul; turn all your genius into cunning; prefer your wages to your work; study not what you can do for your country, but what your country can do for you." […] (Mieder 2005c: 172–173).

But here then are a few shortened examples from our collection that are in fact rather straight-forward regarding their first appearance in a written or oral communication by a known person of considerable consequence:

If it (If the glove) doesn't fit, you must acquit. (1995, 81). The saying entered oral tradition as a proverb from its use as a mantra by the defense lawyer Johnnie Cochran, Jr., in his closing argument at the murder trial of O. J. Simpson (27 Sep.). […] The proverb means "You must reject, abandon, or discard a belief or plan that does not 'fit' with realities, goals, or purposes." The proverb is less commonly applied jurisprudentially. (Winick 2003: 587–588, Prahlad 2006: II,1026).

You can't go home again. (1940, 123). The saying probably entered oral tradition as a proverb from the title of Thomas Wolfe's novel, published posthumously (Wolfe died in 1938). […]

Love means never having to say you're sorry. (1970, 152). The saying entered oral tradition as a proverb from Erich Segal's best-selling novel *Love Story* (New York: Harper & Row), which first appeared (somewhat condensed) in *Ladies Home Journal* 87, no. 2 (Feb.) 124: "She cut off my apology, then said very quietly, 'Love means not ever having to say you're sorry.'" In the popular motion picture, "never" replaces "not ever." The novel was written after Segal's screen play but published before the release of the movie in Dec. 1970. [...]

Pain is (Tough times are) temporary; failure (quitting) is forever. (2003, 188). Lance Armstrong (with Sally Jenkins), *Every Second Counts* (New York: Random House) 3–4: "But the fact is I wouldn't have won a single Tour de France without the lesson of illness. What it teaches is this: pain is temporary. Quitting lasts forever." [...]

Speak (Talk, Walk) softly and carry a big stick. (1900, 238). Theodore Roosevelt, letter to Henry Sprague (26 Jan.): "I have always been fond of the West African proverb: 'Speak softly and carry a big stick; you will go far.' If I had not carried the big stick the organization would not have gotten behind me ..."; *Letters*, edited by Elting E. Morison (Cambridge MA: Harvard UP, 1951–54) 2: 1141. On several occasions Roosevelt uttered the saying, without the last clause and without the West African connection. In oral tradition, the proverb often varies the first verb. [...] An interesting prior analog: 1882 C. H. Spurgeon, "Colportage a Want of the Age," in *Booksellers and Bookbuyers*, by Spurgeon et al. (London: Passmore and Alabaster) 12: "Amid abundant laughter, our friend [an evangelist] declared that he had not fought wild beasts at Ephesis, but ... he had found it well to trust in God *and carry a big stick*" (italics as shown).

War will cease when men refuse to fight. (1933, 271). Albert Einstein, *The Fight against War*, edited by Alfred Lief (New York: John Day) 37 (excerpted from Einstein's interview with George Sylvester Viereck, Jan. 1931): "I am not only a pacifist but a militant pacifist. I am willing to fight for peace. Nothing will end war unless the peoples themselves refuse to war [sic]." [...] Cf. "Some day they will give a WAR and nobody will come."

It has long been established that advertising slogans have given rise to new proverbs (Mieder and Mieder 1977 [1981], Prahlad 2004, Winick 2011), but the 17 (1.2%) texts in our collection are certainly not an overwhelming number. Many slogans are simply too specifically oriented towards a certain product to take on the nature of a general proverb. In addition, over time the association with the original advertising campaign is lost, making it difficult to establish clear-cut connections. In other words, proverbs starting as advertising slogans have a tendency of becoming anonymous traditional sayings, as is, of course, the very nature of real proverbs. The complexity of all of this, including variants building on such slogans, can readily be seen from this one reference from our collections cited in its entirety:

> What happens (goes on) in Las Vegas stays in Las Vegas. (2002, 137). *Las Vegas Review-Journal* 25 Nov.: "The Las Vegas Visitors and Convention Authority, meanwhile, continued its saucy come-to-Vegas-baby advertising campaign with six new spots filmed over a three-day period last week. Depicting the theme 'what happens in Las Vegas stays in Las Vegas,' the national commercials, produced by Hungry Man Productions, feature Vegas visitors indulging fantasies in locations ranging from a limousine to a tattoo parlor." 2002 Kellye M. Garrett et al., "Everything the Top Football Stars Can't Live Without," *Vibe* Nov. 62 (quoting the football player Adam Archuleta): "Favorite city: Las Vegas … You party and have a good time with your friends. What happens in Vegas stays in Vegas." Whether the advertising campaign originated the saying or merely employed an existing proverb, "What happens in Las Vegas stays in Las Vegas" has become, by far, the most common of the popular sayings that follow the formula; it is widely assumed to be the prototypical version, and currently it can be uttered (figuratively) in reference to any site of conduct that calls for non-disclosure. However, it was anticipated—at least as early as the 1970s—by parallel sayings about secrecy or discretion of various sorts: "What's said (What happens) at home stays at home," an expression sometimes used to lament the secrecy of child abuse or spousal abuse; the clinical or psychotherapeutic adage "What happens in the group (at the meeting, at the session) stays …"; the professional baseball maxim "What happens in the clubhouse stays …" Even in the dissipated-vacation usage, other versions are apparently older: 1996 *San Antonio Express-News* 13 Nov.: "But there was one condition. Drill sergeants told them repeatedly: 'Whatever happens in Mexico stays in Mexico.'" 1998 *Orlando Sentinel* 30 Mar.: "'What happens in Daytona, stays in Daytona,' he tells the others."

But here then are once again a few shortened examples of advertising slogans turned proverb, with only one text actually maintaining the name of a company (Delta Airlines). Nevertheless, a certain amount of cultural literacy and knowledge about the commercial world belong at least in part to the proper understanding of some of these texts (Mieder 1992 [1994], see also Haas 2008):

Where is the beef? (1984, 18). The saying entered oral tradition as a proverb from an advertising slogan for Wendy's hamburgers. [...] In the proverb, the word *beef* is understood to mean 'substance' in various senses. (Barrick 1986). It's what's up front that counts. (c1957, 45). The saying entered oral tradition as a proverb from an advertising slogan for Winston cigarettes—playing on the older proverb "It's what inside that counts." [...]

Say it with flowers. (1917, 82). The saying entered oral tradition as a proverb from an advertising slogan of the Society of American Florists. [...]
Number two tries harder (When you're number two, you try harder). (1962, 182). The proverb probably entered oral tradition from an advertising campaign for Avis: "We're Number Two. We try harder" (Avis was second to Hertz in the car-rental business).

Reach out and touch someone. (1970, 214). Eliot Tiegel, "Reach Out and Touch Someone," *Billboard* (15 Aug.) 26; the title of the review of a live performance by Diana Ross presumably alludes to Ross's song "Reach Out and Touch Somebody's Hand." [...] Beginning in 1978 the proverb was featured in an advertising campaign for AT&T's long-distance phone service. [...]

As can be seen from two of these examples, proverb-like one-liners from the world of advertising and popular music can actually work hand in hand in creating and spreading new proverbs. With music playing such a large role on the modern entertainment scene, it should not be surprising that songs have given rise to ample modern proverbs, with our collection containing 65 (4.6%) texts. It should be noted, however, that this is nothing new as far as the creation of proverbs is concerned (Bryan 2001, Mieder 1988). Religious hymns, anonymous folksongs, operettas, and musicals have long given rise to proverbs, with the song texts of Gilbert and Sullivan being prime examples in the nineteenth and early twentieth centuries (Bryan 1999). Nothing in this regard has changed on the modern scene, as can be seen by country songs, blues, reggae, or rap music (Folsom 1993, Prahlad 2001, Taft 1994). In fact, songs by famous lyricists and musicians like the Beatles, Bob Dylan, and Bruce Springsteen have led to new proverbs. Here then are at least a few examples from the treasure trove of proverbs stemming from popular songs. Of course, let me also state for the record that lyric poets also employ traditional proverbs and formulate lines that later become proverbs, as can be seen from many such proverb poems (Sobieski and Mieder 2005):

> There's no business like show business. (1946, 30). The saying entered oral tradition as a proverb from the title and first line of a song by Irving Berlin. [...] Diamonds are (A diamond is) a girl's best friend. (1949, 55). The saying entered oral tradition as a proverb from the title and refrain of a song by Leo Robin. [...]

> It's not easy being green. (1970, 65). The saying entered oral tradition as a proverb from a song by Joe Raposo, sung by the character Kermit the Frog of the Muppets. It applies to the difficulty of efforts to save the environment and perhaps to other kinds of figurative "greenness."

> Everybody wants to go to heaven, but nobody wants to die. (1950. 119). The proverb originated with—or gained popularity from—the title of Tommy Dorsey's song "Everybody Wants to Go to Heaven (But No One Wants to Die)."

> Life is (just) a cabaret. (1966, 142). The saying entered oral tradition as a proverb from the featured song in the musical *Cabaret*, lyrics by Fred Ebb (music by John Knader). [...] The proverb updates the venerable Elizabethan commonplace of the world as a stage (and men and women merely players).

> It takes two to tango. (1952, 266). The saying entered oral tradition as a proverb from the song "It Takes Two to Tango," by Al Hoffman and Dick Manning. [...] The proverb may have originated as an anti-proverb based on "It takes two to quarrel." (Mieder and Bryan 1983, Mieder 1985: 151–154)

Motion pictures are not surprisingly also a fruitful ground for spreading laconic insights to large segments of the population who in turn help to distribute them by frequent repetition as new proverbs of the folk (Krummenacher 2007). Our collection assembles 19 (1.3%) such proverbs whose origin can be traced back to popular films:

> If you build it, they will come (Build it and they will come). (1979, 28). The saying probably entered oral tradition as a proverb—or at least gained popularity—from W. P. Kinsella's story "Shoeless Joe Jackson Comes to Iowa" and the motion picture based on it, *Field of Dreams* (1989). [...]

Keep your friends close and (but) your enemies closer. (1974, 87). The proverb probably entered oral tradition from a speech in the motion picture *The Godfather, Part II*: "There are many things my father taught me here in this room. He taught me: Keep your friends close, but your enemies closer." Occasionally it is referred to as an ancient Chinese proverb.

If (When) you've got it, flaunt it. (1968, 96). The saying may have entered oral tradition as a proverb from the motion picture *The Producers*: "That's it, baby! When you got it, flaunt it!" (or the character in the movie may have been uttering a proverb). Most frequently the proverb refers to the display of an individual's sexuality.

Life is like (is just) a box of chocolates (chocolate). (1994, 143). The saying entered oral tradition as adapted from the motion picture *Forrest Gump*: "Life is a box of chocolates, Forrest. You never know what you're going to get." The proverb sometimes intends to *satirize* the sententious utterance of Forrest Gump's mother.

There are no rules in a knife fight. (1969, 221). The entered oral tradition as a proverb, garbled, from dialog in the motion picture *Butch Cassidy and the Sundance Kid*: "[Butch:] 'No, no, not yet. Not until me and Harvey get the rules straightened out.' [Harvey Logan:] 'Rules? In a knife fight? No rules!'" (at which instant Butch kicks Harvey in the groin). [...]

Turning now to the realia of modern proverbs, it is perhaps surprising that various animals continue to appear with considerable frequency. Obviously the modern age still relates well to animals, especially such domesticated animals as cats, cows, dogs, horses, and pigs. But wild animals as birds, elephants, fish, frogs, monkeys, and others are also employed to express human behavior and attitudes via animal metaphors. There is, of course, also the telling British modern proverb "All animals are (created) equal, but some are more equal than others" (1945. 6) that entered oral tradition from George Orwell's *Animal Farm* (1945), expressing in metaphorical wording an unfortunate aspect of human life. In any case, our proverb collection contains 116 (8.2%) so-called animal proverbs, among them:

A bird may love a fish, but where would they live (build a home, build a nest)? (1964, 21; Mahoney 2009)
You can't run with the (big) dogs if you pee like a pup. (1986, 59)

If it looks like a duck, walks like a duck, and quacks like a duck, it's a duck. (1948, 64)

It is possible to swallow (You can eat) an elephant—one bite at a time. (1921, 67)

You have to kiss a lot of frogs (toads) to find a prince. (1976, 89; Mieder 2014)

When you hear hoofbeats, think horses, not zebras (When you hear hoofbeats, don't look for zebras). (1969, 123–124; Dundes, Streiff, and Dundes 1999)

Always ride the (your) horse in the direction it's going (it wants to go). (1975,124–125)

You can put lipstick on a pig but it's still a pig (A pig wearing lipstick is still a pig). (1985, 148, Mieder 2009b: 83–85)

Only monkeys work for peanuts (If you pay peanuts, you get monkeys). (1953, 171)

Old rats like cheese too. (1977, 214)

Just as animal metaphors have not disappeared from modern proverbs, the same is also true for somatisms, with such nouns as ass (behind), eye, hand, head, heart, mouth, and nose being the most frequent among the 49 (3.4%) texts.

Your arms are too short (not long enough) to box (fight, spar) with God. (1912, 7)

If you're too open-minded, your brains will fall out. (1960, 26)

Every shut eye is not asleep. (1900, 70)

It is better to die on your feet than to live on your knees. (1924, 84)

Busy hands are happy hands. (1956, 115)

You can't measure heart. (1967, 119)

Never take more on your heels than you can kick off with your toes. (1925, 120)

A moment (minute) on the lips, a lifetime (forever) on the hips. (1940, 168)

A closed (shut) mouth gathers (catches) no feet. (1956, 173)

Keep your nose clean. (1903, 179)

The toes you step on today may be attached (connected) to the ass you have to kiss tomorrow. (1999, 261)

Today's preoccupation with business, finance, and more specifically money has left its mark on modern proverbs as well, with 47 (3.3%) texts showing up in our corpus. They all reflect the pecuniary aspects of modern life, stressing the importance of business, the power of money, the rights and expectations of customers, the hope for prosperity, etc.:

Buy the best and you only cry once. (1959, 19)

Business goes where it is invited and stays where it is well-treated. (1910, 30)

The customer is always right. (1905, 48–49; Taylor 1958)
Another day, another dollar. (1907, 50)
Never give anything away that you can sell. (1953, 98)
Put your money where your mouth is. (1913, 170)
You pay now (You can pay) or pay later (with interest). (1974, 192)
If you have to ask the price (the cost, how much it costs), you can't afford it.
(1926, 207)
No one ever went bankrupt (went broke, lost money) taking (making) a profit.
(1902, 208)
Prosperity is always just around the corner. (1936, 208)
The best way to make money is to save it (is not to lose it). (1922, 272)

Speaking of modern preoccupations, it certainly comes as no surprise that at least 39 (2.7%) proverbs relate to the ever-present and fascinating world of sports. There are several more general proverbs referring to games as such or balls, but it is indeed striking that the majority of sports proverbs are based on the American national sport of baseball (Frank 1983). While these proverbs relate literally to that very sport, their figurative meanings are, of course, much broader and can be applied to situations far removed from the actual game of baseball. Yet popular as these proverbs might be especially in American folk language, they are also the ones that will give people not acquainted with the lingo of this sport certain comprehension difficulties. But here then are a few striking examples:

You can't hit the ball (get a hit) if you don't swing (the bat). (1943, 12)
You can't score unless you have the ball. (1907, 13)
Nobody bats a thousand. (1930, 14–15)
You can't steal first base. (1915, 78)
It isn't whether you win or lose (that counts); it's how you play the game.
(1913, 92–93)
Don't hate the player, hate the game. (1992, 201)
If you have two quarterbacks, you don't have one (any). (1993, 211)
You can't score if you don't shoot. (1965, 223)
You can't steal second base while your foot is on first base (if you keep one
foot on first). (1942, 224)
You miss 100 per cent of the shots you don't take. (1991, 229–230)
Three strikes and you're out. (1901, 241)

In comparison to the importance of sports for the origin of modern proverbs, it is surprising that our corpus includes but 24 (1.7%) texts that exhibit at least some relationship to technology by way of certain words. It is here where we might want to look for new proverbs in the future. Of course, there are some modern proverbs like "Garbage in, garbage out" that come from the world of computers, but they do not show by the choice of words any immediate relationship to technology. The entry with its contextualized references makes this connection perfectly clear:

> Garbage in, garbage out. (Often abbreviated with the acronym GIGO.) (1957, 94; Winick 2001). Ernest E. Blanche, "Applying New Electronic Computers to Traffic and Highway Problems," *Traffic Quarterly* 11: 411: "When the basic data to be used by a computer are of questionable accuracy or validity, our personnel have an unusual expression—GIGO—to characterize such information and the answers the computer produces. It simply means 'garbage in—garbage out.'" 1959 B. A. Wilson, "Operations Research and Management," *Business Quarterly* 24, no. 4 (Winter) 215: "The attempt to use existing records and data in O.R. studies may eventually indicate the inadequacy or inconsistency of existing data, but any results derived from using such data can be no better than the basic data. As one consultant puts it, 'Garbage in, Garbage out.'" […].

In any case, here are some additional proverbs that indicate that technology is playing at least a small role in the creation of modern proverbs, with more to be found or to come in the foreseeable future:

> You never forget how to ride a bicycle. (1933, 20)
> There will always be another bus (streetcar). (1925, 30)
> Nobody washes (We don't wash) a rental (rented) car. (1985, 33)
> You can't judge a car by its paint (job). (1908, 33–34)
> Dot-com, dot-bomb. (2000, 60–61)
> Dynamite comes in small packages. (1937, 64)
> Gasoline and whiskey (Alcohol and gasoline, etc.) do not mix. (1915, 94)
> You cannot tell which way the train went (is going) by looking at the tracks. (1977, 262–263)
> Sometimes (Some days) you're the windshield, and sometimes you're the bug (bird). (1981, 277)

Even though our collection has no texts that indicate by certain word choices that they were coined in Australia, Great Britain, or elsewhere where English is spoken, there are 16 (1.1%) modern proverbs in our collection that refer explicitly to American matters, with a text like "What is good for General Motors is good for America" needing an explanatory comment:

> What is good for General Motors is good for America (the country). (1953, 95). The proverb originated as a misquotation from US Senate testimony of Charles E. Wilson (former president of General Motors): "For years I thought what was good for our country was good for General Motors, and vice versa. The difference did not exist." [...] The proverb most often satirizes the concept that the well-being of giant corporations is inextricably and benevolently connected with the welfare of the nation and its populace.

Such comments are also added to some of the following proverbs that might not necessarily be clear to non-native speakers of American English:

> Never (Don't) sell America short. (1922, 5–6)
> The business of America is business. (1928, 30)
> As California goes, so goes the nation. (1940, 32)
> Don't mess with Texas. (1985, 251)

The meager number of proverbs referring to American matters is a clear sign that our collection is in many ways a compilation of texts that is in general use in the United States, Great Britain, Canada, and elsewhere. This is, of course, also true for those proverbs that have very common keywords. The most popular word is "life", and it is hardly surprising that modern humankind has much wisdom about existence. Altogether 46 (3.2) proverbs contain "life" as a keyword, with most of them following the structural and definitional pattern "Life is X". While some of them in two or four words refer to life being problematic, that is, "Life sucks" (1979, 145) and "Life is a bitch" (1940, 141), others look at life much more positively, as for example "Life begins at forty" (1932, 141) and "If life hands you lemons, make lemonade" (1910, 140). Some additional representative examples are:

Life comes at you fast. (2004, 141)
Life is a journey, not a destination. (1941, 142)
Life is a picture; paint it well. (1956, 142–143)
Life is not a spectator sport. (1958, 143)
Life is what happens while you are making other plans. (1957, 145)
To lengthen your life, lessen your meals. (1947, 146)
You get out of life (the world) what you put into it. (1901, 146)

Next in high-frequency keywords is "man/men", with 34 (2.3%) dealing positively or negatively with the male species. Some texts also contrast men with women, of course, and there are some texts that use this keyword in its generic meaning, thus somewhat inflating this group of "male" proverbs:

Every man to his own poison (To every man his own poison). (1922, 156–157)
Men are from Mars, women are from Venus. (1992, 157)
No man is above the law, and no man is below it. (1903, 161)
Old men make wars, and young men fight them (pay the price). (1912, 161)
The best man for the job may be a woman. (1974, 156)
The man most down on a thing is he who is least up on it. 1909, 158–159)

Proverbs with "woman/women" as the keyword are smaller in number with but 8 (not even .56%), but do notice that none of them refer to men as well. As wisdom about women, they are pretty much split between positive and negative characterizations, quite in keeping with traditional proverbs that often express misogynous generalizations (Kerschen 1998, Schipper 2003):

A woman should be (kept) barefoot and pregnant (an in the kitchen). (1947, 279)
A woman without a man is like a fish without a net. (1993, 280)
A woman's place is any place she wants to be. (1918, 279)
Never run after a woman or a streetcar; if you miss one, another will come along soon. 1910, 278–279)
Well-behaved women rarely (seldom) make history. (1976, 279)

But here are a few more lists for a number of relatively high-frequency keywords, with "God"-proverbs perhaps reflecting the religious preoccupation of parts of the American society. Proverbs about friends, time, age, love, beauty, knowing, pain, success, children, luck, and winning are nothing new as far as Anglo-American proverbs and those of other languages and cultures are concerned, but there are now texts that contain references that identify them as proverbs that could only have originated in more recent times, such as the drug-related "A friend with weed is a friend indeed" (1968, 86) as an anti-proverb to the traditional "A friend in need is a friend indeed" (Mieder, Kingsbury, Harder 1992: 233) or "Act your age, not your IQ" (1995, 3) with its reference to the score of an intelligence test. Above all, it should be noticed that most of these modern proverbs are rather literal statements of basic truths of modern life without couching them into expressive metaphors. Folklorists obviously will delight in the proverb "Every beauty needs her beast" (1973, 17) which is a proverbial allusion to the fairy tale of "The Beauty and the Beast":

God (19)
God can make a way out of no way. (1922, 102; Mieder 2010a: 171–186)
God doesn't make junk (trash). (1975, 103)
God is good, but don't dance in a small boat. (1995, 103)
God sends no cross that you cannot bear. (1985, 104)
Kill them all, and let God sort them out. (1932, 104–105; Russell 1999)
Let go; let God. (1923, 105)

friend (15)
A (true, good) friend walks in when (all) others walk out. (1994, 86)
A true friend is one who knows all your faults and still loves (likes) you. (1917, 87–88)
Fast pay (payment) makes (for) fast friends. (1980, 85–86)
If you want a friend, get (buy) a dog. (1941, 86–87)
Little friends may prove (become) great friends. (1903, 87)
You cannot use your friends and have them too. (1954, 88)

time (11)
Time flies when you're having fun. (1939, 259)
Time spent wishing is time wasted. (1922, 259)
The time to shoot (catch) bears is when they are out. (1914, 259)
Time wounds all heels. (1938, 259)
Tough times don't last, tough people do. (1983, 260)
When it's time to go, it's time to go. (1936, 260)

age (8)
Act your age, not your shoe size. (1967, 3)
Age (Old age) is a high price (too high a price) to pay for maturity. (1969, 3)
Age is just a number. (1957, 4)
Old age (Getting old) is better than the alternative. (1960, 4)
Old age is hell. (1952, 4)

love (8)
If you love something, let it go (set it free); if it comes back to you, it is yours.
(1972, 151)
Love is (just, only, nothing but) a four-letter word. (1937, 151–152)
Love is where you find it. (1938, 152)
Love it or leave it. 1901, 152)

beauty (7)
Beauty does not buy happiness. (1989, 16)
Beauty is only skin.(1963, 17)
Beauty is pain. (1978, 17)

know (7)
If you don't know what it is, (then) don't mess with (fool with, touch, eat) it.
(1950, 134)
You can't know where you're going unless you know where you've been.
(1937, 134)
You have to know when to hold them [cards] and know when to fold them.
(1977, 135)

pain (7)
Don't tell me about the pain (labor pains); just show me the baby. (1979, 187)
Pain (Fatigue) is nature's way of telling you to slow down (you need a rest).
(1920, 187–188)
Pain is the price of glory. (2005, 188)

success (7)
Success (Victory) has many (a hundred) fathers, but failure (defeat) is an
orphan. (1961, 244)
Success is always preceded by preparation. (1981, 244)
Success is never final (and failure is never fatal). (1920, 245)
children (5)
Children (Our children, The children) are our future. (1920, 38)
Children should be seen and not had. (1928, 38)

Teach your (Parents must teach their) children to walk then to walk away. (1964, 38)

luck (5)
Luck (Good luck, Bad luck) does not just happen. (1965, 153)
Luck is the residue of design. (1946, 153).
You can't trust luck. (1928, 153–154)

win (5)
You can't win if you don't play. (1940, 276)
You can't win them all. (1918, 276)
You win a few, you lose a few. (1912, 76)

Proverbs from these groups organized according to various dominant keywords perhaps show at least in a generalized way some of the pre-occupations of modern society. People at times appear to be obsessed with matters of age, beauty, love, luck, success, winning, and of course also the element of time (Lau 1996 [2003]). While it is problematic to deduce the worldview of masses of people from different countries by way of a corpus of proverbs (Dundes 1972 [2007], White 1987), there is no way of denying that there are some themes that permit us to draw some tentative conclusions about the nature of modern proverbs. Continuing along these lines, it can then also be said that people are concerned about pain and anxieties of various types, that they look for friendships in an ever more segmented and chaotic modern life, and that they continue to find solace in knowing that God might assist them in coping with modernity.

With this said, we can turn to one last major group of 83 (5.8%) proverbs that belong to the realms of sexuality, obscenity, and scatology. Looking at earlier proverb collections, one might well get the impression that the folk has no so-called "dirty" proverbs. Even though paremiographers usually have included at least some such proverbs, they have in general been reluctant to collect them or their publishers did not consent to publish them. And yet, some specialized collections have been published along these lines separately from major collections. Thus Ignace Bernstein in Poland followed his massive collection *Jüdische Sprichwörter und Redensarten* (1908 [1969]) up with a published manuscript of *Proverbia Judaeorum Erotica et Turpia. Jüdische Sprichwörter erotischen und rustikalen Inhalts* (1918 [1971]). And Edwin Miller Fogel augmented his important collection *Proverbs of the Pennsylvania Germans* (1929 [1995]) by a privately distributed *Supplement to Proverbs of the Pennsylvania Germans* (1929) which I had the audacity of including in the reprint of the major collection in 1995. Numerous smaller collections of obscene proverbs have been published in books, journals, and above all in three serial publications dedicated explicitly to taboo folkloric matters, that is, *Anthropophyteia* (1904–1913), *Kryptadia* (1883–1911 [1970]), and *Maledicta* (1977–2004). Today, with a more open attitude, popular collections of erotic proverbs and proverbial expressions are more readily available, to wit Marinus A. van den Broek's *Erotisch Spreekwoordenboek. Spreekwoorden en zegswijzen* (2002).

In any case, we have not shied away from including suggestive or obscene proverbs of which some are rather explicit and literal, while others are metaphorical and figurative to the point that many native speakers might have difficulty understanding them. But the fact remains that these proverbs exist, and they are part and parcel of the proverbial speech among the initiated, as our Google searches have proven beyond any doubt. They are part of the world of slang, graffiti, latrinalia (Dundes 1966 [2007]) and the so-called "vulgar tongue", with Francis Grose's *A Classical Dictionary of the Vulgar Tongue* (1785 [1931, 1992]) in the eighteenth century having set the stage for a rich tradition of compendia dealing with obscenities of the underworld and "upperworld". Proverbs deal with all aspects of life, and they certainly have always commented on such basic issues as sexuality. It should then not be surprising that in an age that is dealing quite openly with sex in particular that proverbs will be involved as well. Of course, it is exactly the way that proverbs comment on sexuality in a metaphorical way that makes these texts especially interesting.

The word "shit", less taboo in fine society than in former times, is quite prevalent in this type of proverbs. But this scatological term does not really refer to feces as such in most of these proverbs but rather to something bad or unpleasant. This is also the case for the slang term "bullshit" (often cited in its abbreviated form as B.S.) with the meaning of "nonsense, lies, or exaggeration". A few examples, with the short proverb "Shit happens" (1944, 228; Rees 2005) and its clean variant "Stuff happens" being very popular indeed, will illustrate this:

> Shit (Piss) or get off the pot. (1935, 204)
> Don't shit where you eat. (1953, 227)
> If you stir (up) shit, it will stink (you raise a stink). (1982, 227–228)
> Shit flows (runs, rolls) downhill. (1971, 228)
> Shit rubs off. (1997, 229)
> You can't kill shit (Shit never dies). (1997, 229; Winick 2004)

A few other proverbs dealing with urination, flatulence, and feces (i.e., turds) are clear indications that people at least at times rely on this more or less crassly expressed wisdom as a summary of some of the unpleasant aspects of human interaction:

> The one who smelt it dealt it. (1971, 185)
> It's better to be pissed off than pissed on. (1974, 198)
> Don't eat yellow snow [reference to urine]. (1971, 236)
> Don't kick a (fresh) turd on a hot day. (1980, 265–266)

Male genitalia, that is, testicles and the penis, appear in various slang transmutations, with "balls" in the two proverbs listed below usually not being thought of as testicles by speakers. In other words, the metaphorical proverb legitimizes a slang word so that the proverb "Take the bull by the balls" (1954, 28–29) with the meaning of taking charge of a situation becomes quite innocuous.

> Grab them (If you've got them) by the balls, their hearts and minds will follow. (1967, 12)
> Big car, small dick (prick). (1991, 33)
> Chicks [girls] before dicks.
> Don't let your meat [penis] loaf. (1969, 164–165)
> Big mouth, small pecker (dick, prick). (1993, 173)

As can be seen from these texts, males showing off with big cars or a big mouth are quickly ridiculed by the claim that their apparent wealth and boisterousness is but a psychological cover-up for a small penis size that in this case serves as a weakening of their masculinity. Only the proverb "Don't let your meat loaf" actually has a sexual meaning in that it gives the advice that a man ought not to let his meat (penis) be inactive. Of course, it is a well-known fact that males as well as females have had their questions about the matter of penis size, and this concern has found its way into modern proverbs as well. As sex surveys have shown, the feeling about the importance of penis size for sexual satisfaction differs considerably, and this is mirrored in the conflicting proverbs about this topic as well:

> It's not the meat, it's the motion. (1951, 165)
> It's not the size of the boat (ship) but the motion of the ocean (that matters). (1968, 232)
> Size does matter. (1964, 232–233)
> Size doesn't matter (it's what you do with it, it's how you use it). (1903, 233)

In any case, sexual intercourse appears to be the talk of the town everywhere, with some of the proverbs dealing with this matter being quite crude. But not just that, for they also show that their male originators unfortunately at times express an aggressive or even violent attitude toward women seen as mere sex objects:

> Old enough to bleed, old enough to breed (butcher, stick, etc.). (1971, 22–23)
> Fuck them (Find them, fuck them) and forget them. (1922, 89–90)
> If there's grass on the field [woman's pubic area], (you can) play ball. (1998, 111)
> If she smokes, she pokes [fornicates]. (1996, 235)

Much more positive are the two related proverbs "The blacker the berry (meat), the sweeter the juice" (1929, 19) and "The blacker the meat, the sweeter the bone (piece)" (1935, 164) that are part of the rich African-American proverb tradition (Daniel, Smitherman-Donaldson, and Jeremiah 1987, Prahlad 1996). While they are clearly sexual metaphors, they do look positively at black women, as we documented in the following entry:

> The blacker the berry (meat), the sweeter the juice. 1929 *Chicago Defender* 2 Mar.: "They tell me that 'The blacker the berry, the sweeter the Juice:' is that so?" 1929 Wallace Thurman, *The Blacker the Berry* (New York: Macaulay) [3]; an epigraph to the novel gives the full form, presented as verse: "The blacker the berry / The sweeter the juice"—identifying it as a "Negro folk saying."

1934 Zora Neale Hurston, *Jonah's Gourd Vine* (Philadelphia: J. B. Lippincott) 234: "Ah could uh married one uh dem French women but shucks, gimme uh brown skin eve'y time. Blacker de berry sweeter de juice." [...] Cf. "The blacker the MEAT, the sweeter the bone." The proverb praises blackness, usually in regard to sexual desirability. (Prahlad 1996: 209–210)

Little wonder that modern Anglo-American proverbs also include cautionary texts that warn against sex at an early age, advocate safe sex, and also declare that people have the right to refuse a sexual encounter:

Keep your dress down and your panties (drawers) up. (1975, 62–63)
No glove, no love. (1982, 99)
No means "no." (1980, 178–179)

And what is the proverbial wisdom on sex in general, with the short word "sex" finally also appearing in a proverb collection? Once again we have conflicting attitudes, and the proverb "Everybody lies about sex" (1973, 226) most likely has a solid truth claim to it: "Bad sex is better than no sex" (1969, 226) and "No sex is better than bad sex" (1984, 226; *Sunday Times [London]*). As the extremely short proverb "Sex sells" (1926, 226) states, sexuality has become a commodity in the modern world obsessed with this topic. These sexual games have little to do with love about which many traditional proverbs comment much more positively without forgetting that love has its problems too (Mieder 1989b).

In conclusion, let me reiterate that Charles Doyle, Fred Shapiro, and I have done our level best to register as many modern Anglo-American proverbs as possible. We have assembled 1422 richly annotated proverbs, of which 731 (51.4%) have never been recorded in paremiographical or paremiological publications before. Regarding the other 691 (48.6%) proverbs, they were located text by text in numerous collections and scholarly books and articles. We have thus unearthed and registered an impressive proverbial corpus for the first time in one and the same place in our *Dictionary of Modern Proverbs* (2012), and we hope that other proverb scholars will follow suit by compiling collections of modern proverbs for their languages and cultures. Regarding our collection, I can offer two more statistics that might be of considerable interest. Regarding the distribution of our 1422 texts over the eleven decades from 1900 to 2010, it can be stated that the number of new proverbs appearing on the scene is quite constant, albeit with a noticeable drop-off during the two most recent decades:

```
1900–1909: 155 proverbs
1910–1919: 169
1920–1929: 152
1930–1939: 149
1940–1949: 124
1950–1959: 139
1960–1969: 154
1970–1979: 152
1980–1989: 116
1990–1999: 86
2000–2009 26
(2010/11)  0
total      1422
```

With time and more research, I would imagine that more proverbs will be identified for the period from 1990 to 2010 and beyond (see now the three supplements by Doyle and Mieder 2016, 2018, and 2020), and since proverbs will surely be created as time goes on, the immediate presence will also yield proverbs that will be discovered in due time. And here then is the last statistical information with the caveat that it is at times difficult to decide whether a certain proverb is metaphorical or not. But keeping such questionable cases in mind, 676 (47.5%) of our 1422 proverbs are clearly metaphorical, with slightly more than half of our corpus (746, 52.5%) being literal statements. In order to draw definitive conclusions from this data, statistical information concerning the metaphorical—non-metaphorical dichotomy of traditional proverbs would have to be obtained. For now, it is reasonable to state that modern Anglo-American proverbs might well be less metaphorical than the proverbs from earlier periods. But that is not to say that such eminently American proverbs as "Different strokes for different folks" (1945, 241–242; McKenzie 1996, Mieder 1989a: 317–332, 2006), "The grass is always greener on the other side of the fence" (1913, 110–111; Mieder 1993b [1994]), and "A picture is worth a thousand words" (1911, 196;

Mieder 1990a [1993a], 2005a) with their international dissemination in English or loan translations are not as metaphorical as proverbs usually come (Mieder 2005b, 2005c)! One thing is for certain, proverbs are well and alive in the modern age (Mieder 1993a), and as folk wisdom they express the attitudes, beliefs, mores, and values of the people who use them. As such they are indeed "monumenta humana" (Kuusi 1957: 52) and warrant the attention of paremiographers and paremiologists throughout the world who, in order to identify and interpret them, must, to speak proverbially, "Think outside the box."

Bibliography

This chapter was first published as "'Think Outside the Box': Origin, Nature, and Meaning of Modern Anglo-American Proverbs." *Proverbium*, 29 (2012), 137–196. It has been revised so that all the examples given are of American and not British origin.

Anthropophyteia. 1904–1913. *Anthropophyteia. Jahrbuch für ethnologische, folkloristische und kulturgeschichtliche Sexualforschungen*. Ed. Friedrich S. Krauss. 10. vols. Leipzig: Ethnologischer Verlag.

Arora, Shirley L. 1988 "'No Tickee, No Shirtee': Proverbial Speech and Leadership in Academe." *Inside Organizations: Understanding the Human Dimension*. Eds. Michael Owen Jones, Michael Dane Moore, and Richard Christopher Snyder. Newbury Park, CA: Sage Publishers. 179–189.

Barbour, Frances M. 1963. "Some Uncommon Sources of Proverbs." *Midwest Folklore*, 13: 97–100.

Barrick, Mac E. 1979. "Better Red than Dead." *American Notes and Queries*, 17: 143–144.

Barrick, Mac E. 1986. "Where's the Beef?" *Midwestern Journal of Language and Folklore*, 12: 43–46.

Bernstein, Ignace. 1908. *Jüdische Sprichwörter und Redensarten*. Warschau: Kauffmann; rpt. ed. Hans Peter Althaus. Hildesheim: Georg Olms, 1969; rpt. again Wiesbaden: Fourier, 1988.

Bernstein, Ignace. 1918. *Proverbia Judaeorum Erotica et Turpia. Jüdische Sprichwörter erotischen und rustikalen Inhalts*. Als Manuskript gedruckt. Wien and Berlin: R. Löwit; rpt. Haifa: "Renaissance" Publishing, 1971.

Bertram, Anne, and Richard Spears. 1993. *NTC's Dictionary of Proverbs and Clichés*. Lincolnwood, IL: National Textbook Company.

Bloch, Arthur. 1979. *Murphy's Law and Other Reasons Why Things Go Wrong*. Los Angeles, CA: Price, Stern, Sloan Publishers.

Bloch, Arthur. 1982a. *Murphy's Law. Book Two. More Reasons Why Things Go Wrong*. Los Angeles, CA: Price, Stern, Sloan Publishers.

Bloch, Arthur. 1982b. *Murphy's Law. Book Three. Wrong Reasons Why Things Go More*. Los Angeles, CA: Price, Stern, Sloan Publishers.

Broek, Marinus A. van den. 2002. *Erotisch Spreekwoordenboek. Spreekwoorden en zegswijzen*. Antwerpen: L.J. Veen.

Bryan, George B. 1999. "The Proverbial W.S. Gilbert: An Index to Proverbs in the Works of Gilbert and Sullivan." *Proverbium*, 16: 21–35.

Bryan, George B. 2001. "An Unfinished List of Anglo-American Proverb Songs." *Proverbium*, 18: 15–56.

Bryan, George B., and Wolfgang Mieder. 2005. *A Dictionary of Anglo-American Proverbs & Proverbial Phrases Found in Literary Sources of the Nineteenth and Twentieth Centuries*. New York: Peter Lang.

Chlosta, Christoph, and Peter Grzybek. 1995. "Empirical and Folkloristic Paremiology: Two to Quarrel or to Tango?" *Proverbium*, 12: 67–85.

Chlosta, Christoph, and Torsten Ostermann. 2002. "Suche *Apfel* Finde *Stamm*. Überlegungen zur Nutzung des Internats in der Sprichwortforschung." *"Wer A sägt, muss auch B sägen": Beiträge zur Phraseologie und Sprichwortforschung aus dem Westfälischen Arbeitskreis*. Eds. Dietrich Hartmann and Jan Wirrer. Baltmannsweiler: Schneider Verlag Hohengehren. 39–56.

Colson, Jean-Pierre. 2007. "The World Wide Web as a Corpus for Set Phrases." *Phraseology. An International Handbook of Contemporary Research*. Eds. Harald Burger, Dmitrij Dobrovol'skij, Peter Kühn, and Neal R. Norrick. 2 vols. Berlin: Walter de Gruyter. II, 1071–1077.

Daniel, Jack L., Geneva Smitherman-Donaldson, and Milford A. Jeremiah. 1987. "Makin' a Way Outa No Way: The Proverb Tradition in Black Experience." *Journal of Black Studies*, 17: 482–508.

Doyle, Charles Clay. 1996. "On 'New' Proverbs and the Conservativeness of Proverb Dictionaries." *Proverbium*, 13: 69–84. Also in *Cognition, Comprehension, and Communication: A Decade of North American Proverb Studies (1990–2000)*. Ed. Wolfgang Mieder. Baltmannsweiler: Schneider Verlag Hohengehren, 2003. 85–98.

Doyle, Charles Clay. 2001. "Is the Third Time a Charm? A Review of *The Concise Oxford Dictionary of Proverbs*." *Proverbium*, 18: 453–468.

Doyle, Charles Clay. 2007a. "A Good Man Is Hard to Find: The Proverb." *Flannery O'Connor Review*, 5: 5–22.

Doyle, Charles Clay. 2007b. "Collections of Proverbs and Proverb Dictionaries: Some Historical Observations on What's in Them and What's Not (with a Note on Current 'Gendered' Proverbs)." *Phraseology and Culture in English*. Ed. Paul Skandera. Berlin: Mouton de Gruyter. 181–203.

Doyle, Charles Clay. 2009. "'Use It or Lose It': The Proverb, Its Pronoun, and Their Antecedents." *Proverbium*, 26: 105–118.

Doyle, Charles Clay, and Wolfgang Mieder. 2016. "*The Dictionary of Modern Proverbs*: A Supplement." *Proverbium*, 33: 85–120.

Doyle, Charles Clay, and Wolfgang Mieder. 2018. "*The Dictionary of Modern Proverbs*: Second Supplement." *Proverbium*, 35: 15–44.

Doyle, Charles Clay, and Wolfgang Mieder. 2020. *"The Dictionary of Modern Proverbs*: Third Supplement." *Proverbium*, 37: 53–86.

Doyle, Charles Clay, Wolfgang Mieder, and Fred R. Shapiro. 2012. *The Dictionary of Modern Proverbs*. New Haven, CT: Yale University Press.

Dundes, Alan. 1966. "Here I Sit—A Study of American Latrinalia." *The Kroeber Anthropological Society Papers*, 34: 91–105. Also in A. Dundes, *The Meaning of Folklore. The Analytical Essays of Alan Dundes*. Ed. Simon J. Bronner. Logan, UT: Utah State University Press, 2007. 360–374.

Dundes, Alan. 1972. "Folk Ideas as Units of Worldview." *Towards New Perspectives in Folklore*. Eds. Américo Paredes and Richard Bauman. Austin, TX: University of Texas Press. 93–103. Also in A. Dundes, *The Meaning of Folklore. The Analytical Essays of Alan Dundes*. Ed. Simon J. Bronner. Logan, UT: Utah State University Press, 2007. 179–192.

Dundes, Alan. 1975. "On the Structure of the Proverb." *Proverbium*, no. 25: 961–973. Also in *The Wisdom of Many. Essays on the Proverb*. Eds. W. Mieder and Alan Dundes. New York: Garland Publishing. 43–64.

Dundes, Alan, and Carl R. Pagter. 1987. *When You're Up to Your Ass in Alligators: More Urban Folklore from the Paperwork Empire*. Detroit, MI: Wayne State University Press.

Dundes, Lauren, Michael Streiff, and Alan Dundes. 1999. " 'When You Hear Hoofbeats, Think Horses, Not Zebras': A Folk Medical Diagnostic Proverb." *Proverbium*, 16: 95–103. Also in *Cognition, Comprehension, and Communication: A Decade of North American Proverb Studies (1990–2000)*. Ed. Wolfgang Mieder. Baltmannsweiler: Schneider Verlag Hohengehren, 2003. 99–107.

Flavell, Linda, and Roger Flavell. 1993. *Dictionary of Proverbs and Their Origins*. London: Kyle Cathie.

Fogel, Edwin Miller. 1929. *Proverbs of the Pennsylvania Germans*. Lancaster, PA: Lancaster Press; rpt. ed. Wolfgang Mieder. Bern: Peter Lang, 1995.

Fogel, Edwin Miller. 1929. *Supplement to Proverbs of the Pennsylvania Germans*. Fogelsville, PA: Americana Germanica Press.

Folsom, Steven. 1993. "A Discography of American Country Music Hits Employing Proverbs: Covering the Years 1986–1992." *Proceedings for the 1993 Annual Conference of the Southwest-Texas Popular Culture Association*. Ed. Sue Poor. Stillwater, OK: Southwest-Texas Popular Culture Association. 31–42.

Frank, Lawrence. 1983. *Playing Hardball. The Dynamics of Baseball Folk Speech*. New York: Peter Lang.

Grose, Francis. 1785. *A Classical Dictionary of the Vulgar Tongue*. London: S. Hooper, 1785; rpt. ed. Eric Partridge. London: Scholartis Press, 1931; rpt. once again New York: Dorset Press, 1992.

Grzybek, Peter. 2000. "Zum Status der Untersuchung von Satzlängen in der Sprichwortforschung: Methodologische Vor-Bemerkungen." *Slovo vo vremeni i prostranstve. K 60-letiiu professora V.M. Mokienko*. Eds. G.A. Lilich, A.K. Birikh, and E.K. Nikolaeva. Sankt-Peterburg: Folio-Press. 430–457.

Haas, Heather H. 2008. "Proverb Familiarity in the United States: Cross-Regional Comparisons of the Paremiological Minimum." *Journal of American Folklore*, 121: 319–347.

Hernadi, Paul, and Francis Steen. 1999. "The Tropical Landscape of Proverbia: A Crossdisciplinary Travelogue." *Style*, 33: 1–20. Also in *Cognition, Comprehension, and Communication: A Decade of North American Proverb Studies (1990–2000)*. Ed. Wolfgang Mieder. Baltmannsweiler: Schneider Verlag Hohengehren, 2003. 185–204.

Higbee, Kenneth L., and Richard J. Millard. 1983. "Visual Imagery and Familiarity Ratings for 203 Sayings." *American Journal of Psychology*, 96: 211–222.

Hoffman, Robert R., and Richard P. Honeck. 1987. "Proverbs, Pragmatics, and the Ecology of Abstract Categories." *Cognition and Symbolic Structures: The Psychology of Metaphoric Transformation*. Ed. Robert E. Haskell. Norwood, NJ: Ablex Publishing. 121–140.

Honeck, Richard P., and Jeffrey Welge. 1997. "Creation of Proverbial Wisdom in the Laboratory." *Journal of Psycholinguistic Research*, 26: 605–629. Also in *Cognition, Comprehension, and Communication. A Decade of North American Proverb Studies (1990–2000)*. Ed. Wolfgang Mieder. Baltmannsweiler: Schneider Verlag Hohengehren, 2003. 205–230.

Jente, Richard. 1931–1932. "The American Proverb." *American Speech*, 7: 342–348.

Kerschen, Lois. 1998. *American Proverbs about Women. A Reference Guide*. Westport, CT: Greenwood Press.

Kirshenblatt-Gimblett, Barbara. 1973. "Toward a Theory of Proverb Meaning." *Proverbium*, no. 22: 821–827. Also in *The Wisdom of Many. Essays on the Proverb*. Eds. Wolfgang Mieder and Alan Dundes. New York: Garland Publishing. 111–121.

Kleinberger Günther, Ulla. 2006. "Phraseologie und Sprichwörter in der digitalen Öffentlichkeit—am Beispiel von Chats." *Phraseology in Motion I. Methoden und Kritik. Akten der Internationalen Tagung zur Phraseologie (Basel, 2004)*. Eds. Annelies Häcki Buhofer and Harald Burger. Baltmannsweiler: Schneider Verlag Hohengehren. 229–243.

Krummenacher, Adrian. 2007. " 'To Live and Let Die': Sprichwörter, Redensarten und Zitate in den James-Bond-Filmen." *Sprichwörter sind Goldes wert. Parömiologische Studien zu Kultur, Literatur und Medien*. Ed. Wolfgang Mieder. Burlington, VT: The University of Vermont. 127–152.

Kryptadia. 1883–1911. No editor given. *Kryptadia. Recueil de documents pour servir à l'étude des traditions populaires*, 12 vols. Paris: H. Welter; rpt. Darmstadt: J.G. Bläschke, 1970.

Kuusi, Matti. 1957. *Parömiologische Betrachtungen*. Helsinki: Suomalainen Tiedeakatemia.

Lau, Kimberly J. 1996. " 'It's about Time': The Ten Proverbs Most Frequently Used in Newspapers and Their Relation to American Values." *Proverbium*, 13: 135–159. Also in *Cognition, Comprehension, and Communication. A Decade of North American Proverb Studies (1990–2000)*. Ed. Wolfgang Mieder. Baltmannsweiler: Schneider Verlag Hohengehren, 2003. 231–254.

Lau, Kimberly J., Peter Tokofsky, and Stephen D. Winick, eds. 2004. *What Goes Around Comes Around: The Circulation of Proverbs in Contemporary Life. Essays in Honor of Wolfgang Mieder*. Logan, UT: Utah State University Press.

Lauhakangas, Outi. 2001. "How to Avoid Losing a Needle in a Haystack. Challenges and Problems of Compiling Paremiological Databases." *Tautosakos Darbai/Folklore Studies* (Vilnius, Lithuania), 22: 93–102.

Litovkina, Anna T. 2000. *A Proverb a Day Keeps Boredom Away*. Pécs-Szekszárd, Hungary: IPF-Könyek.

Litovkina, Anna T., and Carl Lindahl, eds. 2007. *Anti-proverbs in Contemporary Societies*. Budapest: Akadémiai Kiadó. (*Acta Ethnographica Hungarica* 52).

Litovkina, Anna T., and Wolfgang Mieder. 2006. *Old Proverbs Never Die, They Just Diversify: A Collection of Anti-proverbs*. Burlington, VT: The University of Vermont; Veszprém, Hungary: Pannonian University of Veszprém.

Mahoney, Dennis F. 2009. "'The Bird and the Fish Can Fall in Love …': Proverbs and Anti-proverbs as Variations on the Theme of Racial and Cultural Intermingling." *The Proverbial "Pied Piper." A Festschrift Volume of Essays in Honor of Wolfgang Mieder on the Occasion of His Sixty-Fifth Birthday* Ed. Kevin J. McKenna. New York: Peter Lang, 245–256.

Maledicta. 1977–2004. *Maledicta. The International Journal of Verbal Aggression*. Ed. Reinhold Aman. 13 vols. Waukesha, WI: Maledicta Press.

Manser, Martin H. 2002. *Facts on File Dictionary of Proverbs*. New York: Facts on File.

McKenzie, Alyce M. 1996. "'Different Strokes for Different Folks': America's Quintessential Postmodern Proverb." *Theology Today*, 53: 201–212.

Mieder, Barbara, and Wolfgang Mieder. 1977. "Tradition and Innovation: Proverbs in Advertising." *Journal of Popular Culture*, 11: 308–319. Also in *The Wisdom of Many. Essays on the Proverb*. Eds. W. Mieder and Alan Dundes. New York: Garland Publishing, 1981. 309–322.

Mieder, Wolfgang. 1982. "'Eine Frau ohne Mann ist wie ein Fisch ohne Velo.'" *Sprachspiegel*, 38: 141–142.

Mieder, Wolfgang. 1985. *Sprichwort, Redensart, Zitat. Tradierte Formelsprache in der Moderne*. Bern: Peter Lang.

Mieder, Wolfgang. 1987. "The Proverb in the Modern Age: Old Wisdom in New Clothing." *Tradition and Innovation in Folk Literature*. Ed. W. Mieder. Hanover, NH: University Press of New England. 118–156 and 248–255 (notes). Also in W. Mieder, *Proverbs Are Never Out of Season: Popular Wisdom in the Modern Age*. New York: Oxford University Press. 58–96.

Mieder, Wolfgang. 1988. "Proverbs in American Popular Songs." *Proverbium*, 5: 85–101.

Mieder, Wolfgang. 1989a. *American Proverbs: A Study of Texts and Contexts*. Bern: Peter Lang.

Mieder, Wolfgang. 1989b. *Love. Proverbs of the Heart*. Shelburne, VT: New England Press.

Mieder, Wolfgang. 1990a. "'A Picture Is Worth a Thousand Words': From Advertising Slogan to American Proverb." *Southern Folklore*, 47: 207–225. Also in W. Mieder,

Proverbs Are Never Out of Season: Popular Wisdom in the Modern Age. New York: Oxford University Press, 1993. 135–151.

Mieder, Wolfgang. 1990b. "Prolegomena to Prospective Paremiography." *Proverbium*, 7: 133–144.

Mieder, Wolfgang. 1992. "Paremiological Minimum and Cultural Literacy." *Creativity and Tradition in Folklore*. Ed. Simon J. Bronner. Logan, UT: Utah State University Press. 185–203. Also in *Wise Words: Essays on the Proverb*. Ed. W. Mieder. New York: Garland Publishing, 1994. 297–316.

Mieder, Wolfgang. 1993a. *Proverbs Are Never Out of Season: Popular Wisdom in the Modern Age*. New York: Oxford University Press; rpt. New York: Peter Lang, 2012.

Mieder, Wolfgang. 1993b. "'The Grass Is Always Greener on the Other Side of the Fence." *Proverbium*, 10: 151–184. Also in *Wise Words: Essays on the Proverb*. Ed. W. Mieder. New York: Garland Publishing, 1994. 515–542.

Mieder, Wolfgang, ed. 1994. *Wise Words: Essays on the Proverb*. New York: Garland Publishing.

Mieder, Wolfgang. 1996. "'No Tickee, No Washee': Subtleties of a Proverbial Slur." *Western Folklore*, 55: 1–40. Also in W. Mieder, *The Politics of Proverbs. From Traditional Wisdom to Proverbial Stereotypes*. Madison, WI: The University of Wisconsin Press, 1997. 160–189 and 227–235 (notes).

Mieder, Wolfgang. 1997. *The Politics of Proverbs. From Traditional Wisdom to Proverbial Stereotypes*. Madison, WI: The University of Wisconsin Press.

Mieder, Wolfgang. 2000. "'Proverbs Bring it to Light': Modern Paremiology in Retrospect and Prospect." *Strategies of Wisdom. Anglo-American and German Proverb Studies*. Ed. W. Mieder. Baltmannsweiler: Schneider Verlag Hohengehren. 7–36

Mieder, Wolfgang, ed. 2003a. *Cognition, Comprehension, and Communication: A Decade of North American Proverb Studies (1990–2000)*. Baltmannsweiler: Schneider Verlag Hohengehren.

Mieder, Wolfgang. 2003b. *English Proverbs*. Stuttgart: Phillip Reclam.

Mieder, Wolfgang. 2004. *Proverbs: A Handbook*. Westport, CT: Greenwood Press; rpt. New York: Peter Lang, 2012.

Mieder, Wolfgang. 2005a. "'A Proverb Is Worth a Thousand Words': Folk Wisdom in the Modern Mass Media." *Proverbium*, 22: 167–233.

Mieder, Wolfgang. 2005b. "American Proverbs as an International, National, and Global Phenomenon." *Tautosakos Darbai/Folklore Studies* (Vilnius, Lithuania), 30: 57–72. Also in W. Mieder, *Proverbs Are the Best Policy: Folk Wisdom and American Politics*. Logan, UT: Utah State University Press, 2005. 1–14 and 244–248 (notes).

Mieder, Wolfgang. 2005c. *Proverbs Are the Best Policy: Folk Wisdom and American Politics*. Logan, UT: Utah State University Press.

Mieder, Wolfgang. 2006. "'Different Strokes for Different Folks.'" *Encyclopedia of African American Folklore*. Ed. Sw. Anand Prahlad. 3 vols. Westport, CT: Greenwood Press. I: 324–327.

Mieder, Wolfgang. 2009a. "New Proverbs Run Deep: Prolegomena to a Dictionary of Modern Anglo-American Proverbs." *Proverbium*, 26: 237–274.

Mieder, Wolfgang. 2009b. *"Yes We Can"*. *Barack Obama's Proverbial Rhetoric.* New York: Peter Lang.

Mieder, Wolfgang. 2010a. *Making a Way Out of No Way: Martin Luther King's Sermonic Proverbial Rhetoric.* New York: Peter Lang.

Mieder, Wolfgang. 2010b. "The Golden Rule as a Political Imperative for the World: President Barack Obama's Proverbial Messages Abroad." *Millî Folklor,* 22: 26–35.

Mieder, Wolfgang. 2010c. "'The World Is a Place': Barack Obama's Proverbial View of an Interconnected Globe." *Sopostavitel'naia filologiia i polilingvizm.* Eds. A.A. Aminova and N.N. Fattakhova. Kazan': G. Ibragimova An RT. 192–196.

Mieder, Wolfgang. 2011. "'It Takes a Village to Change the World': Proverbial Politics and the Ethics of Place." *Journal of American Folklore,* 124: 4–28.

Mieder, Wolfgang. 2014. "'You Have to Kiss a Lot of Frogs (Toads) Before You Meet Your Handsome Prince': From Fairy-Tale Motif to Modern Proverb." *Marvels & Tales: Journal of Fairy-Tale Studies,* 28: 104–126.

Mieder, Wolfgang, and Alan Dundes, eds. 1981. *The Wisdom of Many. Essays on the Proverb.* New York: Garland Publishing.

Mieder, Wolfgang, and George B. Bryan. 1983. "'Zum Tango gehören zwei'." *Der Sprachdienst,* 27: 100–102 and 181. Also in W. Mieder, *Sprichwort, Redensart, Zitat. Tradierte Formelsprache in der Moderne.* Bern: Peter Lang, 1985. 151–154.

Mieder, Wolfgang, and George B. Bryan. 1997. *The Proverbial Harry S. Truman. An Index to Proverbs in the Works of Harry S. Truman.* New York: Peter Lang.

Mieder, Wolfgang, and Janet Sobieski, ed. 2006. *"Gold Nuggets or Fool's Gold?" Magazine and Newspaper Articles on the (Ir)relevance of Proverbs and Proverbial Phrases.* Burlington, VT: The University of Vermont.

Mieder, Wolfgang, Stewart A. Kingsbury, and Kelsie B. Harder, eds. 1992. *A Dictionary of American Proverbs.* New York: Oxford University Press.

Nierenberg, Jess. 1983. "Proverbs in Graffiti: Taunting Traditional Wisdom." *Maledicta,* 7: 41–58. Also in *Wise Words: Essays on the Proverb.* Ed. Wolfgang Mieder. New York: Garland Publishing. 543–561.

Nussbaum, Stan. 2005. *American Cultural Baggage [i.e., Proverbs]. How to Recognize and Deal with It.* Maryknoll, New York: Orbis.

Petrova, Roumyana. 1996. "Language and Culture: One Step Further in the Search for Common Ground." *Europe from East to West. Proceedings of the First International European Studies Conference.* Eds. Martin Dangerfield, Glyn Hambrook, and Ludmilla Kostova. Varna, Bulgaria: PIC. 237–248.

Pickering, David. 2001. *Cassell's Dictionary of Proverbs.* 2nd ed. London: Cassell.

Pickering, David, Alan Isaacs, and Elizabeth Martin. 1992. *Brewer's Dictionary of 20th-Century Phrase and Fable.* Boston: Houghton Mifflin.

Prahlad, Sw. Anand. 1994. "'No Guts, No Glory': Proverbs, Values and Image among Anglo-American University Students." *Southern Folklore,* 51: 285–298. Also in *Cognition, Comprehension, and Communication. A Decade of North American Proverb*

Studies (1990–2000). Ed. Wolfgang Mieder. Baltmannsweiler: Schneider Verlag Hohengehren, 2003. 443–458.

Prahlad, Sw. Anand. 1996. *African-American Proverbs in Context*. Jackson, MS: University Press of Mississippi.

Prahlad, Sw. Anand. 2001. *Reggae Wisdom: Proverbs in Jamaican Music*. Jackson, MS: University Press of Mississippi.

Prahlad, Sw. Anand. 2004. "The Proverb and Fetishism in American Advertisements." *What Goes Around Comes Around: The Circulation of Proverbs in Contemporary Life. Essays in Honor of Wolfgang Mieder*. Eds. Kimberly J. Lau, Peter Tokofsky, and Stephen D. Winick. Logan, UT: Utah State University Press. 127–151.

Prahlad, Sw. Anand, ed. 2006. *Encyclopedia of African American Folklore*. 3 vols. Westport, CT: Greenwood Press.

Ratcliffe, Susan. 2006. *Oxford Dictionary of Phrase, Saying, and Quotation*. 3rd ed. Oxford: Oxford University Press.

Rees, Nigel. 1984. *Sayings of the Century. The Stories Behind the Twentieth Century's Quotable Sayings*. London: Allen & Unwin.

Rees, Nigel. 1991. *Bloomsbury Dictionary of Phrase & Allusion*. London: Bloomsbury.

Rees, Nigel. 1995. *Phrases & Sayings*. London: Bloomsbury.

Rees, Nigel. 2005. "'Shit Happens'." *"Quote … Unquote" Newsletter*, 14, no. 2: 6.

Rees, Nigel. 2006. *A Word in Your Shell-Like: 6,000 Curious and Everyday Phrases Explained*. London: HarperCollins.

Rittersbacher, Christa, and Matthias Mösch. 2005. "A Haystack Full of Precious Needles—The Internet and Its Utility for Paremiologists." *Proverbium*, 22: 337–362.

Room, Adrian. 2000. *Brewer's Dictionary of Modern Phrase & Fable*. London: Cassell.

Russell, Melissa Anne. 1999. "Kill 'Em All and Let God Sort 'Em Out: The Proverb as an Expression of Verbal Aggression." *Proverbium*, 16: 287–302.

Schipper, Mineke. 2003. *"Never Marry a Woman with Big Feet": Women in Proverbs from Around the World*. New Haven, CT: Yale University Press.

Sevilla Muñoz, Julia. 2009. "The Challenges of Paremiology in the XXI. Century." *Proceedings of the Second Interdisciplinary Colloquium on Proverbs, 9th to 16th November 2008*. Eds. Rui J.B. Soares and Outi Lauhakangas. Tavira: Tipografia Tavirense. 438–448.

Shapiro, Fred. 2006. *Yale Book of Quotations*. New Haven, CT: Yale University Press.

Sobieski, Janet, and Wolfgang Mieder, eds. 2005. *"So Many Heads, So Many Wits". An Anthology of English Proverb Poetry*. Burlington, VT: The University of Vermont.

Speake, Jennifer. 2008. *The Oxford Dictionary of Proverbs*. 5th ed. Oxford: Oxford University Press.

Stevenson, Burton. 1948. *Home Book of Proverbs, Maxims and Familiar Phrases*. New York: Macmillan.

Taft, Michael. 1994. "Proverbs in the Blues: How Frequent Is Frequent?" *Proverbium*, 11: 227–258.

Taylor, Archer. 1931. *The Proverb*. Cambridge, MA: Harvard University Press; rpt. ed. Wolfgang Mieder. Bern: Peter Lang, 1985.

Taylor, Archer. 1939. "The Study of Proverbs." *Modern Language Forum*, 24: 57–83. Also in A. Taylor, *Selected Writings on Proverbs*. Ed. Wolfgang Mieder. Helsinki: Suomalainen Tiedeakatemia. 40–47 (co-authored with Bartlett Jere Whiting, Francis W. Bradley, Richard Jente, and Morris Palmer Tilley).

Taylor, Archer. 1958. "'The Customer Is Always Right'." *Western Folklore*, 17: 54–55.

Taylor, Archer. 1969. "How Nearly Complete Are the Collections of Proverbs?" *Proverbium*, no. 14: 369–371.

Titelman, Gregory. 2000. *Random House Dictionary of America's Popular Proverbs and Sayings*. 2nd ed. New York: Random House.

Tóthné Litovkina, Anna. 1998. "An Analysis of Popular American Proverbs [found in the Folklore Archive at UC Berkeley] and Their Use in Language Teaching." *Die heutige Bedeutung oraler Tradition: Ihre Archivierung, Publikation und Index-Erschließung*. Eds. Walther Heissig and Rüdiger Schott. Opladen: Westdeutscher Verlag. 131–158.

Umurova, Gulnas. 2005. *Was der Volksmund in einem Sprichwort verpackt ... Moderne Aspekte des Sprichwortgebrauchs—anhand von Beispielen aus dem Internet*. Bern: Peter Lang.

Valdaeva, Tatiana. 2003. "Anti-proverbs or New Proverbs: The Use of English Anti-proverbs and Their Stylistic Analysis." *Proverbium*, 20: 379–390.

White, Geoffrey M. 1987. "Proverbs and Cultural Models: An American Psychology of Problem Solving." *Cultural Models in Language and Thought*. Eds. Dorothy Holland and Naomi Quinn. Cambridge: Cambridge University Press. 151–172.

Whiting, Bartlett Jere. 1989. *Modern Proverbs and Proverbial Sayings*. Cambridge, MA: Harvard University Press.

Wilson, F.P. 1970. *Oxford Dictionary of English Proverbs*. 3rd ed. Oxford: Clarendon Press.

Winick, Stephen D. 1998. *The Proverb Process: Intertextuality and Proverbial Innovation in Popular Culture*. Diss. University of Pennsylvania.

Winick, Stephen D. 2001. "'Garbage In, Garbage Out,' and Other Dangers: Using Computer Databases to Study Proverbs." *Proverbium*, 18: 354–364.

Winick, Stephen D. 2003. "Intertextuality and Innovation in a Definition of the Proverb Genre." *Cognition, Comprehension, and Communication. A Decade of North American Proverb Studies (1990–2000)*. Ed. Wolfgang Mieder. Baltmannsweiler: Schneider Verlag Hohengehren. 571–601.

Winick, Stephen D. 2004. "'You Can't Kill Shit': Occupational Proverb and Metaphorical System Among Young Medical Professionals." *What Goes Around Comes Around: The Circulation of Proverbs in Contemporary Life. Essays in Honor of Wolfgang Mieder*. Eds. Kimberly J. Lau, Peter Tokofsky, and Stephen D. Winick. Logan, UT: Utah State University Press. 86–106.

Winick, Stephen D. 2011. "Fall into the (Intertextual) Gap: Proverbs, Advertisements and Intertextual Strategies." *Proverbium*, 28: 339–380.

Chapter Two

"The Journey Is the Reward"

Worldview of Modern American Proverbs

There exists an impressive amount of scholarship that has looked at proverbs as expressions of national character, various types of stereotypes, and other types of generalizations (Mieder 2009). In the still useful book *The Wisdom of Many. Essays on the Proverb* (1981) its editors Wolfgang Mieder and Alan Dundes included three essays that reflect this preoccupation in its different manifestations, to wit A.A. Parker's "The Humor of Spanish Proverbs," Matti Kuusi's "Fatalistic Traits in Finnish Proverbs," and F.N. Robinson's "Irish Proverbs and Irish National Character." This enumeration could easily be multiplied by many other studies of this type. While they do have their value, there are also considerable problems with them that put some of their generalized conclusions into question. Basically, all of them do not consider the origin of the proverbs that are cited as examples (Ayas 2001, Honeck and Welge 1997). For example, how can an internationally disseminated classical proverb like "One hand washes the other" have anything to do with the Russian national character where the proverb is also frequently used. Another problem is that the proverbs are discussed without any consideration whether they are still in use and with what frequency. In other word, a misogynous proverb like "A woman's tongue is like a lamb's tail" that has been traced back to the sixteenth-century has long since passed out of use. So how can it be cited today to prove how proverbs spread anti-feminism the modern age? And there is a third issue that complicates and invalidates such studies to a certain degree. The proverbs are almost always given without any contextual information that would reveal the function and actual meaning in a particular situation. All of this adds up to a word of caution with studies that look at proverbs as expressions of cultural or sociological worldview. No matter what, such investigations can only be part of a general view of the world that is, to be sure, in flux in any case and does not belong to every member or group of a given society (Naugle 2002, Nedeva 2014, Norwine and Smith 2000).

As can be imagine, so-called American proverbs represent a particularly vexing problem in this regard. What really is an American proverb? Many American proverbs go back to classical antiquity, the Bible, the Middle Ages with its Latin lingua franca, and to British and other national proverbs brought to the United States. There are also Native American, African-American and many other proverbs from various groups of people (Mieder 1989 and 2015a, Prahlad 1996). In other words, even the massive *Dictionary of American Proverbs* (1992) edited by Wolfgang Mieder, Stewart A. Kingsbury, and Kelsie B. Harder has a highly questionable title. After all, it implies to a certain degree that it contains but proverbs that originated in the United States. And yet, nothing could be further from the truth, with many of the proverbs being of British origin or appearing as loan translations languages and cultures from around the world. In fact, generally speaking, American proverbs are a regional, national, international. and now also global phenomenon in that American proverbs are being spread with English as the lingua franca of the world today (Mieder 2005 and 2015c).

But there is a way out of this mixed-bag background of American proverbs. Both paremiography (proverb collections) and paremiology (proverb studies) have entered the modern age (Mieder 2014). Valerii M. Mokienko in Russia has published his book *Novaia russkaia frazeologiia* (2003) that contains for the first time modern Russian phraseological units. For the Anglo-American language Charles Clay

Doyle, Wolfgang Mieder, and Fred R. Shapiro have done the same in their *Dictionary of Modern Proverbs* (2012) that includes 1422 proverbs. Every two years Doyle and Mieder have published supplements in *Proverbium* (2016, 2018, 2020; identified in parentheses as S1, S2, and S3) that have included 85, 57, and 53 newly registered proverbs. These 195 proverbs plus the 1422 original texts amount to 1617 modern proverbs whose origins are not older than the year 1900. While some of them are slightly older than one hundred year, others have been coined but a few years ago in the twenty-first century. Each text is cited with its first occurrence in print, and there are usually also several additional contextualized references plus explanatory notes included. All of this adds up to a truly unique collection of modern proverbs of which the vast majority is of proven American origin! They represent the proverbial wisdom established during the past twelve decades, and as such they can reveals something about the beliefs, concerns, mores, and thoughts of Americans today. Without wanting to overemphasize the general picture of an American worldview from just about one and a half thousand proverbs, a few careful conclusions can be reached, as can be seen from the 298 (18.4% of the total of 1617) modern American proverbs cited as examples in the following pages. Anthropologists, cultural historians, folklorists, linguists, sociologists, and others can add to this general picture (Dundes 1972, Hakamies 2002, Profantova 1996). Proverbs can help in looking for something like the vague idea of a general worldview if the textual corpus is controlled as it happens to be with these exclusively modern proverbs. As such, they also disprove some unfounded claims that the time for the use of traditional and the creation of new proverbs has passed (Albig 1931, Stewart 1991). There simply is no doubt that "Proverbs are never out of season" (Mieder 1993a).

At this point it is important to mention Stan Nussbaum's interesting book *American Cultural [and Proverbial] Baggage. How to Recognize and Deal with It* (2005). An earlier and smaller version appeared with the more telling title *The ABC of American Culture: First Steps toward Understanding the American People though Their Common Sayings and Proverbs* (1998). In any case, Nussbaum would have done well to have included the adjective "proverbial" [as has been done here] in the expanded edition to indicate that he is presenting a picture of American culture by way of its proverbs (Tierney 2016). The book begins with a discussion of "The 'Ten Commandments' of American Culture":

1. You can't argue with success. (Be a success.)
2. Live and let live. (Be tolerant.)
3. Time flies when you're having fun. (Have lots of fun.)
4. Shop till you drop.
5. Just do it.
6. You are only young once. (Do whatever you can while you have the chance.)
7. Enough is enough. (Stand up for your rights.)
8. Rules are made to be broken. (Think for yourself.)
9. Time is money. (Don't waste time.)
10. God helps those who help themselves. (Work hard.)

On the next 125 pages these commandments are explained by way of citing and discussing close to 250 proverbs that are more or less current in the United States but for the most part not of American origin. Many of the proverbs have entered the English languages through loan translations of proverbs form classical antiquity, the Bible, the Latin Middle Ages, etc. Most of them are of English origin, of course. The point here is that these proverbs are used in other societies as well and do not necessarily say that much about the American culture or worldview even. Nevertheless, it is fair to say that since they are used in large part by Americans today, some conclusions of value can be drawn. Altogether, the proverbs cited by Nussbaum do fall under the ten commandments that reflect American attitudes in general. And to be sure, the modern truly American proverbs fit into some of these categories as well. But since they were all coined on American soil in modern times, they might present an even more valid idea of what makes Americans klick, to put it proverbially.

Charles Doyle in his article "On 'New' Proverbs and the Conservativeness of Proverb Dictionaries" (1996) and Wolfgang Mieder in his analysis " 'Think Outside the Box': Origin, Nature, and Meaning of Modern Anglo-American Proverbs" (2012) have dealt with some of these aforementioned issues. They argue for the importance of collecting and studying modern proverbs that at least in part are considerably different in language and message from older proverbs. One noticeable difference is that modern proverbs are often straight-forward non-metaphorical statements following no particular structure and exhibiting no poetic features like rhyme, parallelism, etc. Might this be the result of a rather realistic, matter of fact, and prosaic language use if not attitude of Americans? The following proverbs certainly allow such a generalization (lists of proverbs are cited in chronological order with their first date of occurrence in print and the page number in *The Dictionary of Modern Proverbs*):

> It pays to pay attention. (1902, 10)
> Think big (big thoughts, big things). (1907, 255)
> There are no foolish (stupid, silly) questions. (1915, 211)
> There are no final answers (solutions). (1916, 6)
> Keep it simple (Keep it short and simple). (1919, 132)
> Tell it like it is. (1939, 251)
> Never say never or always. (1967, 178)
> Keep it real. (1975, 132)

The shortness of several of these proverbs might also reflect the American penchant towards terseness and abbreviation that avoids any metaphorical "beating around the bush." Of note is also the fascinating proverb "Eat it up (Use it up), wear it out, make it do, or do (go) without" (1933, 66) that certainly did not need a metaphor at its most popular use during the difficult times of the thirties and forties when people had to make do with what they had available. But, of course, there is modern proverbial wisdom that is couched into metaphorical language. There are two proverbs in particular that have become so popular that they have also become current in other English-speaking countries and as loan translations in other languages throughout the world. In fact, considering the ever-expanding visualization process in the American society, one can well argue that the proverb "One Picture is worth a thousand words" (1911, 196; Mieder 1990) had to have its start in the United States. Here are a few additional examples of metaphorical proverbs:

Little apples (always) go to the bottom of the barrel. (1912, 6–7)

The grass is always greener on the other side of the fence. (1913, 110–111; Mieder 1993b)

There was never a horse that couldn't be ridden. (1921, 125)

Mud thrown is lost ground. (1923, 175)

Even a blind squirrel can sometimes find a nut (an acorn). (1928, 238–239)

Life is (just) a bowl of cherries. (1931, 141–142)

The nail that sticks out gets pounded (hammered down). (1969, 177)

The sun doesn't shine on (up) the same dog's ass every day. (1976, 246)

Show me a fifty-foot fence, and I'll show you a fifty-one-foot ladder. (1986, 76)

The toes you step on today may be attached to the ass you have to kiss tomorrow. (1999, 261)

The second to the last proverb is of special interest in light of President Donald Trump's fence-building obsession at the Mexican American border to control drug trafficking and illegal immigration. It is also noteworthy that the seventeenth-century British proverb "There's more than one way to skin a cat" has been replaced by the more humane metaphorical proverb "There's more than one way to peel an orange (banana, egg)" (1954, 273–274). Considering Americans' love for felines, this switch makes perfect sense.

As one would expect, coiners of modern proverbs continue to be interested in giving very basic advice by telling their compatriots what not to do. In so doing, they follow the long-established proverbial formula "Don't ..." for the didactic message. In some cases this has resulted in making a proverb out of an older proverbial expressions, as for example "Don't compare apples and oranges" (1949, 6, "to compare apples and oranges") and "Don't reinvent the wheel" (1970, 275; also as proverbial expression: "to reinvent the wheel"). The following examples show the already observed split between literal and figurative proverbs:

Don't let the same bee sting you twice. (1911, 18)

Don't start something you can't finish. (1915, 239–240)

Don't advertise what (if) you cannot fulfill (deliver). (1919, 2–3)

Don't start a fight you can't finish. (1921, 77)

Don't dish it out if you can't take it. (1930, 57)

Don't judge someone till you have walked a mile in his shoes (moccasins). (1930, 166)

Don't make waves. (1934, 271; also as proverbial expression: "to make waves")

Don't use a sledgehammer (hammer) to kill a fly. (1941, S1, 114–115)

Don't get caught with your pants down. (1944, 189)

Don't sweat the small stuff (shit). (1960, 242)

Don't knock it till you've tried it. (1960, 133)

Don't take (tear) down a fence (wall) unless you are sure why it was put up. (1964, 75z0

Don't play with fire if you don't want to get burned. (1977, S3, in print)

There is clearly a predominance of such more or less straight forward advice to proper American behavior based on the individual and his/her relationship to others. The following three texts deserve special comments: Thus, it is interesting to note that the proverb "Don't sweat the small stuff" also exists in the scatological variant "Don't sweat the small shit." In fact, there are numerous modern proverbs that deal with excrements and urination, a sign that such vocabulary is more accepted in the United States in modern times (Mieder 2020). The proverb "Don't burn your bridges in front of you (before you get to them)" (1917, 27) might have originated as an anti-proverb as a blending of the older "Don't burn your bridges behind you" with "Don't cross your bridges before you get to them" (Mieder, Kingsbury, Harder 1992: 71). The proverb "Don't rearrange the deck chairs on the *Titanic*" (1991, 36) is based on the cultural knowledge of the ship catastrophe of 1912 and expresses the idea that one should not undertake futile tasks. And there is also the proverb "Don't miss the donut by looking through the hole" (1999, 6) that is a rephrasing of the older but modern proverb "Keep your eyes on the donut and not on the hole" (1908, 71). Their food-metaphor relates to the lover of Americans for donuts and tells them to emphasize major matters and not get lost in irrelevant matters. Finally, then. there is the all-important proverb "Don't sell America short" 1922, 5–6) that originated on the stock market but that expresses in general terms the problematic view of Americans that their country is exceptional in all matters. The belief in this uncritical exceptionalism is without doubt part of the American worldview and needs correction to be sure.

There are some proverbs that address Americans directly by employing the "you" pronoun. They tell people to face the challenges of their lives squarely and to deal with them in an engaged manner. This pragmatic worldview is rather obvious in the following examples:

> You get out of life (the world) what you put into it. (1901, 146)
> You must fight one battle at a time. (1903, 15)
> You can only spend a dollar (money) once. (1913, 60)
> You can't fight city hall. (1933, 40)
> You cannot push a string (of spaghetti). (1935, 241)
> You never know what you have till it's gone (you've lost it). (1952, 135)

These proverbs encourage Americans to stick to their pragmatic approach to the challenges of life, asking them to realize that there are limits even in the land of unlimited possibilities. Since Americans in general are great sports fans, it should come as no surprise that the proverb "You can't steal first base" (1915, 38) from the national sport of baseball has been current for about one hundred years. Its metaphor expresses with much authority that there is a limit to everything, no matter how good one might be. One thing is for certain for Americans as they face new demands "Can't never could" (1952, 33)

That does not mean that modern proverbs do not have solid advice for establishing positive character traits. Here too the proverbs address people directly by way of the "you" pronoun, stressing above every-thing else the view that Americans don't give up the fight, that they are willing to get engaged, and that they face challenges head-on. These proverbs reflect the positive attitudes about life's challenges that American people have in general. Especially the popular and already hundred years old proverb "If life hands you lemons, make lemonade" (1910, 140) and the much more recent proverb "If life hands (gives) you scraps, make a quit" (1992, 140; MacDowell and Mieder 2010) with the same message couched into a different metaphor exhibiting this char-acter building message. But there are other proverbs that give advice for socially responsible living with the proverb "There is no such thing as a free lunch" (1917, 253) having steadily increased in popularity during the past two decades:

You can disagree without being disagreeable. (1927, 56–57)

If you can't stand the heat, get out of the kitchen. (1931, 119; one of President Harry S. Truman's favorite proverbs; see Mieder and Bryan 1997: 59–61)

When you're down (at the bottom) the only way is up. (1933, 274)

To see the view, you have to climb the mountains. (1945, 268)

If you don't stand for something, you will fail for anything. (1945, 239)

There is no such thing as a free ride. (1949, 253)

You never get a second chance to make a first impression. (1952, 36)

It's not how many times you get knocked down that matters but how many times you get back up. (1954, 258)

When the going gets tough, the tough get going. (1954, 106)

You can do anything you want to if you want to (badly) enough. (1961, 57)

When you fall off a horse (bicycle), you have to get (right) back on. (1962, 125)

If you can dream it, you can do it (be it, have it). (1970, 62)

If you aren't the lead dog, the scenery (view) never changes. (1980, 58)

If you're going to dream, dream big (you might as well dream big). (1984, S1, 93)

If (When) you're going through hell, keep going (don't stop). (1990, S1, 102)

How can anybody not be encouraged by the proverbial advice. It expresses both literally and figuratively that Americans can achieve almost anything if they put their mind and energy to it. Many proverbs encourage people to keep going no matter what obstacles might stand in the way. After all, "Nothing comes to a sleeper but a dream" (1968, 233–234), so keep moving and pay attention to personal ethics that will enhance a meaningful career:

Push can get you there, but it takes character to stay there. (1935, 210)

Ability (Talent) can take you to the top, but character is what will keep you there. (1980, 1)

Beauty may open doors but only virtue (strength) enters. (2000, 17)

The third very recent proverb comes as somewhat of a surprise, and it might well be an anti-proverb enlarging on the old "Beauty opens locked doors" (Mieder, Kingsbury, Harder 1992, 41). Virtuous character traits continue to be valued, as can be seen from such proverbs as "Manners matter (much)" (1909, 163), "Courtesy pays dividends [of all types]" (1922, 46), "Give (Show) respect, get (gain) respect" (1925, 216), and "You can delegate authority but not responsibility" (1945, S2, 18).

This brings to mind the ultimate American proverb relating to responsibility: "The buck stops here" (1942, 28; Mieder and Bryan 1997: 62–64). It was one of President Harry S. Truman's favorite proverbs that resulted in people claiming that he originated it despite his making it clear that he did not come up with it. Be that as it may, here is an example of Truman's moralistic modus operandi as president exemplified by this proverb:

> You know, it's easy enough for the Monday morning quarterback to say what the coach should have done, after the game is over. But when the decision is up before you—and on my desk I have a motto which says "The buck stops here"—the decision has to be made. That decision may be right. It may be wrong. If it is wrong, and it has been shown that it is wrong, I have no desire to cover it up. I admit it, and try to make another decision that will meet the situation. And that is what any President of the United States has to do. Just bear that in mind. (Mieder and Bryan 1997: 63)

Little wonder that Truman was nicknamed to be a straight shooter, a person who called things the way they are and who took responsibility for his decisions and actions. One can indeed only wish that modern presidents would keep this ethical attitude in mind. As far as President Donald Trump is concerned, he obviously does not adhere to this proverbial motto. In fact, during his impeachment hearings during the spring of 2020 he should have been reminded of the proverb "No man is above the law, and no man is below it" (1903, 161) that goes back to a message that President Theodore Roosevelt delivered to Congress on December 7, 1903. While the proverb "No man is above the law"—quoted repeatedly by the Democrats pushing for Trump's impeachment—was recorded at the United States Supreme Court in 1867 (Shapiro 2006: 648), it might have been worthwhile to cite Roosevelt's longer version as well, especially since he was a Republican president.

Speaking of this important president, the popular proverb "Speak (Talk, Walk) softly and carry a big stick" (1900, 238) might be mentioned here. Its first written reference occurs on January 26, 1900 in a letter by President Theodore Roosevelt who called it a "West African proverb." However, the proverb has not been found in any of the many African proverb collections, and it is possible that Roosevelt, who uttered it on other occasions without that clause, coined it himself. The stress on virtue, manners, courtesy, and kindness can also be seen in proverbs like "It's the thought that counts" (1907, 256–257), "A true friend is one who knows all your faults and still loves (likes) you" (1917, 87–88), and "To make a friend, be a friend" (1977, S2, 22). Two proverbs in particular stand out: "You can't measure heart" (1967, 119) and "Love trumps hate" (1996, S2, 30–31), The first proverb brings to mind the remarkable commitment of Americans to all philanthropy that is definitely part of a generally held worldview. The other proverb is a rather obvious piece of wisdom, but it has taken on a special significance as a political slogan against the ill-advised policies of President Donald Trump. There are people who think it started during Trump's presidency, but the proverb is actually over two decades older. This might serve as another example of how proverbs can become actualized with new sociopolitical developments. As a general rule the proverb states the obvious, of course, and that is the love for one's fellow human beings is incredibly more important that hate.

This is not to say that Americans do not also want to excel and cab be impatient with people who knight be holding them back. Based on the word "turkey" in the slang meaning of a foolish, inept, or stupid person, there are two related animal proverbs that compare successful people (eagles) with such turkeys, as it were: "In any group (flock) of eagles, there will be at least one turkey" (1979, 111–112) and "It is hard to soar with the eagles when you are surrounded by turkeys" (1980, 65). Such driven people in their frustration might well cite the proverb "Don't mess with success" (1978, S1, 116–117), followed by such terse admonitions as "No guts, no glory" (1945, 112–113), "Go big or go home" (1965, 99), "Go all the way or don't go at all" (1968, 99), "Go hard or go home" (1990, 99), and "Go strong or don't go at all (or go home)" (1995, 99). These proverbs are obviously interrelated, but they are each current as individual proverbs in their own right. They express a certain impatient character trait than is also part of the general go-getting attitude of Americans. "The show must go on" (Mieder, Kingsbury, Harder 1992: 8), to cite a nineteenth-century American proverb, and "Failure is not falling down but staying down" (1936, 73). The message is clearly that Americans can master almost anything, again express-ing a certain exceptionalistic mentality. And yet, it must not be forgot-ten that the "failure"-proverb can also be uttered to lend support and encouragement. It is utterly important that proverbs without context do not really reveal their significance that becomes clear only by con-sidering their polyfunctionality, polysituativity, and polysemanticity (Mieder 2004: 9).

The idea of being good, successful or even perfect is yet another stone in the multifaceted mosaic of what one may call the American worldview. This is certainly borne out by a barrage of modern proverbs that have become current during the past century. It is good that people don't have to listen them all in one day for otherwise this overemphasis on perfection might well lead to psychological problems. Young people in particular could well suffer by feeling inept while actually trying to do their level best:

> Good enough (Sometimes good enough) is not good enough. (1907, 108)
> Almost (Close, Nearly, About) is not good (close) enough. (1921, 5)
> Be good or be gone. (1932, S1, 101)
> You're only as good as your last performance. (1935, S1, 112)
> Be good or be good at it. (1995, S1, 101)

It is quite fascinating that there are two proverbs from 1946 that are the opposite of each other: "The good is the enemy of the perfect" (1946, S1, 101–102) and "The perfect is the enemy of the good" (1946, S1, 111–112). They both make sense and will be employed depending of the situation to which they are applied. But in any case, there are also other "good"-proverbs of a more general message in that they point out the advantage or disadvantage of something: "If something sounds (seems) too good to be true, it (probably) is" (1908, 237), "Get while the getting is good" (1911, 97–98), "Go while the going is good" (1911, 105–106), and "Take while the taking is good" (1921, 249). And owing to the American optimistic outlook on life, there is finally the hopeful proverb that "Good things happen (come) to good people" (1980, S1, 117).

The (over)emphasis of being good or even perfect can be seen to a large degree also in the American fascination if not obsession with sports and the desire to win that comes with it. It is of considerable interest that while the proverb "Winning isn't everything" (1912, 277–278) was coined early in the twentieth century, its anti-proverb "Winning isn't everything, it's the only thing" (1950, 278) came about in mid-century as a reflection of the American culture with being first wherever possible. Here then are a few "winning"-proverbs of which at least a couple recognize that winning really is not everything. Part of it all ought to be the joy of the game itself, since after all, "You can't win them all" (1918, 276:

> It isn't whether you win or lose (that counts); it's how you play the game. (1913, 92–93)
> A winner never quits, and a quitter never wins. (1922, 277)
> Play to win or don't play (at all). (1938, 201)
> Every game (contest) has (to have) a winner (and a loser). (1943, 91)
> Play big to win big. (1978, 201)

Some fifty years after the coinage of the first proverb in this list its anti-proverb "It isn't how you play the game that counts; it's whether you win or lose" (1967, 92) was coined. This newer proverb clearly stresses the importance of winning whereas the original proverb is more concerned about the gamesmanship.

If a society is that taken by sports, be it as virtual observers of games or sitting on the couch at home watching them or reading about them in the papers, it should come as no surprise that the various sports have led to a number of proverbs that have become current in the general population. These proverbs also express the rather typical American attitude of stepping up to new challenges:

> You can't score unless you have the ball. (1907, 13)
> You can't hit the ball (get a hit) if you don't swing (the bat). (1943, 12)
> Step up (You have to step up) to the plate. (1965, 200; also as proverbial expression: "to step up to the plate")
> You can't score if you don't shoot. (1965, 223)
> You miss 100 percent of the shots you don't take. (1991, 229–230)

Baseball has been particularly productive in bringing about "sports"-proverbs, but many of them can apply to other sports as well. Of course, there are also more general proverbs like "Don't change the rules in the middle of the game" (1921, 220) and "When you change the rules, you change the game" (1945, 221). Special credit should go to the originator of the proverb "There is no *I* (*me*) in *team*" (1960, 128) that does not only relate to sports teams as a collective but to any other group of people working together. Finally, there is one of the ultimate American proverbs stating "Life is not a spectator sport" (1958, 143) that goes from watching games to playing an active role in societal matters. The message is clearly to get involved in making this a better world.

Team work and cooperation belong to basic American values, with the following two proverbs being somewhat of a leitmotif: "Teamwork makes a (the) dream work" (1995, S2, 40) and "If you don't believe in cooperation, watch what happens to a wagon (car) when one wheel comes off" (1921, 43–44). The following proverbs of the twentieth century give rather straight forward advice of how to be part of the solution and not part of the problem. The proverb "If you're not part of the solution (answer), you're part of the problem" (1937, 190) is actually older than one might have surmised with its fifty years younger more metaphorical anti-proverb "If you're not part of the steamroller, you're part of the road" (1987, 190) expressing the same idea in a rather drastic fashion. In any case, the following proverbs certainly have not lost any significance in the American way of life:

> Everyone must pull his own weight. (1902, 274–275)
> Push, pull, or get out of the way. (1909, 273)
> A candle loses nothing by lighting another candle. (1918, 32)
> Give a hand up, not a handout. (1938, 115)
> You've got to go along to get along. (1952, 101)
> Go with the flow. (1962, 82)
> If you want to talk the talk, you've got to walk the walk. (1967, 250)

The last proverb started about fifty years ago among the African-American population and has gained currency throughout the country as an expression of getting involved in a cooperative way in sociopolitical problems. After all, as another modern proverb has it, "If you are not at the table, you may be on the menu" (1993, 248). The slightly older proverb "It takes two to tango" (1952, 266) says all of this in a much more concise way. It had its origin in a song by Al Hoffman (author) and Dick Manning (composer) that became an international hit by way of the famous African-American singer Pearl Bailey.

> *Takes Two to Tango*
> Takes two to tango, two to tango,
> Two to really get the feeling of romance.
> Let's do the tango, to the tango,
> Do the dance of love.
>
> You can sail a ship by yourself,
> Take a nap of a nip by yourself.
> You can get into debt on your own.
> There are lots of thigs that you can do alone.
> (But it)
> Takes two to tango (etc.)
> (Mieder 2004: 233)

Little wonder that this proverb has conquered the world in English or in translations (Mieder 2019a: 225–226). It is, of course, a wonderfully positive anti-proverb of the much older proverb "It takes two to quarrel" (Mieder, Kingsbury, and Harder 1992: 493) and shows how new proverbs are created on the basis of older ones (Litovkina and Mieder 2006, Valdaeva 2003). But there is also the hopeful proverb "A rising tide lifts all boats (ships)" (1915, 258) whose maritime metaphor has given hope for a more cooperative American society for about one hundred years and which has gained a renewed currency in very recent times as America is facing serious social problems.

Hopeful optimism is without doubt a major part of the American composite worldview. At its extreme stands the proverb "The sky is the limit" (1909, 233) that somewhat surprisingly is over one hundred years old. One might have thought that it is much more recent claim in view of its popularity today. Then there is also the equally popular proverb "The glass is either half empty or half full" (1930, 98) with the idea that a pessimist looks at his glass and says it is half empty whereas the optimist looks at it and says it is half full. When the proverbial push comes to shove, most Americans will lean towards the glass being half full. And do note that there is also the dry-cut proverb "Accentuate the positive, eliminate the negative" (1944, 204). In any case, quite a few

modern proverbs give positive advice following the pattern "If you ..."
to individuals:

> If you can see it, you can be (achieve) it. (1973, 225)
> If you build it, they will come. (1979, 28)
> If you sift through enough dirt (mud, crap), you may find gold (a diamond).
> (1997, 56)

The last example with its somewhat earthy metaphor is somewhat of a
surprise in that it is of only recent origin. Most of the optimistic proverbs tend toward rather straight forward declarations with "It costs
nothing to dream" (1920, 44–45) changing little of this fact:

> Any chance is better than no chance. (1901, S2, 19–20)
> Down is not (always) out. (1910, 61–62)
> What a difference a day makes (can make)! (1914, 56)
> Half a chance beats (is better than) none. (1968, S1, 90)
> Eighty percent of life (success) is (just) showing up. (1977,140)

Never mind looking back! It is the future with all of its chances, ideas,
and challenges that is of greatest importance, leaving the past as a
matter of bygones. A number of short proverbs make this perfectly
clear, with "There is no future like the present" (1909, 90) being an
anti-proverb to the sixteenth-century proverb "There is no time like
the present" (Mieder, Kingsbury, Harder 1992: 598). Other proverbs are
"The future is not (no longer) what it used to be" (1948, 90), "The past
is not what it used to be" (1950, 192), and "The past does not equal the
future" (1991, 191). And to be sure, the proverb "You can't kill an idea"
(1908, S1, 103) also signals that future changes will surely come.

This positive outlook on life can also be seen in several problems
that succeed in rationalizing crises or tragedies into challenging opportunities to deal with in a positive and optimistic way. These texts are
perfect examples for proverbs being able to serve as guideposts to
overcome obstacles of any type:

> A crisis is an opportunity. (1900, 47)
> There are no problems, only opportunities (challenges). (1948, 207)
> In the middle of difficulty lies (there is) opportunity. (1975, 165–166)

Don't waste a crisis (Never let a crisis go to waste). (1976, 47–48)
Tragedy (Every tragedy) is an opportunity. (1978, 262)

The second text is of special interest, as can be seen from a reference in *Newsweek* magazine of March 12, 1979: "There are three additional rules of [Albert] Einstein's work that stand out for use in our science, our problems, our times. First, out of clutter find simplicity. Second, from discord make harmony. Third, in the middle of difficulty lies opportunity" (p. 67). The proverb has indeed commonly been credited to Einstein even though nothing like it has been found in his published writings. In a light-hearted fashion someone reacted to these matters with the wisdom "No risk, no fun" (1953, 218) that might have come about as an anti-proverb to the more serious and several decades older "No risk, no reward" (1907, 218). It should be noted that the proverbial structure "No X, no Y" has been popular at least since the sixteenth-century with proverbs like "No pain, no gain" (Mieder, Kingsbury, Harder 1992: 447). In any case, Americans are risk takers, as the two additional proverbs "The thrill (rush) is worth the risk" (1936, 257) and the very recent "You have to risk it to get the biscuit" (2010. S1, 88–89) make perfectly clear. But now there is also the proverb "Risk is the price you pay for opportunity" (1 981, 218) that encourages people to move forward no matter what. Never mind that "Nothing comes easy in this world" (1900, 180), just keep plugging along remembering the metaphorical proverb "Knock on the door often enough, and it will open" (1993, S1, 93). After all, "Everybody has to start somewhere" (1926, 240) and who would not agree with the proverb that "To grow is to change" (1908, 112) whose message for modern existence is so very appropriate. The only surprise here is that it is over one hundred years old, indicating that perhaps the old Bible proverb "There is nothing new under the sun" (Ecclesiastes 1:9) has its continued value.

Speaking of the sun brings to mind a little anonymous poem called "The Robin" that contains the earliest reference of the proverb "The sun will come out tomorrow" (1938, 246):

It is raining.
The wind blows.
There is snow on the fence.
But the sun will come out tomorrow.

A more modern proverb changing the nature metaphor to one of technology expresses a similar optimistic point of view: "There's always (a) light at the end of the tunnel" (1971, 147). And yet, the folk is well aware of the fact that at times a reality check is necessary even if just as a warning against exaggerated optimism: "The light at the end of the tunnel may be a train" (1974, 147). This is also mindful of the cautionary proverb that "Hope is not a plan" (1948, 124).

With this said, the question arises whether something like fatalism can be found in modern American proverbs. Is there a counterweight to the overwhelming optimism found in the American society? The answer is an expected "yes" since proverbs do contain insights into all aspects of life that is not void of disappointments and anxieties. Such matters do get expression in proverbs that portray a certain among of resignation or fatalism, as for example in these texts addressing life as such: "Nobody ever said life is fair" (1929, 146) and "Nobody ever said life is easy" (1965, 126). In fact, "Nothing in life is simple" (1901, 180) or more generally expressed "Nothing is as easy (simple) as it looks (seems, appears" (1905, 181). From these "nobody/nothing"-proverbs it is a small step to "everyone/everything"-proverbs with similar all-inclusive claims: "Everything (that happens) happens for a reason" (1916, 214), "Everything is not (all) peaches and cream" (1928, 193), and "Everyone can't be first" (1955, 78). Not even the pragmatic and optimistic Americans can master everything as the proverb "You can't fix everything" (1933, 81) states so fittingly to awaken people to that fact.

Once in a while resignation is unavoidable as three proverbs originating from the well-established pastime of playing cards point out: "You play the hand (the cards) you are dealt" (1953, 116), "A card laid is a card played" (1975, 34), and "Life deals us each a hand" (1997, 141). Staying with the game metaphor, there is, of course, also the proverb "You win a few, you lose a few" (1912, 76). But here are a few more fatalistic proverbs of which some are literally stated while others couch their resigned messages into animal metaphors that add to their expressiveness:

A rooster one day, a feather duster the next. (1907, 219–220)
You either have (got) it or you don't (1921, 118)

When you have nothing, you have nothing to lose. (1965, 182)

   (popularized by Bob Dylan's song "Like a Rolling Stone" of 1965)

When you're hot, you're hot (and when you're not, you're not). (1969, 125–126)

Sometimes (Some day) you get the bear, sometimes the bear gets you. (1970, 16)

You pay now or you pay later (with interest). (1974, 192)

Sometimes the dragon wins. (1981, 62; Dundes and Pagter 1996: 58–61)

The last proverb, perhaps based on a dragon-slaying movie scene based on a medieval epic, shows how modern proverbs can contain motifs from times long passed. Such a metaphor is certainly more expressive than the nondescript proverbial statement "No good deed goes unpunished" (1938, 52) which is, however, had its start as a splendid anti-proverb of the older moralistic proverb "No bad deed goes (remains) unpunished." A certain fatalism is also contained in the message of the African-American proverb "What goes around comes around" (1961, 100; Prahlad 1996: 205–206) that is employed frequently to express a certain unavoidable repetition. Of course, depending on the context, this proverb can also be employed in a positive way. This is also true to a certain degree with the negative proverb "If anything can go wrong, it will" (1908, 102) that is commonly known as "Murphy's Law." It is another example of how a proverb as become attributed to a certain individual for which there is no proof. Proverbs like this one are covered with considerable detail in the *Dictionary of Modern Proverbs*:

If anything can go wrong, it will (Anything that can go wrong, will go wrong Anything that can possibly go wrong usually does). 1908 Nevil Maskelyne, "The Art in Magic," *The Magic Circular* (Jun.) 25: "It is an experience common to all men to find that, on any special occasion, such as the production of a magical effect for the first time in public, everything that *can* go wrong *will* go wrong. Whether we must attribute this to the malignity of matter or to the total depravity of inanimate things, whether the exciting cause is hurry, worry, or what not, the fact remains" (italics as shown). 1951 Anne Roe, "Child Behavior, Animal Behavior, and Comparative Psychology," *Genetic Psychology Monographs* 43 (May) 204: "As for himself he realized that this was the inexorable working of the second law of the thermodynamics which stated Murphy's law 'If anything can go wrong it will.' I always liked Murphy's law." 1955 Lee Corey, "Design Flaw," *Astounding Science Fiction* 54 (Feb.) 54: "'Reilly's Law,' Guy Barclay said cryptically. 'Huh?' 'Reilly's Law,' Guy repeated. 'It states that in any scientific or engineering endeavor, anything that can go wrong *will* go wrong" (italics as shown). [...] In popular legend, Murphy's Law originated in 1949 at Edwards Air Force Base in California, coined by project manager George E. Nichols after hearing Edward A. Murphy Jr. complain about a wrongly wired rocket-sled experiment. However, there is no documentation of that connection until 1955. The idea embodied in Murphy's Law (less often, "Reilly's Law" or "O'Reilly's Law") has appeared in numerous forms, in reference to a variety of activities, from antiquity forward [...]. For example: 1878 Alfred Holt, "Review of the Progress of Steam Shipping during the Last Quarter of a Century," *Minutes of Proceedings of the Institution of Civil Engineers* 51: 8: "It is found that anything that can go wrong at sea generally does go wrong sooner or later." 1941 George Orwell, "War-time Diaries," in *Collected Essays, Journalism and Letters*, edited by Sonia Orwell and Ian Angus (New York: Harcourt, Brace & World, 1968) 2: 400–401: "Iraq, Syria, Morocco, Spain, Darlan, Stalin, Raschid Ali, Franco—sensation of utter helplessness. If there is a wrong thing to do, it will be done, infallibly. One has come to believe in that as if it were a law of nature." The term "Murphy's Law" has come to designate a range of seemingly reasonable but often paradoxical or absurd propositions.

Little wonder that such frustration with the imperfections of life in all of its appearances has led to the shortest fatalistic proverb of them all. The relatively new scatological proverb "Shit happens" (1991, 228) says it all, with its expanded equivalent "Shit happens, and then you die" (1991, 228–229) carrying its message to the extreme. One can hear the shorter proverb in polite society, but there is always the euphemistic variant "Stuff happens" that can be cited but with the caveat that everybody will know what really is meant!

So, what then is a good American individual to do to master life? First of all, there is plenty of proverbial wisdom that provides encouragement. There is first of all the quintessential American proverb "Pick yourself up and dust yourself off" (1915, 196) that was popularized by the song "Pick Yourself Up" (lyrics by Dorothy Fields, music by Jerome Kern) that was part of the film *Swing Time* (1936) staring Fred Astaire and Ginger Rogers. It starts with this uplifting message:

Nothing's impossible I have found,
For when my chin is on the ground,
I pick myself up,

Dust myself off,
Start all over again.

"Pick yourself up, / Dust yourself off, / Start all over again" is repeated in subsequent stanzas assuring the memorability of the proverb. Nevertheless, it had fallen somewhat out of use, replaced to a certain degree by the proverbial expression "to pull oneself up by one's bootstraps." This happens to be President Barack Obama's favorite phrases (Mieder 2009: 177–178), but even more importantly, he remembered the song "Pick Yourself Up" when he prepared his first inaugural address that he delivered on January 20, 2009: "But our time of standing pat, of protecting narrow interests and putting off decisions—that time has surely passed. Starting today, we must pick ourselves up, dust ourselves off, and begin again the work of remaking American" (Mieder 2009: 140–141). Obama, known for his likes of popular music, gave the proverb a shot in the arm, so to speak. It serves as another indication of the great influence that major public figures and the media have in the dissemination of proverbs.

Other positive proverbial admonitions for coping in a typically constructive American way follow suit, often in very concise straightforward language:

You have to (be able to) live with yourself. (1902, 149)
Take what life gives you. (1908, 146)
Live what you love. (1926, S1, 106)
Do your own thing. (1929, 252)
Happiness is where you find it. (1937, 116–117)
Clean up your own backyard (first). (1943, 12)
Think big, be big. (1951, S2, 40–41)
Be all (the best) that you can be. (1956, 4–5)
If it feels good, do it. (1968, 75)
Think outside the box. (1971, 25)
Follow your (own) bliss. (1971, 23)
Choose (Pick) your battles wisely. (1972, 15)
Live (Live life) like you mean it. (1972, 148)
Whatever floats your boat. (1981, 23)
Check yourself before you wreck yourself. (1994, S1, 90–91)

The "floating your boat" text that asserts that one should or may do whatever one wishes or is interested in has spawned such humorous or ridiculous analogous phrases as "Whatever tickles your pickle," "Whatever butters your biscuit," and "Whatever blows your skirt up." But whatever, the American emphasis on individual self-determination is rather obvious in these short texts expressed in positive imperatives. All of this can, of course, also be expressed in equally short and also longer proverbs that employ telling metaphors. There is no doubt that the appeal of modern proverbs is in part due to the imagery. The first proverb in the following list is a fascinating contradiction to Ralph Waldo Emerson's proverb "Hitch your wagon to a star" (Mieder, Kingsbury, Harder 1992: 637) from 1862 in that it asserts that it might be better to do the pulling oneself and travel in the direction of the star:

> You have to pull your own (little red) wagon. (1907, 269)
> Wake up and smell the coffee. (1943, 41)
> Stop and smell the flowers. (1951, 82)
> If you shoot (aim) for the stars, maybe at least you will hit the moon. (1955, 239)
> Bloom (Grow) where you are planted. (1971, 23)
> Labels are for cans (not people). (1984, 136)
> A closed mouth does not get fed. (1989, 173)

The last text with the meaning that one must speak up in order to be noticed or rewarded is reminiscent of a somewhat earlier proverb "A closed mouth gathers no feet" (1956, 173). It is an ingenious folk proverb that is probably a combination of the sixteenth-century British proverb "A closed mouth catches no flies" (Mieder, Kingsbury, Harder 1992: 420), the fourteenth-century proverb "The rolling stone gathers no moss" (Mieder, Kingsbury, Harder 1992: 565) and the somatic proverbial expression "to put one's foot in one's mouth."

American individualism carries with it the obligation to be true to oneself that is so convincingly expressed in the proverb "Don't try to be someone you are not" (1956, 265). It suffices to "Be all (the best) that you can be" (1956, 4–5) as another proverb from the mid-fifties offers as solid advice. Forty years later one finds the significant proverb "Be the change you want (wish) to see (in the world" (1995, S1, 90) that has been attributed to Gandhi without substantiation. No matter, it is a proverb that has come about as Americans and people throughout the world have become aware not only of regional and national but also of global sociopolitical issues like the environment, immigration, poverty, etc. All of this is summarized in the proverb "Think globally, act locally" (1942, 256) that somewhat surprisingly was put forth during the Second World War already but which in the twenty-first century has become a world-wide proverbial slogan.

But to return to America's love-affair with individualism that incorporates the concept of independence, it is time to consider the quintessential American proverb "Different strokes for different folks" (1945, 241–242; Prahlad 1996: 253) that has a less metaphorical pendant as "Different ways for(on) different days" (1971, 272). Both proverbs started among the African-American population with the "stroke"-proverb entering into mainstream American parlance by way of the extremely popular song "Everyday People" (1968) be Sly and the Family Stone. It can honestly be stated that the proverb and the lyrics of the song have become somewhat of a national credo for individual freedom in particular but also human rights in general (McKenzie 1996, Mieder 1989: 317–332, 2006). With the proverb as a leitmotif the lyrics of the song say all of this the best:

Everyday People
Sometimes I am right,
Then I can be wrong.
My own beliefs are in my song.
The butcher, the baker, the drummer and then,
Makes no difference what group I'm in.
I am everyday people.

There is a blue one who can't accept the green one
For living with the fat one, trying to be a skinny one.
Different strokes for different folks.
And so on and so on and scooby dooby dooby.
We've got to live together.
I am no better and neither are you.
We are the same in whatever we do.
Love me or hate me; get to know me and then
You can figure out what bag I'm in.

I am everyday people.

There is a long hair who doesn't like the short hair
For being such a rich one who will not help the poor one.
Different strokes for different folks.
And so on and so on and scooby dooby dooby.
We've got to live together.

There is a yellow one that won't accept the black one
That won't accept the red one that won't accept the white one.
Different strokes for different folks.
And so on and so on and scooby dooby dooby.
I am everyday people.

Acceptance and tolerance of differences are certainly part of the modern American worldview that accepts the modern wisdom that "Our choices define us" (1985, 39). The challenges facing the society might seem insurmountable, but the modern proverb "There is no day but today" (1979, 51) calls for immediate action no matter if "Every solution creates new problems" (1920, 237). Indeed, Americans believe in a *vita activa* more than a *vita contemplativa* that is geared towards progressive action with hopefully positive results. Many proverbs underscore this engaged philosophy of life, not the least of which is "Caring is (means) sharing" with its equally relevant reversal "Sharing is caring" (1924, S2, 19).

The concept of "action" belongs unequivocally to the American mindset that advocates for everybody to "Live life to the fullest" (1934, 146). Some proverbs don't beat about the bush metaphorically and come straight to the point regarding a life full of activity: "Action (Activity) is worry's worst enemy" (1930, 2), "There are no second acts (in American lives)" (1941, 2), "Act first, think later (afterward)" (1965, 2), and the often heard "Get your act together" (1972, 2). Delays of any sort should not be tolerated, as two proverbs declare without relying on metaphors: "If you fail to prepare, you prepare to fail" (1919, 73), "Delay is the deadliest form of denial" (1966, 53), and "If you stay ready, you won't have to get ready" (1994, S1, 116). The proverb "Wait broke the wagon down (broke the mule's back, broke the camel's back)"

(1936, 269) says all of this in a more descriptive way. It is usually stated as a punning (wait—weight) objection of being asked to wait. The variant with the "camel's back" probably alludes to the seventeenth-century proverb "The last straw will break the camel's back" (Mieder, Kingsbury, Harder 1992: 567). It may serve as a small example of how traditional proverbs can play a role in the creation of new proverbs.

It is interesting to note that quite a few modern proverbs rely on animal metaphors to stress the fact that one must be ready for action and know where to execute it. In this regard it can also be mentioned that technology plays a minimal role in the modern proverbs that have been registered thus far. Animals on the other hand have always been part of didactic proverbs, something that is obvious also from the long tradition of animal fables that are based on or include such proverbs (Carnes 1988):

> Fish where the fish are. (1901, 79)
> You can't catch a fish without baiting a hook. (1921, 79)
> You've got to fish while they are biting. (1921, 80)

The proverb "Go hunting where the ducks are" (1930, 64) obviously belongs to this wisdom from outside activities with the advice of "Get your ducks in a row" (1956, 63–64) having become very popular both as an imperative sentence and the older proverbial expression "to get one's ducks in a row." Regarding this matter, it must be pointed out that many proverbs can be formed from proverbial expressions by making indicative sentences out of the latter. A telling example is the proverbial pair "Don't throw the baby out with the bathwater" and "to throw the baby out with the bathwater" with the problem of not being able to ascertain conclusively which phrase came first (Mieder 1991).

Some of the modern non-metaphorical proverbs calling people to action are rather harsh in equating lack of action, evolution, and innovation with dying:

> Innovate or die. (1967, S1, 104)
> Get busy living or get busy dying. (1973, 30–31)
> Evolve or die. (1991, S3, in print)

Such short proverbs like "Move it or lose it" (1973, S3, in print) and "Do it once, do it right" (1975, S1, 92) are less aggressive, with the frequently cited proverb "Shape up or ship out" (1953, 227) expressing a certain impatience in the American mind if things do not quite proceed with the expected efficiency and speed. Of course, this sentiment can also be expressed with the somewhat older scatological proverb "Shit (Piss) or get off the pot" (1935, 204). Over the years this proverb has gained considerable currency in American parlance, although care should be taken where and when it might be acceptable and in what manner.

No such worries with the proverbs "Tough (Hard, Difficult) times call for tough (hard, difficult) decisions" (1955, 259–260) and "Tough times don't last; tough people do" (1983, 260) that express American resolve for courageous action in the face of need or tragedy. And yet, the coiners of modern American proverbs are also aware of the fact that there are good and easy times, as the proverb "Time flies when you're having fun" (1939, 259) declares by expanding the classical proverb "Tempus fugit" or "Time flies" just a bit. In any case, now the proverb "Ask not what your country can do for you—ask what you can do for your country" (1961, 45–46) has been reached that every American knows well. It became part of the American psyche by way of President John F. Kennedy's inaugural address on January 20, 1961:

> In the long history of the world, only a few generations have been granted the role of defending freedom in its hour of maximum danger. I do not shrink from this responsibility—I welcome it. I do not believe that any of us would exchange places with any other people or any other generation. The energy, the faith, the devotion which we bring to this endeavor will light our country and all who serve it—and the glow from that fire can truly light the world. And so, my fellow Americans, as not what your country can do for you; ask what you can do for your country. My fellow citizens of the world: Ask not what American will do for you, but what together we can do for the freedom of man. (Mieder 2000:)

Kennedy's name will forever be associated with this antithetical phrase, but it does have a precursor of sorts in an address delivered on May 30, 1884, by Oliver Wendell Holmes: "It is now the moment when by common consent we pause to become conscious of our national life and to rejoice in it, to recall what our country has done for each of us, and to ask ourselves what we can do for our country in return" (Mieder 2000:). It is hard to imagine that Kennedy and his sophisticated speech writers (primarily Theodore C. Sorenson) were not aware of this statement that morphed into Kennedy's famous civic slogan. Be that as it may, as a modern proverb it epitomizes the hands-on pragmatic and philanthropic mindset of many Americans.

Surely Benjamin Franklin with his commitment to the common sense of solid puritan work ethics would have agreed with this mindset. The many proverbs he included in the twenty-five years of his *Poor Richard's Almanack* (1733–1758) and the 105 proverbs he assembled from the 1044 proverbs in them for his famous essay on "The Way to Wealth" (1758) provide much traditional wisdom for a successful life based on serious work (Mieder 2004: 216–224, Manders 2006: 137–168). Not much has changed during two and a half centuries except for the fact that modern times have come up with some of their own proverbs. Some of them come right out and address work directly in both positive and negative ways:

> The best way to kill time is to work it to death. (1914, 271)
> Dreams can't (won't) come true unless you wake up (and go to work). (1928, 62)
> Working (Trying) hard is not (good) enough. (1934, 265)
> The harder (more) you work, the luckier you get. (1940, 280)
> Miracles take (a lot of) hard work. (1946, 167)
> The only place where success comes before work is in a dictionary. (1955, 199)
> If you love your job, you don't have to work (a day in your life). (1991, 130)

The admonitions for wasting time or sleeping too much—in other words being unproductive—come across as almost un-American in their rigid word choices:

> Time spent wishing is wasted. (1922, 259)
> You can sleep when you are dead (Sleep is for the dead). (1931, S2, 38)
> Life (Time) is too short (precious) to waste sleeping. (1944, 145)
> You snooze, you lose. (1950, 236)

The "sleep"-text is similar to Benjamin Franklin's much older proverb creation "There will be sleeping enough in the grave" (Mieder, Kingsbury, Harder 1992: 546) that he included in his *Poor Richard's Almanack* for the year 1741. One gets the feeling that there is nothing but work and that there is "No rest for the weary" (Mieder, Kingsbury, Harder 1992: 507) as the nineteenth-century proverb states. Thank God that a couple of metaphorical proverbs put at least a positive spin on the unavoidability of work: "The bee that gets (makes) the honey doesn't hang (loaf) around the hive" (1906, 18) and "It is possible to swallow (You can eat) an elephant—one bite at a time" (1921, 67–68). In other words, the job might be a lengthy and bothersome one, but eventually it will get done knowing the "apparent" truth that "Busy hands are happy hands" (1956, 115). Proverbs have for long been employed for rationalizing processes and that is how this proverb can function as well.

But how about the "busy hands" becoming "praying hands" in the mind of Americans that consider their society being informed by religion. True, there is the modern wisdom that "When all else fails, pray (try prayer)" (1957, 73), but seemingly that will not do by itself, as can be seen from the proverb "When you pray, move your feet" (1936, 84–85) that calls for virtuous action to complement prayer. The proverb "Courage is fear that has said its prayers" (1922, 46) also argues that praying might not always bring desired results. Very much accepted is the apparent truth of the proverb "The family that prays together stays together" (1947, 74) that is used with such frequency that it has been widely parodied, to wit "The family that stays together probably has only one car" (1968), "Comes autumn, the family that rakes together aches together" (1980), "The family that prays together stays together—thank God my mother-in-law's an atheist" (1981), "The family that pulls taffy together sticks together" (1997), and "Mafia—the family that preys together" (1997) with its verbal pun (Litovkina and Mieder 2006: 282–283). With all this praying and gospel singing, it perhaps comes as no surprise that there is the proverb "Even God gets tired of too much hallelujah" (1936, 102) which is doubtlessly calling people to stand on their own two feet and get moving ahead. But there are truly uplifting modern proverbs that help people along on life's challenging paths, as for example "God sends no cross that you cannot bear" (1985, 104). Many Americans would also agree with the cautionary proverb "Your arms are too short (not long enough) to box (fight, spar) with God" (1912, 7) that calls for humble acceptance of God's designs. The importance of religion is driven home by a proverb that originated among American soldiers during the horrors of the Second World War, and there is no doubt that "There are no atheists in foxholes" (1942, 9–10) has maintained its currency in the mentality of a country that has thousands of troops fighting undeclared wars abroad.

Of special interest is the seemingly absurd proverb "A man without faith (religion, God) is like a fish without a bicycle" (1958, 160) with its ridiculous comparative metaphor. It is an unexpectedly irreligious statement from the nineteen-fifties when religion certainly had a stronghold in American society. It is somewhat surprising that it caught on without, however, becoming overwhelmingly current. But it is of importance for the creation of the feminist proverb "A woman without a man is like a fish without a bicycle" (1976, 279–280) that was modeled on not quite two decades later. It has been attributed to Gloria Steinem, but it is now believed to have been coined in 1970 by the Australian educator, journalist, and politician Irina Dunn. But no matter, by the mid-1970s it had caught on in the United States as well and has been translated into other languages as well.

This leaves one more proverb to mention that in a serious and uplifting way shows the religious worldview of Americans. Its earliest found reference contains not only God as an active participant in their lives but also calls for prayers to find guidance: "God can make a way out of no way. Pray to him, and he will open a way" (1922, 102; Doyle 2014). It originated among the religious African-Americans and became popular as "God can make a way out of no way" with its secular variant "Making a way out of no way" having also established itself. Both texts became solidly ingrained in the American mindset by way of Martin Luther King's use of them in his struggle for civil rights. In fact, it was the proverb of hope, as can be seen from King's speech of August 16, 1967:

When our days become dreary with low-hovering clouds of despair, and when our nights become darker than a thousand midnights, let us remember that there is a creative force in this universe, working to pull down the gigantic mountains of evil, a power that is able to make a way out of now way and transform dark yesterdays into bright tomorrows. Let us realize that the arc of the moral universe is long but it bends toward justice. (Mieder 2010: 186, also 524–526; the last sentence is a quotation of the abolitionist Theodore Parker)

King's struggle for freedom and equality moved forward in many ways, and as he spoke about the various paths taken, he relied on proverbs and proverbial expressions that contain the "way"-noun. They are by their nature usually future oriented and thus are perfectly suited to describe and reflect upon the way to progress. despite setbacks and defeats, he never faltered in his struggle, citing the proverbial phrase "to have come a long way" to emphasize the progress that had been made while at the same time stressing with the proverbial phrase "to have a long way to go" that much work was still lying ahead (Mieder 2020: 171–180). Of course, without taking anything away from King's future orientation, he is adhering to the fundamental futuristic mindset of Americans that Alan Dundes has analyzed in his seminal studies "Thinking Ahead: A Folkloristic Reflection of the Future Orientation in American Worldview" (1969) and "'As the Crow Flies': A Straightforward Study of Lineal Worldview in American Folk Speech" (2004).

This aspect of the American worldview is contained in several modern proverbs that look at life as a journey towards a goal, to wit the fascinating terse proverb "The way is the goal" (1992, S2, 42–43) registered for the first time not even two decades ago. Even if one is not sure whether to advance or retreat, there is a middle way towards an achievable goal: "The only way out (Sometimes the only way out) is through" (1918, S2, 42). And once there is the desired momentum, the following metaphorical proverb—for once containing a reference to a machine—explains that there is no way to halt the forward movement: "There's no stopping the train (once it leaves the station)" (1915, 262). Somehow the proverb "You can't go home again" (1940, 123) comes to mind here which had its start as the title of one of Thomas Wolfe's novel published posthumously in 1940. It might then be a few years older than that date since Wolfe had died two years earlier. Be that as it may, this well-known proverb—nowadays often cited about college students wanting to move back home to save money and to find employment— carries with it the forward-looking philosophy of Americans.

Other proverbs carry the same message, as for example "Being born is only (just) the beginning" (1919, 18). The proverb "There is no such thing as a definitive study" (1936, 252–253) is also projecting into the future, since research and scholarship are bound to make new discoveries. Obviously it is also true that "Success is never final" (1920, 245), with progress having to be made even if just in small steps or ever so slowly as pronounced in the proverbs "Progress comes in small steps (one step at a time)" (1935, 208) and "Slow progress (Even slow progress) is (still) progress" (1971, S2, 36). Some thirty years earlier the proverb "Slow motion is better than (beats) no motion" (1938, S2, 33) expressed the same idea that inertia must be prevented at all costs so that matters can move forward. And yet, folk wisdom is aware that the past or presence cannot be completely left out of this picture, as can be seen from the two proverbs "You can't know where you're going unless you know where you've been" (1937, 134) and "In order to get where you want to go, you have to start from (know) where you are now" (1965, 96). It is good to know that historical and present-day accomplishments are not forgotten with this emphasis on the future. But America looks at the future as a priority, as expressed in the proverb "You can't create the future by clinging to the past" (1988, S1, 97–98). And yet, there are some voices who warn against the blind faith in the future since it really cannot be forecast with accuracy and might in fact be an elusive dream. The proverb "The future is a moving target" (1975, S2, 22–23) certainly has plenty of wisdom in it that should give people pause to reflect upon the uncertainties and vicissitudes of times to come.

One thing is for certain, the journey of life goes on. Interestingly enough, Americans have found a proverbial structure (Dundes 1975) to express their view that life is future oriented and ever changing. The concept of a journey without a definite destination has been compacted into the lineal formula "X is a journey, not a destination" where the variable can stand for various life shaping aspects:

Success (Accomplishment) is a journey, not a destination. (1933, 244)
Education is a journey, not a destination. (1936, 66)
Happiness is a journey, not a destination. (1937, 116)
Marriage is a journey, not a destination. (1943, 163)

One wonders what proverb based on this pattern will be next. But not to worry, the expected modern American proverb "Life is a journey, not a destination" (1941, 142) has been around for some eighty years to summarize the forward-looking worldview of Americans who for the most part look optimistically into the future with its challenges and hopes. As a mobile society, they are constantly on the move looking for new ways to master life. Of course, there is also a relatively new proverb to express this view as American wisdom: "The journey is the reward (its own reward)" (1978, S2, 28–29). The variant "The journey is its own reward" brings to mind the early sixteenth-century proverb "Virtue is its own reward" (Mieder, Kingsburg, Harder 1992: 634), showing that proverbial wisdom, both old and new, are interconnected. May they continue in their own small way to guide the American people on their hopefully virtuous life journey.

Bibliography

Albig, William. 1931. "Proverbs and Social Control." *Sociology and Social Research*, 15: 527–535.

Ayaß, Ruth. 2001. "On the Genesis and the Destiny of Proverbs." *Verbal Art across Cultures: The Aesthetics and Proto-Aesthetics of Communication*. Eds. Hubert Knoblauch and Helga Kotthoff. Tübingen: Gunter Narr. 237–254.

Carnes, Pack. 1988. *Proverbia in Fabula. Essays on the Relationship of the Fable and the Proverb*. Bern: Peter Lang.

Doyle, Charles Clay. 1996. "On 'New' Proverbs and the Conservativeness of Proverb Dictionaries." *Proverbium*, 13: 69–84.

Doyle, Charles Clay. 2014. "'A Way Out of No Way': A Note on the Background of the African American Proverbial Saying." *Proverbium*, 31: 193–198.

Doyle, Charles Clay, and Wolfgang Mieder. 2016. "*The Dictionary of Modern Proverbs*: A Supplement." *Proverbium*, 33: 85–120.

Doyle, Charles Clay, and Wolfgang Mieder. 2018. "*The Dictionary of Modern Proverbs*: Second Supplement." *Proverbium*, 35: 15–44.

Doyle, Charles Clay, and Wolfgang Mieder. 2020. "*The Dictionary of Modern Proverbs*: Third Supplement." *Proverbium*, 37: 53–86.

Doyle, Charles Clay, Wolfgang Mieder, and Fred R. Shapiro. 2012. *The Dictionary of Modern Proverbs*. New Haven, CT: Yale University Press.

Dundes, Alan. 1969. "Thinking Ahead: A Folkloristic Reflection of the Future Orientation in American Worldview." *Anthropological Quarterly*, 42: 53–72.

Dundes, Alan. 1972. "Folk Ideas as Units of Worldview." *Towards New Perspectives in Folklore*. Eds. Américo Paredes and Richard Bauman. Austin, TX: University of Texas Press. 93–103.

Dundes, Alan. 1975. "On the Structure of the Proverb." *Proverbium*, no. 25: 961–973.

Dundes, Alan. 2004. " 'As the Crow Flies': A Straightforward Study of Lineal Worldview in American Folk Speech." *"What Goes Around Comes Around": The Circulation of Proverbs in Contemporary Life. Essays in Honor of Wolfgang Mieder*. Eds. Kimberly J. Lau, Peter Tokofsky, and Stephen D. Winick. Logan, UT: Utah State University Press. 171–187.

Dundes, Alan, and Carl R. Pagter. 1996. *Sometimes the Dragon Wins: Yet More Urban Folklore Form the Paperwork Empire*. Syracuse, NY: Syracuse University Press.

Haas, Heather A. 2008. "Proverb Familiarity in the United States: Cross-Regional Comparisons of the Paremiological Minimum." *Journal of American Folklore*, 212: 319–347.

Hakamies, Pekka. 2002. "Proverbs and Mentality." *Myth and Mentality: Studies in Folklore and Popular Thought*. Ed. Anna-Leena Siikala. Helsinki: Finnish Literature Society. 222–230.

Honeck, Richard P., and Jeffrey Welge. 1997. "Creation of Proverbial Wisdom in the Laboratory." *Journal of Psycholinguistic Research*, 26: 605–629.

Litovkina. Anna T., and Wolfgang Mieder. 2006. *Old Proverbs Never Die, They Just Diversify. A Collection of Anti-proverbs*. Burlington, VT: The University of Vermont; Veszprém, Hungary: The Pannonian University of Veszprém.

MacDowell, Marsha, and Wolfgang Mieder. 2010. "When Life Hands You Scraps, Make a Quilt': Quiltmakers and the Tradition of Proverbial Inscriptions." *Proverbium*, 27: 113–172.

Manders, Dean Wolfe. 2006. *The Hegemony of Common Sense. Wisdom and Mystification in Everyday Life*. New York: Peter Lang.

McKenzie, Alyce M. 1996. " 'Different Strokes for Different Folks': America's Quintessential Postmodern Proverb." *Theology Today*, 53: 201–212.

Mieder, Wolfgang. 1989. *American Proverbs: A Study of Texts and Contexts*. Bern: Peter Lang.

Mieder, Wolfgang. 1990. " 'A Proverb Is Worth a Thousand Words': From Advertising Slogan to American Proverb." *Southern Folklore*, 47: 207–225.

Mieder, Wolfgang. 1991. " '(Don't) Throw the Baby Out with the Bath Water': The Americanization of a German Proverb and Proverbial Expression." *Western Folklore*, 50: 361–400.

Mieder, Wolfgang. 1993a. *Proverbs Are Never Out of Season. Popular Wisdom in the Modern Age*. New York: Oxford University Press.

Mieder, Wolfgang. 1993b. " 'The Grass Is Always Greener on the Other Side of the Fence': An American Proverb of Discontent." *Proverbium*, 10: 151–184.

Mieder, Wolfgang. 2000. " 'It's Not a President's Business to Catch Flies': Proverbial Rhetoric in Inaugural Addresses of American Presidents." *Southern Folklore*, 57: 188–232.

Mieder, Wolfgang. 2004. *Proverbs. A Handbook*. Westport, CT: Greenwood Press.

Mieder, Wolfgang. 2005. "American Proverbs as an International, National, and Global Phenomenon." *Tautosakos Darbai/Folklore Studies* (Vilnius), 30: 57–72.

Mieder, Wolfgang. 2006. " 'Different Strokes for Different Folks'." *Encyclopedia of African American Folklore*. Ed. Anand Prahlad. Westport, CT: Greenwood Press. I, 324–327.

Mieder, Wolfgang. 2008. " 'Wisdom Is Better Than Wealth'. Proverbs as Expressions of Culture and Folklore." *"Proverbs Speak Louder Than Words". Folk Wisdom in Art, Culture, Folklore, History, Literature, and Mass Media*. Ed. Wolfgang Mieder. New York: Peter Lang, 9–44.

Mieder, Wolfgang. 2009a. *International Bibliography of Paremiology and Phraseology*. 2 vols. Berlin: Walter de Gruyter.

Mieder, Wolfgang. 2009b. *"Yes We Can": Barack Obama's Proverbial Rhetoric*. New York: Peter Lang.

Mieder, Wolfgang. 2010. *"Making a Way Out of No Way": Martin Luther King's Sermonic Proverbial Rhetoric*. New York: Peter Lang.

Mieder, Wolfgang. 2012. " 'Think Outside the Box': Origin, Nature, and Meaning of Modern Anglo-American Proverbs." *Proverbium*, 29: 137–196.

Mieder, Wolfgang. 2014. "Futuristic Paremiography and Paremiology. A Plea for the Collection and Study of Modern Proverbs." *Folklore Fellows' Network*, no volume given, no. 44 (July): 13–17 and 20–24.

Mieder, Wolfgang. 2015a. *"Different Strokes for Different Folks"*. 1250 authentisch amerikanische Sprichwörter. Bochum: Norbert Brockmeyer.

Mieder, Wolfgang. 2015b. " 'Politics is not a Spectator Sport'. Proverbs in the Personal and Political Writings of Hillary Rodham Clinton." *Tautosakos Darbai/Folklore Studies* (Vilnius), 50: 43–74.

Mieder, Wolfgang. 2015c. "Origin of Proverbs." *Introduction to Paremiology. A Comprehensive Guide to Proverb Studies*. Eds. Hrisztalina Hrisztova-Gotthardt and Melita Aleksa Varga. Berlin: Walter de Gruyter. 28–48.

Mieder, Wolfgang. 2019a. " 'Proverbs Are Worth a Thousand Words': The Global Spread of American Proverbs." *Contexts of Folklore. Festschrift for Dan Ben-Amos on His Eighty-Fifth Birthday*. Eds. Simon Bronner and Wolfgang Mieder. New York: Peter Lang. 217–229.

Mieder, Wolfgang. 2019b.*"Right Makes Might". Proverbs and the American Worldview*. Bloomington, IN: Indiana University Press.

Mieder, Wolfgang. 2020. " 'Love Is Just a Four-Letter Word'. Sexuality and Scatology in Modern Anglo-American Proverbs." *Proceedings of the 13th Interdisciplinary Colloquium on Proverbs, 3rd to 10th November 2019, at Tavira, Portugal*. Eds. Rui J.B. Soares and Outi Lauhakangas. Tavira: Tipografia Tavirense. in print.

Mieder, Wolfgang, and Alan Dundes (eds.). 1981. *The Wisdom of Many. Essays on the Proverb*. New York: Garland Publishing.

Mieder, Wolfgang, and George B. Bryan. 1997. *The Proverbial Harry S. Truman. An Index to Proverbs in the Works of Harry S. Truman.* New York: Peter Lang.

Mieder, Wolfgang, Stewart A. Kingsbury, and Kelsie B. Harder. 1992. *A Dictionary of American Proverbs.* New York: Oxford University Press.

Mokienko, Valerii M. 2003. *Novaia russkaia frazeologiia.* Opole: Uniwersytet Opolski—Instytut Filologii Polskiej.

Naugle, David K. 2002. *Worldview. The History of a Concept.* Grand Rapids, MI: William B. Erdmans.

Nedeva, Svetla. 2014. "Achieving Better Intercultural Communication Through Learning to Interpret Cultural Value of Proverbs in a Language and the Way They Reflect National Character." *Revista Economică*, 66: 105–116.

Norwine, Jim, and Jonathan M. Smith (eds.). 2000. *Worldview Flux. Perplexed Values among Postmodern Peoples.* Lanham, MD: Lexington Books.

Nussbaum, Stan. 1998. *The ABC of American Culture: First Steps toward Understanding the American People though Their Common Sayings and Proverbs.* Colorado Springs, CO: Global Mapping International.

Nussbaum, Stan. 2005. *American Cultural [and Proverbial] Baggage. How to Recognize and Deal with It.* Maryknoll, NY: Orbis Books.

Prahlad, Sw. Anand. 1996. *African-American Proverbs in Context.* Jackson, MS: University Press of Mississippi.

Profantová, Zuzana. 1996. "Worldview, Proverbs, Folk Narrative." *Folk Narrative and World View. Vorträge des 10. Kongresses der Internationalen Gesellschaft für Volkserzählforschung (ISFNR), Innsbruck 1992.* Ed. Leander Petzoldt. 2 vols. Frankfurt am Main: Peter Lang. II, 719–793.

Shapiro, Fred R. 2006. *The Yale Book of Quotations.* New Haven, CT: Yale University Press.

Stewart, Susan. 1991. "Notes on Distressed Genres." *Journal of American Folklore*, 104: 5–31.

Teliya, Veronika N., Natalya Bragina, Elena Oparina, and Irina Sandormirskaya. 1998. "Phraseology as a Language of Culture: Its Role in the Representation of Cultural Mentality." *Phraseology: Theory, Analysis, and Applications.* Ed. A.P. Cowie. Oxford: Oxford University Press. 55–75.

Tierney, John J. 2016. *Conceived in Liberty. The American Worldview in Theory and Practice.* New Brunswick, NJ: Transaction Publishers.

Valdaeva, Tatiana. 2003. "Anti-proverbs or New Proverbs: The Use of English Anti-proverbs and Their Stylistic Analysis." *Proverbium*, 20: 379–390.

White, Geoffrey M. 1987. "Proverbs and Cultural Models: An American Psychology of Problem Solving." *Cultural Models in Language and Thought.* Eds. Dorothy Holland and Naomi Quinn. Cambridge: Cambridge University Press. 151–172.

Chapter Three

"Life Is Not a Spectator Sport"

Proverbial Emotions about Modern Life

There have been voices claiming that proverbs are dropping out of existence in the modern age and that new ones are not created any longer. Already in 1931, the sociologist William Albig made the absurd observation that "it must be clear that the proverb has largely disappeared from our general communicative culture" (Albig 1931: 532). More recently Ruth Ayaß came to the equally questionable conclusion that "proverbs are a communicative fossil and—due to the shape of moral communication in our society—even an endangered species" (Ayaß 2001: 252). And there is also Susan Stewart's claim that proverbs are a distressed genre of verbal folklore: "In its oral form, the proverb is 'worn,' on both the positive and negative senses, because of its status as a transcendent and time-proven form of discourse. A new proverb would be as unimaginable to tradition as an original Aesopian fable or a private fad. Thus, the literary tradition of the proverb takes one of two paths—that of new collections of previously known proverbs, or that of invented proverbs that never survive to be applied to concrete situations" (Stewart 1991: 17–18). Alas, nothing could be further from the truth! As one of my book titles declares, *Proverbs Are Never Out of*

Season: Popular Wisdom in the Modern Age (1993), and traditional folk wisdom survives perfectly well in the twenty-first century, even if the appearance of anti-proverbs, the intentional manipulation and variation of proverbs, is gaining ground (Litovkina and Mieder 2006). But even this is an indication that proverbs are actually doing very well, for innovative anti-proverbs can only be created if the older proverbs are still known. Even more importantly, new proverbs continue to be formulated (Honeck and Welge 1997, Mieder 2015b: 38–43). These modern proverbs are ample proof that the time of proverb making is definitely not over today. People continue to rely on old and new proverbs to express their attitudes, beliefs, emotions, mores, and values in wisdom sayings or, to use a modern term, sound bites of their worldview (Hakamies 2002). And as I have argued at the conclusion of my essay on "Futuristic Paremiography and Paremiology: A Plea for the Collection and Study of Modern Proverbs" (2014), "the polyfunctionality, polysemanticity, and polysituativity of these modern proverbs deserve the attention of paremiographers and paremiologists everywhere, who, proverbially speaking, need to think outside the box as they study the fascinating world of proverbial modernity in the language of their countries" (Mieder 2014: 23).

The scholarly problem is that the study of modern proverbs—let us say any proverb that cannot be referenced before the year 1900—is still very much in its infant stage. For phraseology in general there is Valerii M. Mokienko's book *Novaia russkaia frazeologiia* (2003), but for proverbs in particular Charles Clay Doyle, Fred R. Shapiro, and I have assembled the first *Dictionary of Modern [Anglo-American] Proverbs* (2012). Doyle had published his pioneering article "On 'New' Proverbs and the Conservativeness of Proverb Dictionaries" (1996) in *Proverbium: Yearbook of International Proverb Scholarship*, and we soon realized that we should join forces in trying to find new Proverbs that had not been registered in proverb collections before. Fred R. Shapiro joined us as well, and after many years of identifying and annotating newly found texts, we were able to present 1422 primarily American proverbs in our historically documented and contextualized dictionary. And as can be imagined, the work must go on, with Charles Doyle and I by now having published three supplements with 85, 57, and 53 additional modern Anglo-American proverbs respectively in *Proverbium* (Doyle and Mieder 2016, 2018, and 2020). I have also presented a detailed analysis and characterization in *Proverbium* with the title " 'Think Outside the Box': Origin, Nature, and Meaning of Modern Anglo-American Proverbs" (2012). This is not the place to review all of this, but let me just list the following general observations with but a few examples and their dates of the first occurrence found thus far as well as the page number of where they are registered in the *Dictionary of Modern Proverbs* in parentheses:

1. Modern proverbs do exist in variants
   Don't take (tear) down a fence (wall) unless you are sure why it was put up (1964, 75)
2. Most modern proverbs are straightforward indicative sentences
   A crisis is an opportunity (1900, 47)
3. Some have parallelism and rhyme
   Different strokes for different folks (1945, 241–242; Mieder 1989: 317–332, McKenzie 1996)
4. Prevalent negative patterns:
   You cannot (can't) …
   You can't be a little pregnant (1942, 206)
   Don't …
   Don't believe everything you think (1948, 19)
   Never …
   Never give anything away that you can sell (1953, 98)
5. Prevalent structural patterns:
   No X, no Y
   No guts, no glory (1945, 112–113)
   X is better than Y
   A live soldier is better than a dead hero (1904, 236)
   If you can X, you can Y
   If you can dream it, you can do it (1970, 62)
   When you X, you Y
   When you have nothing, you have nothing to lose (1965, 182)
   There are no X, only (just) Y
   There are no bad students, only bad teachers (1958, 242)

6. Two-word proverbs
   Manners matter (1909, 163)
7. Many four-word proverbs
   Everyone can't be first (1955, 78)
8. There are also longer proverbs, but not very common
   Be nice to people on your way up because you'll meet them on your way down (1932, 193)
9. Proverbs created as so-called laws
   If anything can go wrong, it will (1908, 101–102; Murphy's law)
10. Proverbs attributed to individuals
    Old age is not for sissies (1969, 4; attributed to the actress Bette Davis)
11. Proverbs with known originators
    You can't go home again (1940, 123; title of Thomas Wolfe's novel)
12. Proverbs based on advertising slogans
    It's what's up front that counts (1957, 45; Winston cigarettes)
13. Proverbs from songs
    Diamonds are a girl's best friend (1949, 55; song by Leo Robin)
14. Proverbs form motion pictures
    If you've got it, flaunt it (1968, 96; motion picture *The Producers*)
15. Animal proverbs continue to be popular
    You can put lipstick on a pig but it's still a pig (1985, 148; Mieder 2009: 83–86)
16. Proverbial somatisms are quite prevalent
    Busy hands are happy hands (1956, 115)
17. Proverbs from the world of business
    If you have to ask the price, you can't afford it (1926, 207)
18. The world of sports
    You can't score if you don't shoot (1965, 223)
19. Only a few proverbs dealing with technology
    Garbage in, garbage out (1957, 94; from the world of computers)
20. Scatological proverbs
    Shit happens (1944, 228)
21. Sexual proverbs
    Everybody lies about sex (1973, 226)

It can also be stated that of the 1422 proverbs contained in our dictionary 676 (47.5%) are clearly metaphorical, while slightly more than half the corpus (746; 52.5%) are literal statements. A few of these proverbs have gained a global dissemination as loan translations, as for example the American proverb "One picture is worth a thousand words" (1911, 196) that is current in Russian as "Odna kartina luchshe tysiachi slov" (Mieder 1990).

Regarding the most frequent keywords of the proverbs, it can be seen from the following numbers that the most popular keyword is "life". It is hardly a surprise that modern humankind is preoccupied with various aspects of existence, something that is also true for earlier Anglo-American proverbs (Mieder, Kingsbury, and Harder 1992: 373–376):

life	46 proverbs
man	34 proverbs
God	19 proverbs
time	19 proverbs
friend	15 proverbs
money	12 proverbs
time	11 proverbs
age	8 proverbs
woman	8 proverbs
love	8 proverbs
beauty	7 proverbs
pain	7 proverbs
success	7 proverbs
talk	7 proverbs
hope	5 proverbs
luck	5 proverbs

This shows in a generalized way some of the preoccupations of modern society. People at times appear to be obsessed with matters of age, beauty, love, money, success, and of course time (Lau 1996). But God also plays a considerable role together with hope and luck, somewhat reminiscent of what Alan Dundes has called the "future orientation in American worldview" (1969: 53). It would be difficult to deduce the worldview of masses of people by way of these relatively small numbers (Dundes 1972, White 1987). But the proverbs about life that express various emotional reactions to modernity might well be somewhat indicative of common sentiments. A closer look at them might thus be enlightening indeed, with the following 46 proverbs (with variants in parentheses) being taken from *The Dictionary of Modern Proverbs* (Doyle, Mieder, Shapiro 2012: 139–147) and an additional five proverbs from the two supplements (Doyle and Mieder 2016 and 2018, indicated as S1, S2, and S3). As can be seen, the collection and analysis of new proverbs is an ongoing and never-ending process offering much excitement of discovery for paremiologists—scholars and students alike!

There is no doubt that a majority of the "life"-proverbs follows the definitional pattern of "Life is ..." that is perfectly suitable to express positive as well as negative emotions about modern life without any particular reliance on colorful metaphors. Among the more positive proverbs are the following:

> Life is a treasure hunt. (1924, S3, in print)
> Life is a party (1944, 142)
> Life is (just) a cabaret (1966, 142)
> Life is a dance you can learn as you go (1992, 142)

There is also the jovial proverb "Life is (just) a bowl of cherries" (1931, 141–142) from a popular song by Lee Brown of which the second verse goes like this:

> Life is just a bowl of cherries.
> Don't take it serious,
> Life's too mysterious.
> You work, you save, and you worry so,
> But you can't take your dough when you go, go, go.
> So keep repeating it's the berries,
> The strongest oak must fall.
> The sweet things in life to you were just loaned,
> So how can you lose what you've never owned.
> Life is just a bowl of cherries,
> So live, love, and laugh at all.
> (Sobieski and Mieder 2005: 81)

However, in the same year of 1931 the opposite proverb "Life is not a bowl of cherries" (1931, 143) gained popularity. In 1972 Charles Doyle coined the term "counter-proverb" for such "an overt negation or sententious-sounding rebuttal of a proverb, an explicit denial of the proverb's asserted truth" (Doyle, Mieder, and Shapiro 2012: xi). Such positive/negative proverb pairs are not that rare, with both of them having sufficient currency to be considered proverbs in their own rights. And it might well be that the proverb "Life is like (is just) a box of chocolates" (1994, 143) from the motion picture *Forrest Gump* is an intentional playful manipulation of the "bowl of cherries"-proverb. For this type of new proverb creation Wolfgang Mieder came up with the term anti-proverb, defining it as "an allusive distortion, parody, misapplication, or unexpected contextualization of a recognized proverb, usually for comic or satiric effect" (Doyle, Mieder, and Shapiro 2012: xi). And to be sure, such anti-proverbs can and do become new proverbs if they are accepted and used in oral and written contexts (Valdaeva 2003).

Some anti-proverbs are also created by expanding an existing proverb that adds some revealing fact to its message, as for example:

Life is a bitch (1940, 141)
Life is a bitch, and then you die (1982, 141)
Life is a bitch, and then you marry one (1987, 141)

It is important here to notice that while "bitch" has the basic meaning of "bad" in the first two proverbs, it connotes a "nasty woman" in the misogynous third proverb. Fortunately, there is also the much more complimentary proverb "Life is not life without a wife (There's no life without a wife)" (1952, 143–144).

Here is another pair of basically positive proverbs, with the anti-proverb adding a work component to the pleasant image of life being like a beautiful flower garden. And do notice that their origins are several decades apart with both having their own widespread dissemination:

Life is a garden (1914, 142)
Life is a garden; dig it (1972. 142)

Of interest is also this following pair of proverbs. The earlier longer version has lost its appeal in more recent times and has more or less been replaced with the newer and shorter proverb with a similar meaning:

> Don't take life too seriously; you'll never get out of it alive (1911, 140)
> No one gets out of (this) life alive (1963, S2, 30)

There are also cases where two proverbs are probably variants of each other, but by way of frequency studies it has been established that they both exist as independent proverbs with their origins being years apart:

> Life is hard by the yard, but by the inch it's a cinch (1947, 143)
> Inch-by-inch, life (everything) is a cinch, but yard-by-yard it is hard (1980, S1, 105–106)

> Life is (like) a shit sandwich (without bread) (and every day we take another bite) (1966, 143)
> Life is a shit sandwich: the more bread you have, the less shit you eat (1978, 143)

One of the most popular positive "life"-proverbs instilling hopeful emotions in someone facing some problems has proven itself to be considerably older than one might have suspected. The encouraging message of "If life hands you lemons, make lemonade" (1910, 140) resonates with people for over one hundred years due to its intriguing image. But that does not mean that a small folk group, namely that of blanket quilters, might not have taken its basic structure and changed its realia to "If life hands you scraps, make a quilt" (1992, 140). I still remember when I learned this proverb in 2009 from Marsha MacDowell, a fellow folklorist who happens to be a scholar on the rich world of quilts. I would probably never have discovered this modern proverb on my own, indicating the difficulty of finding hitherto unrecorded proverbs. In any case, both of us subsequently published an article about quilts that contain proverbial inscriptions and we used the proverb as an attention-getting title (MacDowell and Mieder 2010).

One would expect some proverbs that deal with the feeling that life in its shortness passes by too quickly. No wonder that people like to rationalize this emotion by saying "Life begins at forty" (1932, 141). As I am getting older, I have caught myself varying this proverb to

"Life begins at sixty" and now also to "Life begins at seventy". These personal variants have, however, not become proverbial! But here then are three proverbs about the shortness of life that try to put a positive spin on the matter:

> Life is too short (too precious) to waste it sleeping (Don't waste your life sleeping) (1944, 145)
> Life is too short (to wait) for someday (1969, 144)
> Life is too short to drink (too short for) bad wine (1985, 144)

The first proverb is reminiscent of Benjamin Franklin's proverb "There will be sleeping enough in the grave" that he coined in 1741 in his *Poor Richard's Alamanack* (Mieder 2004: 217, and 2015a: 209).

But then there are also proverbs that stress that life is a rather lengthy process that needs to be managed with care, patience, endurance, and good timing (Freund and Baltes 2002):

> Life is a marathon, not a sprint (1915, S2, 29–30)
> Life (The main thing in life) is (about) timing (1919, 144)
> Life is a journey, not a destination (1941, 142)
> Life is a picture; paint it well (1956, 142–143)
> Life is what happened while you are making other plans (1957, 145)
> Eighty (ninety) percent of life (success) is (just) showing up (1977, 140)

A few additional proverbs that follow the "Life is …" pattern concern themselves with the feeling that life is rather mundane with plenty of challenges that can result in depression, frustration, and other types of emotions:

> Life is (just) one (damn) thing after another (1909, 144)
> Life is so daily (1943, 144)
> Life is a funny (strange) dog (1976, 142)
> Life is tough (hard); wear (get) a helmet (1992, 145)

As one would expect, there are also a few "life"-proverbs that do not follow this established pattern. For the most part they look at life as being rather complicated and challenging, even if they intend to be somewhat humorous as in "Anything good in life is either illegal, immoral, or fattening" (1933, 139–140). Speaking of gaining weight, there is of course also this culinary piece of advice: "To lengthen your life, lessen your meals" (1947, 146) that fits well to the modern dietary concerns.

In any case, modern life takes strength and readiness for constant changes, giving people plenty emotional stress:

> It's a good (great) life if you don't weaken (1914, 140–141)
> Life deals us each a hand (1997, 141)
> Life comes at you fast (2004, 141)

That does not mean that modern people should not embrace life to the fullest by facing it head on. It is interesting to note how the proverbs of the following two proverb pairs are quite similar and certainly express the same idea, even though they originated several decades apart. This shows once again how new proverbs are created even though almost identical proverbs already existed. And yet, both proverbs in each case have their own distribution and frequency of use:

> Live life to the fullest (1934, 146)
> Live life like you mean it (1972, 146)
>
> Nobody ever said life is fair (Who ever said life is fair?) (1929, 146)
> Nobody ever said life is easy (Who ever said life is easy?) (1965, 146)

The fact that life is not always fair or easy has also resulted in three related proverbs that became established during a period of a bit more than two decades. The first text is a very simple but rather drastic two-word proverb consisting of a topic and a comment (Dundes 1975: 970), with the slang verb basically meaning "bad, horrible". The second text adds a fatalistic touch to it, while the third and longest proverb argues that while life is problematic, it is still better than death:

> Life sucks (1979, 145)
> Life sucks, and then you die (1984, 145)
> Life sucks, but it's better than the alternative (2002, 145)

So, the best thing to do is to face life squarely and make the best of it since everyone has only one life to live:

You get out of life (the world) what you put into it (1901, 146)
Take (You must take) what life gives you (1908, 146)
You only go around (round) once in life (1966, 146–147)

Since modern proverbs do not shy away from scatological or sexual aspects, a text like "Take (grab) life (the bull) by the balls" (1954,
146) should not be a surprise as a somewhat risqué metaphor for making
the most out of one's life. The proverb had its start as an anti-proverb of
the older innocuous proverb "Take the bull by the horns" and its variant "Take life by the horns". The exchange of "horns" with "balls" adds
an emotional touch of aggression, even though most speakers will not
necessarily think of the balls as testicles when employing this proverb.

Since life in general is considered sacred and valuable, there are
finally also proverbs that express the nobility of saving lives. The following two proverbs are especially appropriate for today's refugee
crisis throughout the world. Remembering this wisdom might help to
provide humanitarian aid to displaced and persecuted people:

The life you save may (could) be your own (1947, 146)
If you save one life, you save the world (1982, S1, 105)

Of course, this is also what the final proverb of this review of modern
"life"-proverbs says in a most appropriate way: "Life is not a spectator
sport" (1958, 143). Former vice president Nelson Rockefeller, as governor of the state of New York, changed the proverb during a news
conference on November 17, 1963, to an anti-proverb: "I think we
would arouse a lot of participation on the part of the public. Politics
is not a spectator sport. We need public participation" (1963, S1, 113).
He might also have been thinking of yet another modern American
proverb that had originated three years earlier and that calls for par-
ticipatory politics in a similar way: "Politics is a contact sport" (1960,
203). In any case, former first lady Hillary Rodham Clinton entitled
a chapter in her acclaimed book *It Takes a Village and Other Lessons
Children Teach Us* (1996) with "Child Care Is not a Spectator Sport" to
express the necessity for people to get involved in improving child
care in the United States (Clinton 1996: 207). And wanting to properly
describe her decades of political engagement as US Senator from the

state of New York and Secretary of State of the United Sates and more, I chose the following proverbial title for my analysis: "'Politics is not a Spectator Sport': Proverbs in the Personal and Political Writings of Hillary Rodham Clinton" (Mieder 2015c). But modern people do not live by politics alone, to paraphrase the Biblical proverb "Man does not live by bread alone" (Deuteronomy 8:3, Matthew 4:4). Much more important is the sapiential insight that "Life is not a spectator sport". This proverb calls for social engagement and compassion, where people join hands in "Making a way out of no way" (1922, 102), as this modern African-American proverb suggests that was Martin Luther King's humanitarian leitmotif (Mieder 2010: 171–186). There can then be no doubt that the modern proverb "Life is not a spectator sport" encapsulates much social wisdom for an interconnected world of peaceful, responsible, and empathetic existence.

Bibliography

This chapter was first published at Moscow, Russia, as "'Life Is not a Spectator Sport'. Proverbial Emotions about Modern Life." *Emotsional'naia sfera cheloveka v iazyke i kommunikatsii: Sinkhroniia i diakhroniia*. Ed. E.R. Ioanesian. Moscow: Institut Iazykoznaniia RAN, 2018. 7–17.

Albig, William. 1931. "Proverbs and Social Control." *Sociology and Social Research*, 15: 527–535.

Ayaß, Ruth. 2001. "On the Genesis and the Destiny of Proverbs." *Verbal Art across Cultures: The Aesthetics and Proto-Aesthetics of Communication*. Eds. Hubert Knoblauch and Helga Kotthoff. Tübingen: Gunter Narr. 237–254.

Clinton, Hillary Rodham. 1996. *It Takes a Village and Other Lessons Children Teach Us*. New York: Simon & Schuster (10th Anniversary Edition with a New Introduction, 2006; the page number refers to this edition).

Doyle, Charles Clay. 1996. "On 'New' Proverbs and the Conservativeness of Proverb Dictionaries." *Proverbium*, 13: 69–84.

Doyle, Charles Clay, and Wolfgang Mieder. 2016. *"The Dictionary of Modern Proverbs*: A Supplement." *Proverbium*, 33: 85–120.

Doyle, Charles Clay, and Wolfgang Mieder. 2018. *"The Dictionary of Modern Proverbs*: A Supplement." *Proverbium*, 35: 15–44.

Doyle, Charles Clay, and Wolfgang Mieder. 2020. *"The Dictionary of Modern Proverbs*: Third Supplement." *Proverbium*, 37: 53–86.

Doyle, Charles Clay, Wolfgang Mieder, and Fred R. Shapiro. 2012. *The Dictionary of Modern Proverbs*. New Haven, CT: Yale University Press.

Dundes, Alan. 1969. "Thinking Ahead: A Folkloristic Reflection of the Future Orientation in American Worldview." *Anthropological Quarterly*, 42: 53–72.

Dundes, Alan. 1972. "Folk Ideas as Units of Worldview." *Towards New Perspectives in Folklore*. Eds. Américo Paredes and Richard Bauman. Austin, TX: University of Texas Press. 93–103.

Dundes, Alan. 1975. "On the Structure of the Proverb." *Proverbium*, no. 25: 961–973.

Freund, Alexandra M., and Paul B. Baltes. 2002. "The Adaptiveness of Selection, Optimization, and Compensation as Strategies of Life Management: Evidence from a Preference Study of Proverbs." *Journal of Gerontology: Psychological Sciences*, 57: 426–434.

Hakamies, Pekka. 2002. "Proverbs and Mentality." *Myth and Mentality: Studies in Folklore and Popular Thought*. Ed. Anna-Leena Siikala. Helsinki: Finnish Literature Society. 222–230.

Honeck, Richard P., and Jeffrey Welge. 1997. "Creation of Proverbial Wisdom in the Laboratory." *Journal of Psycholinguistic Research*, 26: 605–629.

Lau, Kimberly. 1996. "'It's about Time': The Ten Proverbs Most Frequently Used in Newspapers and Their Relation to American Values." *Proverbium*, 13: 135–159.

Litovkina. Anna T., and Wolfgang Mieder. 2006. *Old Proverbs Never Die, They Just Diversify. A Collection of Anti-proverbs*. Burlington, VT: The University of Vermont; Veszprén, Hungary: The Pannonian University of Veszprém.

MacDowell, Marsha, and Wolfgang Mieder. 2010. "When Life Hands You Scraps, Make a Quilt': Quiltmakers and the Tradition of Proverbial Inscriptions." *Proverbium*, 27: 113–172.

McKenzie, Alyce M. 1996. "'Different Strokes for Different Folks': America's Quintessential Postmodern Proverb." *Theology Today*, 53: 201–212.

Mieder, Wolfgang. 1989. *American Proverbs: A Study of Texts and Contexts*. Bern: Peter Lang.

Mieder, Wolfgang. 1990. "'A Proverb Is Worth a Thousand Words': From Advertising Slogan to American Proverb." *Southern Folklore*, 47: 207–225.

Mieder, Wolfgang. 1993. *Proverbs Are Never Out of Season. Popular Wisdom in the Modern Age*. New York: Oxford University Press.

Mieder, Wolfgang. 2004. *Proverbs. A Handbook*. Westport, CT: Greenwood Press.

Mieder, Wolfgang. 2009. *"Yes We Can": Barack Obama's Proverbial Rhetoric*. New York: Peter Lang.

Mieder, Wolfgang. 2010. *"Making a Way Out of No Way": Martin Luther King's Sermonic Proverbial Rhetoric*. New York: Peter Lang.

Mieder, Wolfgang. 2012. "'Think Outside the Box': Origin, Nature, and Meaning of Modern Anglo-American Proverbs." *Proverbium*, 29: 137–196.

Mieder, Wolfgang. 2014. "Futuristic Paremiography and Paremiology. A Plea for the Collection and Study of Modern Proverbs." *Folklore Fellows' Network*, no volume given, no. 44 (July): 13–17 and 20–24.

Mieder, Wolfgang. 2015a. *"Different Strokes for Different Folks". 1250 authentisch amerikanische Sprichwörter*. Bochum: Norbert Brockmeyer.

Mieder, Wolfgang. 2015b. "Origin of Proverbs." *Introduction to Paremiology. A Comprehensive Guide to Proverb Studies*. Eds. Hrisztalina Hrisztova-Gotthardt and Melita Aleksa Varga. Berlin: Walter de Gruyter. 28–48.

Mieder, Wolfgang. 2015c. "'Politics is not a Spectator Sport': Proverbs in the Personal and Political Writings of Hillary Rodham Clinton." *Tautosakos Darbai/Folklore Studies* (Vilnius), 50: 43–74.

Mieder, Wolfgang, Stewart A. Kingsbury, and Kelsie B. Harder. 1992. *A Dictionary of American Proverbs*. New York: Oxford University Press.

Mokienko, Valerii M. 2003. *Novaia russkaia frazeologiia*. Opole: Uniwersytet Opolski—Instytut Filologii Polskiej.

Sobieski, Janet, and Wolfgang Mieder (eds.). 2005. *"So Many Heads, So Many Wits"*. *An Anthology of English Proverb Poetry*. Burlington, VT: The University of Vermont.

Stewart, Susan. 1991. "Notes on Distressed Genres." *Journal of American Folklore*, 104: 5–31.

Valdaeva, Tatiana. 2003. "Anti-proverbs or New Proverbs: The Use of English Anti-proverbs and Their Stylistic Analysis." *Proverbium*, 20: 379–390.

White, Geoffrey M. 1987. "Proverbs and Cultural Models: An American Psychology of Problem Solving." *Cultural Models in Language and Thought*. Eds. Dorothy Holland and Naomi Quinn. Cambridge: Cambridge University Press. 151–172.

Chapter Four

"Age Is Just a Number"

American Proverbial Wisdom about Age and Aging

Proverbs contain generalized wisdom about all aspects of human existence, and it should not be surprising that proverbs about life as such abound in languages throughout the world with new proverbial insights being added as challenges and opportunities change (Ayaß 2001, Honeck and Welge 1997, Mieder 2015b: 38–41). Naturally there are many proverbs about birth and death and various other rites of passage that are part of life with its unavoidable aging process. Every human being faces the multifaceted steps from youth to a hopefully fulfilled old age with proverbs containing much knowledge about getting old in particular. Little wonder that a few paremiologists have looked at these proverbs in some detail, to wit such scholarly contributions as J. Olowo Ojoade's "The Old Woman as Seen through African Proverbs: Fragmentary Remarks about African Society through Sayings" (1985), Ingrid Schellbach-Kopra's "Das Alter im Sprichwort der Deutschen und Finnen—eine kontrastive Betrachtung" (1988), J.O.J. Nwachukwu-Agbada's "The Old Woman in Igbo Proverbial Lore" (1989), Kewzi Ruduri's "Les thèmes de la 'jeunesse' et de la 'vieillesse' dans quelques proverbes Rwanda: Considérations socio-culturelles"

(1993), Wolfgang Mieder's "'Alter schützt vor Torheit und Weisheit nicht': Sprichwörter über das Alter(n) aus Literatur und Massenmedien" (1999), Frank H. Nuessel's "The Depiction of Older Adults and Aging in Italian Proverbs" (2000), José Henrique Barros de Oliveira's "Proverbs about Aging and the Old Ages: Educative Applications" (2008), Carolin Krüger's *Zur Repräsentation des Alter(n)s im deutschen Sprichwort* (2009), and Iu. S. Nazar'vea's "Anglo-amerikanskie aforizmy kak sredstvo ob"ektivatsii kontsepta 'Old Age' ('starost')" (2010). As some of these titles indicate or imply, there are anthropological and socio-cultural differences in the gerontological worldview of people, with the following deliberations taking a look at American proverbial thoughts about getting and being old.

As anthropologists, cultural historians, folklorists, and psychologists have pointed out repeatedly, Americans in general are forward-looking and exhibit a linear and future-oriented worldview (Dundes 1972: 98) that can easily be observed in the "future-orientation in American folk speech" such as "proverbs, folk metaphors, and other traditional linguistic clichés and symbols found throughout the United States" (Dundes 1969: 56). As such, proverbs contain "strategies of life management" (Freund and Baltes 2002: 426) and can together with other indicators "provide relevant and interesting data for mentality studies" (Hakamies 2002: 229). As Geoffrey M. White has shown, certain proverbs can be seen as "cultural models [for] an American psychology of problem solving" (1987: 151) with one of these "problems" being that of advancing age. How then do authentic American proverbs at the intentional exclusion of British proverbs deal with aging as registered in *The Dictionary of Modern Proverbs* (2012), edited by Charles Clay Doyle, Wolfgang Mieder, and Fred R. Shapiro?

In his fascinating book on *The Journey of Life: A Cultural History of Aging in America* (1992) Thomas R. Cole observes that "since the mid-nineteenth century, Americans have come to view aging not as a fated aspect of our individual and social existence but as one of life's problems to be solved through willpower, aided by science, technology, and expertise" (xxii). Citing the modern proverb "There are no second acts in American lives" that had its origin with F. Scott Fitzgerald's "My Lost City" (1932), he points out that "the middle-class American vision of aging has amounted to a kind of perpetual middle age, at once valued above and disconnected from childhood and old age" (241). The proverb, also current in its shortened variant "There are no second acts" (1940: 2; the dates represent the earliest references cited in the *Dictionary of Modern Proverbs* plus the page number therein) contains the message that life must be lived to its fullest before aging sets in or, more extreme, to avoid aging altogether. The considerably older American proverb "You are only young once" from 1804 (Mieder 2015a: 252) expresses a similar attitude, pushing aside aging by stressing that one is always young enough to enjoy life (Mieder 2018). Even the appearance of the anti-proverb turned modern proverb "You're only old once" (1927, 183–184; see also Valdaeva 2003) in the humorous book title *You're Only Old Once. A Book for Obsolete Children* (1986) by the famous Dr. Seuss (Theodor Seuss Geisel, 1904–1991) does not change matters. It still argues for living it up and ignoring age as best as possible. But speaking of anti-proverbs, the American humorist Ogden Nash is supposed to have quipped "You are only young once, but you can stay immature indefinitely", and there are also these additional three parodies: "You are only young once. After that you merely think you are", "You are young only once. If you act foolish after that you'll have to find some other excuse", and "You're only young once, and if you work it right, once is enough" (Litovkina and Mieder 2006: 338).

The quintessential proverb to express this viewpoint is without doubt "Life begins at forty" that had its origin with Walter B. Pitkin's best-selling book title *Life Begins at Forty* (1932) and that was popularized by the 1935 motion picture starring Will Rogers (1932: 141). In a prophetic tone the book starts with: "Life begins at forty. This is the revolutionary outcome of our New Era. This is the supreme reward of the Machine Age, the richest blessing of science. Day before yesterday it wasn't even a dream. Yesterday it was a silly lie. Today it is half a truth. Tomorrow it will be an axiom" (5–6). The anthropologist Stanley Brandes even wrote an entire book on *Forty: The Age and the Symbol* (1985), arguing that this is a "midlife crisis: the widely recognized importance of the age forty" (4), representing "middle age" (18), and "a significant turning point, cutting the life span neatly in two" (21). This turning point might well have to be increased to fifty, as life expectancy is on the increase. But no matter what, the proverb does not really deal with advancing age but rather with staying young and fit for several more decades. After all, the proverb is basically saying that the previous thirty-nine years have not really amounted to real living. In this regard, John Lennon's "little ditty" as he called his short song "Life Begins at Forty" (1980, released in 1998) comes to mind:

> They say life begins at forty
> Age is just a state of mind
> If all that's true
> You know that I've been dead for thirty-nine
>
> And if life begins at forty
> Well, I hope it ain't the same
> It's been tough enough without that stuff
> I don't wanna to be born again
>
> Well, I tried to sweep the slate clean
> With a new broom every day
> If that don't work
> I'll jerk around until my next birthday
>
> Yeah, life begins at forty
> Age is just a state of mind
> Well, if all that's true
> You know that I've been dead for thirty-nine

The Beatles song appeared on the album *Free as a Bird* that contains songs that were recorded between 1977 and 1994 (released in 1998), with Lennon's little song stemming from the year of his death in 1980. It is worthwhile that Lennon also alludes to the classical proverb "New brooms sweep clean" in his song. And then there is "Age is just a state of mind" (1930, S3, in print; S1, S2, and S3 refer to Charles Clay Doyle's and Wolfgang Mieder's three supplements to the *Dictionary of Modern Proverbs*) that has only recently been registered. Doubtlessly it had be added to the growing list of modern proverbs that need to be recorded in new proverb dictionaries (Doyle 1996, Mieder 2014, Mokienko 2003). Its message is also one that rationalizes the fact of getting old into something that can be overcome by a youthful mind-set. This is also the viewpoint of Sylvia Chidi's poem "At Forty Life Begins" (2005) which, like that of Lennon, wants to push aging aside and look forward to a rejuvenated start:

> Relaunching itself
> into a birthless age
> It's a phase
> It's a stage
> It's a case
> a renewed forty year package
>
> The rebirth of youth
> It's time to lose
> all your old fashioned suits

And yet, there are anti-proverbs that question the wisdom of the proverb "Life begins at forty" with its message of pushing aside aging. Clearly the rationalizing proverb is in need of a reality check, as it were:

> It may be true that life begins at forty, but everything else starts to wear out,
> fall out, or spread out.
> Life doesn't begin at forty for those who went weighty when they were twenty.
> Life may begin at forty, but so does rheumatism.
> Life not only begins at forty—it begins to show.
> They tell us that life begins at forty, but they don't say what kind of life.
> (Litovkina and Mieder 2006: 199)

And here then are a few stanzas of the recent poem "Life Begins at Forty" (2015) by Ray Blyde that echo this rather pessimistic view of the proverb:

> Life begins at forty,
> At least that's what they say,
> You'll have to come to terms with it
> In each and every way.
>
> Unfortunately the things you find,
> you'd really like to do,
> Are no longer recommended
> For one as old as you.

[...]

Life begins at forty,
And, when all is said and done,
You'll awaken one fine morning,
To find you're forty-one!

And yet, there is no doubt that the proverb "Life begins at forty" continues to be employed as a highly positive statement that helps to create the mindset that there is much to look forward to after having reached somewhat of a mid-point in life-expectancy. After all, nobody in their right mind wants to be reminded of what the Scottish poet Alan Riddell has expressed in his concise poem "Old Adage" (1965) that is based on the fourteenth-century English proverb "You have to crawl (creep) before you can walk" (Mieder, Kingsbury, Harder 1992: 126):

crawl before you
walk before you
run before you
creep
(Sobieski and Mieder 2005: 189)

This little proverb poem depicts in but a few words what old age might have in store as our minds and bodies decline. The thought of it all leads us to not wanting "to think about aging because the prospect of losing bodily integrity, giving-up our much-prized independence, and nearing the end of life's journey is terrifying to us" (Gillick 2006:266). Muriel R. Gillick's book title *The Denial of Aging. Perpetual Youth, Eternal Life, and Other Dangerous Fantasies* (2006) says it all, but it does not contain any references to the fact that American proverbs are part of this denial.

Of course, not all American proverbs deal with such denial (Mieder 1989). In the *Dictionary of American Proverbs* (1992, abbreviated as *DAP*), edited by Wolfgang Mieder, Stewart A. Kingsbury, and Kelsie B. Harder, one finds the following insights presented here in chronological order of their first recorded appearances:

Age gives good advice when it is no longer able to give bad example. (1828, Ralph Waldo Emerson, *DAP*: 12)
Age before beauty (1843, *DAP*: 12)
The surest sign of age is loneliness (1868, *DAP*: 12)

These three texts from the nineteenth-century are well known, but this dictionary also includes the following texts that were collected between 1945 and 1985 in the United States. However, they only have limited regional distribution and do not belong to the common stock of proverbs. They do not exhibit any age denial but rather present some sensible observations and generalizations:

Age is like love: it cannot hide (*DAP*: 12)
Who honors not age is not worthy of it. (*DAP*: 12)
Old in body, young in spirit. (*DAP*: 437)
The best time to prepare for old age is when you are young. (*DAP*: 437)
We get too soon old and too late smart. (*DAP*: 438)

This dictionary also registers the proverb "You are never older than you think you are" (1946, *DAP*: 438) which might well be a somewhat uncommon variant of the well-known and often cited American proverb "You are as old as you feel" (1907, *DAP*: 438) which in turn most likely goes back to Charles Dickens's statement that "A man is as young as he feels" (Dickens 1851: 3) and the longer and somewhat misogynous English proverb "A man is as old as he feels and a woman is as old as she looks" (1871, Speake 2015: 199). Be that as it may, the proverb definitely belongs to the American worldview of trying to push aging aside by implying that as long as we feel good, advancing age is of no matter. That this strategy does not always work is well expressed by an anonymous writer in a short piece on "Consciousness of Age" (1907) that bears its first printed reference: "Over and again the question has been asked: 'When does old age begin?' And another adage says, 'You are as old as you feel.' Very well, according to that, we have seen fresh looking women, clear-eyed, brown or black-haired, who, after a little siege of rheumatism, have declared they felt a hundred years old. And—we say it with dew reverence—almost any sick man feels and acts old as Methuselah" (Anonymous 1907: 584; May 5, 1907; in Great Britain registered on May 25).

Related to all of this is a proverb that originated with the poem "The Windy City [Chicago]" (1922) by the American poet Carl Sandburg: "It ain't how old you are, / It's how old you look." It is cited today as "It isn't how old you are but how old you look" with variants substituting "look" with "feel" (122, 183). But this somewhat long modern proverb is not in much use any longer since the shorter "You are as old as you feel" expresses basically the same idea.

With this said these deliberations have reached those authentic American proverbs that have been recorded in *The Dictionary of Modern Proverbs* (2012). There are but 27 modern proverbs dealing with age and aging, with the proverb just dealt with and the two proverbs "Life begins at forty" and "You're only old once" having already been discussed above. They contain to a certain degree "the folklore of aging" or "the folklore of the life course" (Sellers 2018: 1–2). While much of this wisdom is applicable to other cultures as well, the proverbs as a group illustrate "the American middle-class mentality to suppose that any state other than that of contentment is somehow untenable" Myerhoff and Simić 1978: 16). Part of that is being young or at least fighting against getting old. Simon Bronner has put his finger on this in a short encyclopedic article on "Old Age": "Particularly in the United States, given the nation's prominent image as youthful and future-oriented, an 'age consciousess' suggests that reaching certain ages carries expectations of cultural behavior, community formation, and social status" (Bronner 2018: 1).

Some of this can readily be seen from this first group of three proverbs that begins with the proverbial imperative "Act your age" (Chudacoff 1989: 117–126) that is followed by two expanded variants that elaborate somewhat sarcastically on this behavioral rule attached to a certain age:

Act your age. (1925, 3)
Act your age, not your shoe size. (1967, 3)
Act your age, not your IQ. (1995, 3)

Another group of four proverbs that all follow the identifying pattern of "Old age is …" proves to be quite telling about attitudes towards the later stage of life. Sure, old age might be better than the alternative, but with its ailments and disabilities it is a high price to pay. Above all, old age is "hell", as one of the proverbs states very negatively. The Russian proverb "Starost' ne radost'" (Old age is no pleasure) is much milder in comparison:

Old age is hell. (1952, 4)
Old age is better than the alternative. (1960, 4)
Old age is a high price to pay for maturity. (1969, 3)
Old age is not for sissies. (1969, 4)

The last proverb is of special interest since it is often attributed to the American actress Bette Davis, with the phenomenon of such false attributions being quite common (Mieder 2012: 159–162).

But there is always hope to make the best of old age, especially if one's health is still robust. This is well expressed in the following metaphorical proverbs:

The older the fiddle, the sweeter the tune. (1909, 76)
Just because there's snow on the roof doesn't mean the fire is out inside. (1943, 236)
Old rats like cheese too. (1977, 214)
The older the moon, the brighter it shines. (1991, 171)

It should be observed that that certainly the "snow [gray hair]" and "rats" proverbs can be interpreted as indirect sexual comments, implying that there is plenty of sexual desire left in old age. There is no doubt that the matter of sexuality is part of age-related proverbs. with "the sexuality of the old, and of the very young, seeming to be particularly disconcerting to our [American] society" (Saporta 1991: 334). Little wonder that there are also several rather disturbing proverbs that refer indirectly to sexual activities at a young age. They were clearly coined by aggressive males having forceful sex and not sincere love in mind:

When they are big enough [in body], they are old enough. (1932, 20)
Old enough to bleed [menstruation], old enough to breed. (1971, 22)
If there's grass [pubic hair] on the field, you can play ball. (1998, 111)

Proverbs are by no means sacrosanct, and some of these modern proverbs express things rather directly as they are, basically saying live now and never mind old age. Live to the fullest and don't worry about the aging process:

> Get them young, treat them rough (and tell them nothing). (1920, 95)
> Live fast, die young, leave a good-looking corpse. (1930, 44)

Of course, ignoring the worries of old age, proverbs also express the thought that life passes by way too quickly. Not reaching a ripe old age certainly means that many experiences and much learning was missed:

> We get old too soon and smart too late. (1942, 183)
> We live too short and die too young. (1991, 148)

Getting old does not necessarily mean that wisdom comes with it. This is fittingly expressed in an American anti-war proverb that originated about two years before the outbreak of the First World War:

> Old men make wars, and young men fight them. (1912, 161)

This proverb brings to mind an additional anti-war proverb which had its start from a couple of verses out of the British soldiers' song "Old soldiers never die" (1916) sung especially during the First World War:

> Old soldiers never die, / They simply fade away. (1916, 236)

This British proverb is nowadays in America associated with its use by General Douglas McArthur in his farewell address to Congress on April 19, 1951: "I still remember the refrain of one of the most popular barracks ballads of that day [from the time of World War I], which proclaimed most proudly that old soldiers never die; they just fade away. I now close my military career and just fade away." But while the common attribution to McArthur is false, this proverb has led to an American variant that in itself has become known as an anti-war slogan of sorts:

> Old soldiers never die, but young ones do. (1951, 236–237)

The same idea is expressed in Raymond Souster's mini-pom "Old Soldiers" (1977) based on this proverb:

> Old soldiers never die—
> they live on to send their sons off
> to other wars.
> (Sobieski and Mieder 2005: 214)

Two years later Souster wrote a short depressing sequel "Old Soldiers Never Die" (1979) to this poetic insight with a painful allusion to retired soldiers finding refuge in alcohol from their horrific war experiences:

> Old soldiers never die,
> never, that is,
> as long as their livers
> can float them home
> from Legion halls.
> (Sobieski and Mieder 2005: 214)

By now the proverb has been reduced to the structure "Old Xs never die; they just …" (Dundes 1975) with literally dozens of jocular parodies ignoring the original seriousness of it all. Here are but a few samples:

> Old accountants never die, they just lose their balance. (1965)
> Old cows never die, they just kick the bucket. (1983)
> Old farmers never die, they just go to seed. (1987)
> Old golfers never die, they just lose their balls. (2004)
> Old physicians never die, they just lose their patients. (1997)
> Old professors never die, they just lose their faculties. (2004)
> Old quarterbacks never die, they just pass away. (1987)
> Old soldiers never die, they just go on television. (2003)
> (Litovkina and Mieder 2006: 244–248)

The original proverb and its parodies comment in a proverbial or more generally folkloric way on "stages of life" or the general "notion of the milestone [implying a] gradual progression, or 'development,' toward a goal" (Hufford 1996: 12). This can well be seen from an American proverb that in its literal sense would refer to the value of a used automobile. It certainly makes sense in this way coming from a society that thrives on cars:

> It's not the years, it's the mileage (miles). (1957, 284)

But there is more to it when the proverb is used metaphorically! In that case it refers to individuals whose physical condition is different from what their age or experience might suggest.

All of this is quite worrisome, especially as yet another birthday serves merely as an unfortunate reminder of life passing by too swiftly. And perhaps a friend even sent a birthday card with the vexing proverbial message:

> Today is the first day of the rest of your life. (1968, 260–261)

And yet, at least more life lies ahead, and perhaps growing old won't be all that bad! At least that is the way how John Denver interprets the proverb in his song "Today is the First Day of the Rest of My Life" (1969):

> Today is the first day of the rest of my life
> I wake as a child to see the world again
> On monarch wings, and birthday wonderings
> Want to put on faces walk in the wet and cold
>
> And look forward to my growing old
> To grow is to change, to change is to be new
> To be new is to be young again
> I barely remember when
>
> My memories are stolen by the morning
> Blotted out by the sun's hypnotic light
> Out by the sun's hypnotic light
>
> Today is the first day of the rest of my life
> I wake as a child to see the world begin
> On monarch wings, and birthday wonderings
> Want to put on faces walk in the wet and cold

Denver clearly puts a positive spin on this proverb by looking at the challenges his future life will entail. So, the proverb does not always have to express the negative view of time having passed too quickly. All of this is clearly a convincing example of the polysituativity, poly-functionality, and polysemanticity of proverbs at their best (Mieder 2004: 9). It is doubtful that John Denver also thought of yet another modern American proverb that expresses a somewhat similar idea:

Inside every old person there is a young one trying to get out. (1973, 195–196)

This clearly encapsulates the American obsession with wanting to be young as long as possible or even forever! So, the best thing is to forget about getting old altogether which is expressed in the frequently cited American proverb that is an attempt to rationalize age and aging away once and for all:

Age is just a number. (1957, 4)

Folklorist Mary Sellers in her enlightening article on "Folklore and Folklife of American Age Groups and Aging" (2019) deals convincingly with this proverb and the already discussed proverb "You are only as old as you feel" as American expressions of defiance (!) as far as old age is concerned:

Folkloristic research on social media should include the context of aging in the ways that traditional rites of passage and processes of mourning and celebration have been adapted for online use. Memes as visual humor can be interpreted for their reinforcement of youth orientation in culture by mocking the technological ineptness of seniors, Memes also circulate within age groups, including seniors, with defiant images containing captions such as "You Are Only as Old as You Feel" or "Age Is Only a Number." (Sellers 2019: 861)

The message is obviously to ignore physical age and to be young at heart and spirit. This idea is contained in Slinger Francisco's (also known as Mighty Sparrow) Calypso song "Age is Just a Number" (2000):

Age is just a number
Dance to the beat of your new life
A life filled with purpose and meaning

Oohoohoo
Stomp your feet and swing those hips

Chorus
Age is just a number
Age is just a number
Oohoohoohoohoohoohoo
Age is just a number
Believe you me
Walk in the glow of your new life
Out of the darkness\
Into the light
You never too old to change
Cos life begins at 50

[*Chorus*]

It's not the way you look
But the way you feel
Life is your oyster
Grab it with both hands

Just as number
Just a number
Oohoohoo tapatararara
Age is just a number
Age is just a number …

Don't despair: Age is just a number

It is interesting to note that in addition to proclaiming that "Age is just a number" the song also changes the proverb "Life begins at forty" to "Life begins at 50" in light of the fact that people are getting older these days. So rather than looking at the mid-life point of forty it has been expanded to fifty.

But there is also Carl Joseph Roberts' proverb poem "Age is Just a Number" (2015) that summarizes the future-oriented American world-view by way of this modern proverb from the 1950s. The author clearly employs the proverb as a liberating piece of wisdom to not give in to age but rather remain youthful to the very end. This is also stressed by the refusal of the proverbial imperative "Act your age":

> Age is just a number
> So refuse to act your age
> Reach that point in your life
> You don't care what others say
>
> Do what makes you happy
> What keeps you young inside
> As long as it hurts no one else
> Just go and live your life
>
> Date those that are younger
> Or older if you choose
> Pick the path that you take
> The one that's best for you
>
> Don't look back and then wonder
> On things you should have done
> Do all the things that you want
> And begin to have some fun
>
> Age is just a number
> So refuse to act your age
> Reach that point in your life
> You don't care what others say

This is basically an argument for the classical advice of "Carpe diem" at the neglect of its opposite warning of "Memento mori". Live for now and ignore the end that eventually must come. After all, there are three American proverbs that contain this youthful and future-oriented wisdom:

> You are as old as you feel. (1907)
> Life beings at forty. (1932)
> Age is just a number. (1957)

Those three proverbs incapsulate to a considerable degree the American mentality concerning age and aging. They are doubtlessly among the most popular age-related proverbs that justify the conclusion that they are part of America's future-oriented, positive, progressive, and hopeful worldview. Since "Proverbs are never out of season" (Mieder 1993) and will not disappear as has sometimes been argued (Albig 1931, Stewart 1991: 17–19), it can be stated with conviction that this view of life will be maintained for the foreseeable future. However, were this forward-looking attitude to change, there will most certainly spring up new proverbs to express that view as well.

Bibliography

This chapter was first published at Moscow, Russia as "'Age Is Just a Number'. American Proverbial Wisdom about Age and Aging." *Emotsional'aia sfera cheloveka v iazyke i kommunikatsii: Sinkhroniia i diakhroniia*. Eds. M.L. Kovshova, H.K. Riabtseva, and P.S. Dronov. Moskva: Instiutut Iazykoznaniia RAN, 2019. 7–23.

Albig, William. 1931. "Proverbs and Social Control." *Sociology and Social Research*, 15: 527–535.

Anonymous. 1907. "Consciousness of Age." *The Christian Work and The Evangelist*, 82, no. 2098 (New York, May 4): 584.

Ayaß, Ruth. 2001. "On the Genesis and the Destiny of Proverbs." *Verbal Art across Cultures: The Aesthetics and Proto-Aesthetics of Communication*. Eds. Hubert Knoblauch and Helga Kotthoff. Tübingen: Gunter Narr. 237–254.

Barros de Oliveira, José Henrique. 2008. "Proverbs about Aging and the Old Ages: Educative Applications." *Proceedings of the First Interdisciplinary Colloquium on Proverbs, 5th to 12th November 2007, at Tavira, Portugal*. Eds. Rui J.B. Soares and Outi Lauhakangas. Tavira: Tipografia Tavirense. 318–324.

Blyde, Ray. 2015. "Life Begins at Forty." http://www.crazyoik.co.uk/spike/selected_poems.htm

Brandes, Stanley. 1985. *Forty: The Age and the Symbol*. Knoxville, TN: University of Tennessee Press.

Bronner, Simon J. 2018. "Old Age." *Encyclopedia of American Studies*. Ed. Simon J. Bronner. Baltimore, MD: Johns Hopkins University Press. 3 pp. (online).

Chidi, Sylvia. 2005. "At Forty Life Begins." https://www.poemhunter.com/poem/at-forty-life-begins/

Chudacoff, Howard P. 1989. *How Old Are You? Age Consciousness in American Culture*. Princeton, NJ: Princeton University Press.

Cole, Thomas R. 1992. *The Journey of Life. A Cultural History of Aging in American*. New York: Cambridge University Press.

Denver, John. 1969. "Today Is the First Day of the Rest of My Life." http://www.metrolyrics.com/today-is-the-first-day-of-the-rest-of-my-life-lyrics-john-denver.html

Dickens, Charles. 1851. "What Christmas Is to a Bunch of People." *Household Words. A Weekly Journal*, Christmas 1851: 3.

Doyle, Charles Clay. 1996. "On 'New' Proverbs and the Conservativeness of Proverb Dictionaries." *Proverbium*, 13: 69–84.

Doyle, Charles Clay, and Wolfgang Mieder. 2016. "*The Dictionary of Modern Proverbs*: First Supplement." *Proverbium*, 33: 85–120.

Doyle, Charles Clay, and Wolfgang Mieder. 2018. "*The Dictionary of Modern Proverbs*: Second Supplement." *Proverbium*, 35: 15–44.

Doyle, Charles Clay, and Wolfgang Mieder. 2020. "*The Dictionary of Modern Proverbs*: Third Supplement." *Proverbium*, 37: 53–86.

Doyle, Charles Clay, Wolfgang Mieder, and Fred R. Shapiro. 2012. *The Dictionary of Modern Proverbs*. New Haven, CT: Yale University Press.

Dundes, Alan. 1969. "Thinking Ahead: A Folkloristic Reflection of the Future Orientation in American Worldview." *Anthropological Quarterly*, 42: 53–72.

Dundes, Alan. 1972. "Folk Ideas as Units of Worldview." *Towards New Perspectives in Folklore*. Eds. Américo Paredes and Richard Bauman. Austin, TX: University of Texas Press. 93–103.

Dundes, Alan. 1975. "On the Structure of the Proverb." *Proverbium*, no. 25: 961–973.

Francisco, Slinger (Mighty Sparrow). 2000. "Life is Just a Number." http://www.metrolyrics.com/age-is-just-a-number-lyrics-mezzo.html

Freund, Alexandra M., and Paul B. Baltes. 2002. "The Adaptiveness of Selection, Optimization, and Compensation as Strategies of Life Management: Evidence from a Preference Study of Proverbs." *Journal of Gerontology: Psychological Sciences*, 57: 426–434.

Geisel, Theodor Seuss. 1986. *You're Only Old Once! A Book for Obsolete Children*. New York: Random House.

Gillick, Muriel R. 2006. *The Denial of Aging. Perpetual Youth, Eternal Life, and Other Dangerous Fantasies*. Cambridge, MA: Harvard University Press.

Hakamies, Pekka. 2002. "Proverbs and Mentality." *Myth and Mentality: Studies in Folklore and Popular Thought*. Ed. Anna-Leena Siikala. Helsinki: Finnish Literature Society. 222–230.

Honeck, Richard P., and Jeffrey Welge. 1997. "Creation of Proverbial Wisdom in the Laboratory." *Journal of Psycholinguistic Research*, 26: 605–629.

Hufford, Mary. 1996. "Folklore and Aging." *American Folklore. An Encyclopedia*. Ed. Jan Brunvand. New York: Garland Publishing. 12–14.

Krüger, Carolin. 2009. *Zur Repräsentation des Alter(n)s im deutschen Sprichwort*. Frankfurt am Main: Peter Lang.

Lennon, John. 1980. "Life Begins at 40." http://www.metrolyrics.com/life-begins-at-40-lyrics-john-lennon.html.

Litovkina. Anna T., and Wolfgang Mieder. 2006. *Old Proverbs Never Die, They Just Diversify. A Collection of Anti-proverbs*. Burlington, VT: The University of Vermont; Veszprém, Hungary: The Pannonian University of Veszprém.

Mieder, Wolfgang. 1989. *American Proverbs: A Study of Texts and Contexts*. Bern: Peter Lang.

Mieder, Wolfgang. 1993. *Proverbs Are Never Out of Season. Popular Wisdom in the Modern Age*. New York: Oxford University Press.

Mieder, Wolfgang. 1999. " 'Alter schützt vor Torheit und Weisheit nicht': Sprichwörter über das Alter(n) aus Literatur und Massenmedien." *Jura Soyfer: Internationale Zeitschrift für Kulturwissenschaften*, 8: 5–16. Also in W. Mieder. *Aphorismen, Sprichwörter, Zitate: Von Goethe und Schiller bis Victor Klemperer*. Bern: Peter Lang, 2000. 95–125.

Mieder, Wolfgang. 2004. *Proverbs. A Handbook*. Westport, CT: Greenwood Press.

Mieder, Wolfgang. 2012. " 'Think Outside the Box': Origin, Nature, and Meaning of Modern Anglo-American Proverbs." *Proverbium*, 29: 137–196.

Mieder, Wolfgang. 2014. "Futuristic Paremiography and Paremiology. A Plea for the Collection and Study of Modern Proverbs." *Folklore Fellows' Network*, no volume given, no. 44 (July): 13–17 and 20–24.

Mieder, Wolfgang. 2015a. *"Different Strokes for Different Folks". 1250 authentisch amerikanische Sprichwörter*. Bochum: Norbert Brockmeyer.

Mieder, Wolfgang. 2015b. "Origin of Proverbs." *Introduction to Paremiology. A Comprehensive Guide to Proverb Studies*. Eds. Hrisztalina Hrisztova-Gotthardt and Melita Aleksa Varga. Berlin: Walter de Gruyter. 28–48.

Mieder, Wolfgang. 2018. " 'Life is not a Spectator Sport': Proverbial Emotions about Modern Life." *Emotsional'naia sfera cheloveka v iazyke i kommunikatsii: Sinkhroniia I diakhroniia*. Ed. E.R. Ioanesian. Moscow: Institut Iazykoznaniia RAN. 7–17.

Mieder, Wolfgang, Stewart A. Kingsbury, and Kelsie B. Harder. 1992. *A Dictionary of American Proverbs*. New York: Oxford University Press.

Mokienko, Valerii M. 2003. *Novaia russkaia frazeologiia*. Opole: Uniwersytet Opolski—Instytut Filologii Polskiej.

Morris, Desmond. 1983. *The Book of Ages*. New York: The Viking Press.

Myerhoff, Barbara G., and Andrei Simić (eds.). 1978. *Life's Career—Aging. Cultural Variations on Growing Old*. Beverly Hills, CA: Sage Publications.

Nazar'eva, Iu. S. 2010. "Anglo-amerikanskie aforizmy kak sredstvo ob"ektivatsii kontsepta 'Old Age' ('starost')." *Nauchnyi vestnik. Seriia: Sovremennye lingvisticheskie i metodiko-didakticheskie issledovaniia*, no volume given, no. 2: 83–92.

Nuessel, Frank H. 2000. "The Depiction of Older Adults and Aging in Italian Proverbs." *Proverbium*, 17: 299–314.

Nwachukwu-Agbada, J.O.J. 1989. "The Old Woman in Igbo Proverbial Lore." *Proverbium*, 6: 75–89.

Ojoade, J. Olowo. 1985. "The Old Woman as Seen through African Proverbs: Fragmentary Remarks about African Society through Sayings." *Folklore* (Calcutta), 26, no. 6: 110–114.

Pitkin, Walter B. 1932. *Life Begins at Forty*. New York: McGraw-Hill.

Roberts, Carl Joseph. 2015. "Age Is Just a Number." https://hellopoetry.com/poem/1074870/age-is-just-a-number/

Ruduri, Kwezi. 1993. "Les thèmes de la 'jeunesse' et de la 'vieillesse' dans quelques proverbes Rwanda: Considérations socio-culturelles." *Proverbium*, 10: 281–295.

Saporta, Sol. 1991. "'Old Maid' and 'Dirty Old Man': The Language of Ageism." *American Speech*, 66: 333–334.

Schellbach-Kopra, Ingrid. 1988. "Das Alter im Sprichwort der Deutschen und Finnen—eine kontrastive Betrachtung." *Jahrbuch für finnisch-deutsche Literaturbeziehungen*, 20: 95–106.

Sellers, Mary. 2019. "Folklore and Folklife of American Age Groups and Aging." *The Oxford Handbook of American Folklore and Folklife Studies*. Ed. Simon J. Bronner. New York: Oxford University Press. 845–866.

Sobieski, Janet, and Wolfgang Mieder (eds.). 2005. *"So Many Heads, So Many Wits". An Anthology of English Proverb Poetry*. Burlington, VT: The University of Vermont.

Speake, Jennifer. 2015. *Oxford Dictionary of Proverbs*. 6th ed. Oxford: Oxford University Press.

Stewart, Susan. 1991. "Notes on Distressed Genres." *Journal of American Folklore*, 104: 5–31.

Valdaeva, Tatiana. 2003. "Anti-proverbs or New Proverbs: The Use of English Anti-proverbs and Their Stylistic Analysis." *Proverbium*, 20: 379–390.

White, Geoffrey M. 1987. "Proverbs and Cultural Models: An American Psychology of Problem Solving." *Cultural Models in Language and Thought*. Eds. Dorothy Holland and Naomi Quinn. Cambridge: Cambridge University Press. 151–172.

Chapter Five

"No Body Is Perfect"

Somatic Aspects of Modern American Proverbs

A glance into any of the major proverb collections of the world reveals immediately that there exists a plethora of somatic proverbs referring to the human body in general as well as its various parts like eye, foot, hand, head, heart, mouth, nose, and others (Mieder 2011). Numerous studies have dealt with such proverbs (Mieder 2009a), among them major monographs like Mirosława Gordy, *Somaticheskaia frazeologiia sovremennykh russkogo i pol'skogo iazykov* (2010), Małgorzata Guławska-Gawkoskwa, *Somatische und emotionale Konzepte in der deutschen und polnischen Phraseologie* (2013), Carmen Mellado Blanco, *Phraseologismos somáticos del alemán. Un studio léxico-semántico* (2004), and Kaifu Zhu, *Lexikographische Untersuchung somatischer Phraseologismen im Deutschen und Chinesischen* (1998). These comprehensive publications and also smaller studies (Aroutunova 1979, Carter 2015, Čermák 1998, Ly 2015, Niemi 2010, Piirainen 2016, Skrypnik 2011) have shown convincingly that references to the body play a major role in traditional proverbs, but they fail for the most part to consider whether new proverbs emphasize somatic matters as well.

The problem is, of course, that paremiologists have paid very little attention to the new proverbs of the modern age. Their serious collection has only started a few decades ago, with Valerii M. Mokienko's *Novaia russkaia frazeologiia* (2003) and *The Dictionary of Modern Proverbs* (2012), edited by Charles Clay Doyle, Wolfgang Mieder, and Fred R. Shapiro, marking the beginnings of the serious paremiographical registration of new Russian and American (also some British) proverbs. It is indeed high time that the conservativeness of proverb collections is overcome and that modern proverbs—texts that are not older than the somewhat arbitrarily chosen year of 1900—are collected and studied (Doyle 1996). This effort has by now been embraced by young scholars in a number of countries, and there is thus a bright future awaiting international paremiography and paremiology (Mieder 2017). In fact, for the 1422 identified and annotated proverbs in *The Dictionary of Modern Proverbs*, some interesting conclusions have been presented in Wolfgang Mieder's analysis with a modern American proverb as its title: "'Think Outside of the Box': Origin, Nature, and Meaning of Modern Anglo-American Proverbs" (Mieder 2014: 80–130). By now he has also looked in more detail at new proverbs that deal with the multifaceted aspects of "life" and "age" (Mieder 2018 and 2019a), trying to see whether they express a certain commonly held worldview in the modern age (Dundes 1972, Hakamies 2002).

But clearly modern people are not only preoccupied with questions of life and the aging process. They are also certainly concerned about the body, as can be seen through the emphasis on appearance and health that might well be called a "body cult" that permeates society, to wit the exercise craze in all of its forms. It should then not be surprising that this obsession in its positive and negative aspects has found expression in modern proverbial wisdom (about 9% of the 1422 proverbs). It is interesting to note right at the outset of the following deliberations that the proverb appearing in the title is a reaction to the overemphasis on the ideal body shape. Based on the much older proverb "Nobody is perfect", the anti-proverb "No body is perfect" (1952, 23; proverbs are cited with the earliest date and page number in the *Dictionary of Modern Proverbs*) originated in the middle of the twentieth century. It is usually employed in connection with anxieties about an unachievable ideal body image. The idea of beauty enters into all of this, and it comes as no surprise that the traditional proverb "Beauty is only skin deep" with its argument against such fantasy has led to the even more extreme anti-proverb "Beauty is only skin (1963, 17). In other words, it is much more important to be a good (beautiful) person inside rather than worrying about outside looks. As expected, there are other new proverbs that react to beauty matters, to wit "Beauty does not buy happiness" (1989, 16) and "No beauty without pain" (1987, 17), with the latter emphasizing that the acquisition and maintenance of physical beauty require hard and perhaps painful exercise.

It should be noted that it is not rare that new proverbs arise as anti-proverbs to established texts that are put into question or played with in order to create wisdom more fitting for modern times (Litovkina and Mieder 2006). Here are a few examples with somatic words included in them:

Absence makes the heart grow fonder.
Absence makes the heart go wander. (1908, 1)

Little pitchers have big ears.
Little rabbits have big ears (1935, 213)

Walls have ears.
Even corn has ears. (1905, 44)

Blood is thicker than water.
Money is thicker than water. (S1, 108–109)

Time heals all wounds.
Time wounds all heels. (1938, 259)

A closed mouth catches no flies.
A closed mouth catches no feet. (1956, 173)

The last example exists, as is often the case with proverbs in general, in a number of variants: "A closed (shut) mouth gathers (catches) no feet." Thus the proverb probably originated as an anti-proverb blending three earlier proverbial phrases: "A closed mouth catches no flies", "A rolling stone gathers no moss", and "to put one's foot in one's mouth."

Related to all of this is also the earlier modern proverb "If you keep your mouth shut, you won't put your foot in it" (1915, 174). Another interesting anti-proverb is "An eye for an eye leaves the whole world blind" (1948, 70–71) that is commonly attributed to Mohandas Gandhi. It is a remarkable and reasonable argument against the Biblical injunction "An eye for an eye, and a tooth for a tooth" (Exodus 21:24) that taken to its extreme would lead to total annihilation.

That most certainly is a very timely anti-proverb turned accepted new proverb in a world confronted with terrorism and war. And there is another "body"-proverb that is equally serious based on the relatively new structural formula "My X, my Y", as for example "My house, my rules" (1983, 126) or "My party, my rules" (2003, 191). The proverb "My body, my choice" (1989, S3, in print [S1–3 refer to the three supplements of the *Dictionary of Modern Proverbs*]) grew out of the feminist movement and was originally used in reference to abortion rights. Its meaning has by now been broadened to include arguments against vaccination as well as for sexual permissiveness and medical suicide. But here is an example of the treatment of this decisive proverb in the third supplement to the *Dictionary of Modern Proverbs*:

> 1989 *Orlando [FL] Sentinel*, 22 Jan.: "The crowd ... carried signs with slogans like ... 'My Body My Choice.'" 1989 *Chicago Tribune*, 21 Apr.: "Two Catholic high school seniors ... hoisted a sign during Bush's appearance .... It read; 'My body. My choice. My right.'" 1992 *Indianapolis Star*, 24 Mar.: "For spring 1991, Moody offered sequined dresses with definite messages: One ... with an all-over 'My Body My Choice.'" 1997 *Orlando [FL] Sentinel*, 9 Jan.: "[Noel] Earley said he is planning his own demise .... 'My body, my choice,' he says ...." 2002 *Hanover [ON] Post*, 8 Jan.: "Yes, I know the arguments against vaccinations: They can't guarantee not getting the flu; there are sometimes side effects; and, of course, the old 'my body, my choice' nugget being trotted out ...." 2014 *Herald Sun [Melbourne, Australia]*, 16 Nov.: "If we feminists truly believe in the adage, 'My body, my choice,' then surely Kim has a right to drop her dacks [i.e. pants] for some easy bucks ...." The saying was originally used in reference to abortion rights, but it has sometimes been applied to sexual permissiveness, to suicide, and to the refusal of certain medical interventions.

This is a clear indication that modern proverbs as well are characterized by their "polyfunctionality, polysemanticity, and polysituativity"

(Mieder 2004: 9). But speaking of pregnancy, there is this disgusting anti-feminist proverb "A woman should be kept barefoot and pregnant" (1947, 279), unfortunately showing that the creation of misogynous proverbs is not over (Schipper 2003). Of interest from the 1940s is also the wisdom "You can't be a little pregnant" (1942, 206) whose meaning has by now been broadened to include various impossibilities. Directly related to the woman's body and a possible pregnancy is the anti-proverb "Better late than pregnant" (1995, 137) with its hidden reference to menstruation. It is not surprising that the traditional proverb "Better late than never" was transformed into this new proverb in an age of sexual freedom.

With sexuality playing such a dominant role in American culture, the proverb "If you've got it, flaunt it" (1968, 96) was bound to appear. Most frequently it refers to the open display of one's own sexuality. The "perfect" body and fashionable as well as noticeable clothes are all part of this exhibitionism. Men and women are exercising to get their bodies in shape, including the build-up of muscles, thus the proverb "Hustle for the muscle" (2013, S3 in print). It can be found on T-shirts and has been used as a ready-made slogan for exercise establishments. This emphasis on physical exercise to the point of exhaustion has found its rationalizing proverb as well: "Pain is just weakness leaving the body" (1991, 187). And there is also the short proverb "Sun's out, guns out" (2007, S2, 39) with its parallel structure. One would have to be in the folk group that enjoys exhibiting their muscles on a sunny day to understand it. The "guns"-term refers to upper-arm (or upper-torso) musculature, and the proverb is reminiscent of the idea of flaunting one's body.

Little wonder that the American society with its problem of obesity also brought forth a number of proverbs dealing with weight gain to the point of being fat. Here are three cautionary proverbs explaining in basic language the widespread problem:

It is not what you like (want) that makes you fat, it is what you eat. (1917, 147)
Anything good (in life) is either illegal, immoral, or fattening. (1933, 106–107)
A moment (minute) on the lips, a lifetime (forever) on the hips. (1940, 168)

Folk wisdom does, however, not stop there but also presents advice on how to retain or attain the ideal thin figure:

> You can't be too rich or too thin. (1974, S1, 113)
> Nothing tastes as good as thin feels. (1989, S1, 111)

It should, however, be recognized that the "fat lady" mentioned in the following three related proverbs is not necessarily a stereotype against corpulent women. It is an allusion to large female opera singers who might conclude a lengthy opera. The proverb "The opera isn't over till the fat lady sings" (1976, 185) was coined by Ralph Carpenter, sports information director of Texas Tech University, on March 10, 1976 during his commentaries on a basketball game. During the same year the proverb "Church is not out till the fat lady sings (1976, 39–40) appeared. It may have started as a variant of the more generic modern proverb "Church is not out till they sing" (1966, 40) of ten years earlier. But then it might also be a conflation (based on wrong memory or intentional wit) of that proverb with "The opera isn't over till the fat lady sings." Finally, there is also the even more recent proverb from the sports world: "The game is not over till the fat lady sings" (1984, 91). The key issue is that all three proverbs have their independent existence and that they do not refer to any particular woman and certainly do not mean to offend anybody with their metaphor.

There are also two related relatively new proverbs that emphasize the dominance of looking good in American culture, namely "It's better to look good than to feel good" (1978, 150) and "It is better to look good than to be good" (1986, 150). A third proverb with its variants of "Feel good, play good" and "Look good, feel good, play good" (1987, S1, 95–96) states convincingly that an attractive or proper appearance can well translate into success. And as expected, there are several proverbs that stress quite directly how important the proper attire might be for getting ahead in the professional world in particular:

> Dress for success. (1933, S2, 39)
> Dress to impress. (1952, S2, 21)
> Dress for the job you want. (1976, S1, 104–105)

Of course, some proverbs counter this wisdom about appearances. As is well known, proverbs are not universally true, and they can be as contradictory as life itself (Mieder 2004: 134). The proverb "A little powder and a little paint makes a woman look like what she isn't" (1908, 205) seems to address the matter of an unnatural insistence on outside appearance. A bit more direct is the proverb "You can put lipstick on a pig but it's still a pig" (1985, 148) with its animal farm imagery. A precursor to this proverb might well be "You can't make a silk purse from a sow's ear" from the sixteenth century. Similar proverbs are "A hog in armor [a person of strange appearance] is still a hog" (eighteenth century) and "A hog in a silk waistcoat is still a hog" (nineteenth century). From the twentieth century there are also such variants as "A pig in a palace is still a pig," "A pig with feathers behind its ears is still a pig," "The pig may have a tuxedo on, but it is still a pig," "A pig painted gold is still a pig," and "A pig in a parlor is still a pig" (Mieder, Kingsbury, Harder 1992). Since the word "lipstick" dates only from about 1880, its appearance in proverbial language had to wait to more modern times, perhaps even until 1985 as its first written reference found thus far. But be that as it may, former President Barack Obama got himself into trouble for using it quite spontaneously at a campaign event on September 9, 2008, to argue against the economic plan of his Republican opponent John McCain:

> John McCain says he's about change too, and so I guess his whole angle is, "Watch out George Bush—except for economic policy, health care policy, tax policy, education policy, foreign policy and Karl Rowe-style-politics—we're really going to shake things up in Washington. " That's no change. That's just calling something that's the same thing something different. You know you can put lipstick on a pig, but it's still a pig. You know you can wrap an old fish in a piece of paper called change, it's still going to stink after eight years. We've had enough of the same old thing. (Mieder 2009b: 83–84)

While it was clear that Obama was speaking about McCain, people claimed that he was referencing Sarah Palin, who was McCain's running mate for the presidency. The result was that Obama had to defend himself against having made a slanderous and sexist statement regarding Palin who by chance had used the word "lipstick" at an earlier occasion. All of this shows that proverbs are never simple or sacrosanct and that they can be manipulated to serve various purposes.

This event caused President Obama a true proverbial pain in the back as he was running a superb campaign to become the first African-American President of the United States. He brought a fresh, innovative, and humane attitude to his candidacy and had to endure at times vicious attacks that included racial slurs. The modern proverb "Pioneers get (take) arrows in their backs" (1972, 198) comes to mind here, and luckily the unfair attacks against him remained verbal. In other words, the proverb "There must be pioneers, and some of them get killed" (1928, 198) as was the case with some astronauts, did not become a terrible reality in his case. Instead Barack Obama had the welcome and appreciated opportunity to serve as a respected president for eight years. His opponents might well have thought of the proverb "If you must strike (hit) a man from behind, slap him on the back" (1955, 157) that appears to be a metaphorical rendering of the Bible proverb "Love your enemies" (Matthew 5:44) that was employed by Martin Luther King innumerable times in his valiant struggle for civil and human rights (Mieder 2010: 281–295). One thing is for certain, the proverb "Strong back, weak mind" (1929, 11–12), often albeit unfairly applied to athletes or body builders, could not possibly apply to the intellectually inclined Barack Obama who, to his credit, was quite an accomplished basketball player.

There is another equally insulting proverb that unfortunately has maintained its currency since the early twentieth century: "No brain, no pain" (1917, 26–27). The implication is that an unintelligent person is not capable of sensing pain or is callous to serious injury. It is based on the popular structure "No X, no Y", as can be seen from the somatic proverb "No body (corpse), no crime" (1947, 23–24) that appears with considerable frequency in detective novels. Regarding corpses, the following proverb is somewhat indicative of an American "carpe diem"-attitude towards life that must be experienced to the fullest at a fast speed: "Live fast, die young, leave a good-looking corpse" (1930, 44). It seems quite an absurd piece of wisdom, but in typical American spirit it leaves the decision to follow its advice up to the individual. Another "brain"-proverb also seems a bit extreme at first: "If you're too open-minded, your brains will fall out" (1960, 26). But it obviously wants to argue that one should not go to extremes in accommodating questionable behavior or attitudes. Of course, there is excellent advice in the proverb "Use your brain before you open your mouth" (1960, 26).

Speaking of the mind or brain, it comes perhaps as somewhat of a surprise to find quite a few modern proverbs addressing that part of the body. One might have thought that the common folk as originators of proverbs would not occupy itself with this matter. But clearly there are people who have generalized thoughts about the human mind into proverbial wisdom that does, alas, usually lack any metaphorical elements. These proverbs are simply too intellectually inclined, something that is true for a little more than 50% of the 1422 proverbs included in the *Dictionary of Modern Proverbs*. It is not known how this relates to older proverbs, but they might well be at least somewhat more metaphorical in nature. Part of the reason might be that newer proverbs often have their start as slogans or aphorisms that are more cerebral as well as shorter and to the point. In any case, here are some straightforward examples that lack the metaphorical charm of more folksy proverbs:

> A mind is a terrible thing to waste. (1972, 167)
> Simple minds, simple pleasures. (1957, S1, 108)
> Minds, like parachutes, function only when they are open. (S2, 1927, 31–32)
> A neat desk is a sign of a sick mind. (1973, 53)
> A messy desk is a sign of a messy mind. (1974, 53)

Regarding the last proverb, there is also the independent variant "A messy (cluttered) desk is a sign of intelligence (brilliance, genius, creativity, productivity, a busy person, etc.)" (1973, 53) that smacks of a professorial excuse for an utterly disorganized office.

The last of these "brain/mind"-proverbs was clearly coined by an intellectual since it employs the term "erogenous zone" (1969, 285) that is somewhat alien to proverbial language. Here is what the *Dictionary of Modern Proverbs* says about it:

> The most important (The most potent, The most) erogenous zone is the brain (mind). 1969 *New York Times* 7 Dec.: "Sometimes [David] Frost simply

manages to bring out somebody in a small way, as when he coaxed out of a shy Raquel Welch ... the notion that 'the mind is the most erogenous zone.'" 1974 *Newsweek* 83, no. 11 (18 Mar.) 43: "There cannot be winners in the battle of erectile tissues. Surely the most erogenous zone in both men and women lies not between the legs but behind the eyes." 1977 *Lawrence [KS] Daily Journal* 24 Oct. ("Ann Landers" advice column): "The most erogenous zone in both male and female is located between the eyebrows and the hairline." 1980 Mike Grace and Joyce Grace, *A Joyful Meeting: Sexuality in Marriage* (St. Paul MN: National Marriage Encounter) 26: "If there is competition from other things—distractions, other feelings—foreplay may have no erotic effect. This is why we emphasize that the most important erogenous zone is the brain."

As can be seen, the dictionary contains plenty of contextualized references, listing the earliest found and a few later ones that exemplify the particular proverb's use and meaning. Such statements are of particular importance for those proverbs that originated in the scholarly realm, as for example the scientific proverb "Genes are not (Genetics is not, Heredity is not) destiny" (1952, S2, 23) that indicate the existence of modern proverbs based on new knowledge. In comparison, such body related proverbs like "A clean cut heals soonest" (1913, 49) and "Coughs and sneezes spread diseases? (1918, 45) from the early twentieth century seem rather mundane. And yet, their simple health messages are of relevance regarding infections and viruses. Of interest is also this quite different proverb "When the United States (U.S., America, Wall Street, etc.) sneezes, the world catches a cold (pneumonia)" (1977, S3, in print). Even though it is a relatively new proverb expressing the unfortunate claim of exceptionalism that has taken a hold in the country, it is noteworthy that the references of it cited in the *Dictionary of Modern Proverbs* start with such introductory formulas as "it was once said," "as the old adage goes," and "the old saying" that are used to add traditional authority to it. Two matters are revealed here, namely that people think that proverbs have to be old and that they for the most part have no idea about the historical origin and dissemination of proverbs.

People with just a fleeting awareness of proverbs might also conclude from most proverb collections that there appear to be only very few sexual, obscene or scatological proverbs relating to the body and its functions. Although they have always existed, with a dominance in the late Middle Ages and the sixteenth century, they have to a large degree been suppressed by puritanical paremiographers of later times. However, today's open discussion of sexuality as well as the prevalent occurrence of obscene and scatological words and phrases has led to a considerable number of modern proverbs of which at least a few might be mentioned here (Mieder 2020). In some instances, it is interesting to note that an old innocuous expression has been turned into a more sexually motivated proverb. Thus the old phrase "to take the bull by the horns" whose metaphor implies a certain measure of control over a strong challenge, has now become the proverb "Take (Grab) the bull by the balls" (1954, 28–29) that most likely started as an anti-proverb to the "horn"-phrase. By now the proverb has become so popular that people employ it without at first thinking of the fact that the "balls" are the bull's testicles. A decade later, during the war in Vietnam, an expanded variant of the proverb took a hold: "Grab them by the balls, their hearts and minds will follow" (1967, 12). It has been attributed to former President Lyndon Johnson who enjoyed using expletives and earthy expressions. The proverb satirizes the Kennedy administrations hope of winning "the hearts and minds" of the Vietnamese people. As it can be cited as a comment for other situations that need to be controlled by some force, the proverb has gained currency without being cited in "polite" society perhaps.

Once testicles made it into modern proverbial language, it is understandable that the penis found its way into modern proverbs as well. In the following two proverbs satirizing boisterous or show-off males, it is important to know that dick, prick, and pecker are slang words for penis: "Big car, small dick (prick)" (1991, 33) and "Big mouth, small pecker (dick, prick)" (1993, 173). Since penis size has been more openly discussed in medical journals and the media since the early twentieth century, a number of proverbs came into being that somewhat *sub rosa* state that penis size has nothing to do with sexual satisfaction:

Size doesn't matter (it's what you do with it, it's how you use it). (1903, 233)
It's not what you've got, it's what you do with it (how you use it). (1934, 96–97)
It's not the size of the boat but the motion of the ocean (that matters). (1968, 232)

From numerous contextualized references cited in the dictionary, it is clear that "it" refers to the penis, and even the third metaphorical text relates to the penis and male sexual proficiency in satisfying a woman. As expected, the counter-proverb "Size does matter" (1964. 232–233) to "Size doesn't matter" has by now become current. Of course, it can also be employed to speak about something far removed from the penis, but there is a good chance that its use will evoke snickers or frowns on account of its perceived sexual allusiveness whether intended or not. Not surprisingly, female sexuality is also to be found in modern proverbs, albeit coined by aggressive males. In the proverb "Old enough to bleed, old enough to breed (butcher, stick)" (1971, 22–23) the verb "bleed" refers to menstruation, while the variant terms allude to dealings with livestock. There is no wordplay here but rather an obvious disrespect for women who are considered like breeding machines. A second metaphorical proverb "If there is grass on the field, (you can) play ball" (1998, 111) is also highly questionable in that it encourages premature sex just because pubic hair (grass) is starting to appear. "Ball' once again refers to the testicles and the phrase "to ball someone" signifies sexual intercourse. Unfortunately the disgusting male proverb coiners also came up with the proverbs "Close your eyes and think of England (the Empire, the queen, Old Glory)" (1943, 70) and the even more insensitive "You don't fuck the face" (1984, 72) that reduce love making to a revolting act.

The word "ass" in the meaning of behind or rump and not donkey has become quite acceptable in American parlance. Thus the proverb "The sun doesn't shine on (up) the same dog's ass every day" (1976, 246) appears slightly varied as "The sun don't shine on a sleepin' dog's ass" without any offense in Bruce Springsteen's proverb song "My Best Was Never Good Enough" (1995) to express that one cannot be lucky every day. And the surprisingly long proverb "When you're up to your ass in alligators, it's hard to remember you're there to drain the swamp" (1971, 8–9; Dundes and Pagter 1987) has gained more popularity in recent years due to the fact that President Trump likes to speak of cleaning out the swamp of Washington politics. Of course, he has not done so but rather has added to it by way of his uncontrolled behavior and aggressive tweets. Referring to people who exhibit unwelcome or ill-advised comments as "assholes" has become widespread as well, but not necessarily in all environments. Be that as it may, the befitting if somewhat direct proverb "Opinions are like assholes (armpits)— everybody's got one (and they all stink)" (1972, 185) has become quite popular in its truncated version "Opinions are like assholes." Based on the proverb, the variant "Excuses are like assholes (armpits); everybody has them (and most of them stink" (1974, 69–70) came into existence two years later and it too is heard quite frequently in its shortened version. There is no doubt that modern proverbs, with some exceptions, are generally on the short side reflecting perhaps the fast-paced life of modernity.

If "asshole" has become somewhat acceptable in American social discourse, it can also be said that the word "shit" has lost much of its taboo character. Several proverbs in the *Dictionary of Modern Proverbs* bear witness of this fact, with the proverb "Shit or get off the pot" (1935, 204) being the most popular. While it also exists in the rare variant "Piss or get off the pot", it has become quite acceptable and one can hear it used in oral discussion, notably at university committee meetings, when someone in utter frustration tries to impress upon people that some decision or action must be undertaken. Three equally short proverbs about this bodily function are so obvious in their meaning that they need no elaboration: "Don't shit where you eat" (1953, 227), "Don't shit on your own doorstep" (1967, 60), and "Everybody shits (poops)" (1968, 227). Their literal meaning is clear enough, but there is at least some figurativeness to these somewhat crass pieces of wisdom. The first two obviously imply that one should not fowl one's own nest that brings to mind the much older and "cleaner" proverb "It's an ill bird that fowls its own nest" (Mieder, Kingsbury, Harder 1992: 52) from the thirteenth century. The two-word proverb "Everybody shits" with its topic and comment so characteristic of proverbs implies that all living creatures have this bodily need of excretion, that is, they are basically all the same despite cultural and social differences. It functions as an equalizing bit of wisdom helping people to cope in a complex modern world.

But enough of these scatological matters by way of this metaphorical "body"-proverb that refers so fittingly to the ups and downs of the professional world with its careerism: "The toes you step on today may be attached (connected) to the ass you have to kiss tomorrow" (1999, 261). Sticking with "toes" for a moment, there is the somewhat rarely heard proverb "Never take more on your heels than you can kick off with your toes" (1925, 120). It is a fine example for the fact that some modern proverbs just as older ones are simply hard to understand without a context. In fact, proverbs in proverb collections that merely list them are often void of clear meaning. In this particular case, the proverb wants to give the reasonable advice that one should not claim or profess more than one can reasonably deliver. The generic proverb "Beware of a smiling man" (1952, 156) and the similar somatic proverb "Beware of a smiling face" (1955, 72) of three years later in origin present a bit of a problem as well. One might well be reminded of the classical proverb "Caveat emptor" that has been current in the English as "Let the buyer beware" or just "Buyer beware" since the sixteenth century (Mieder, Kingsbury, Harder 1992: 78), but two contextualized references in the *Dictionary of Modern Proverbs* provide a semantic clue to be sure: "Beware of a smiling face: A frown could easily take its place" and "Beware of a smiling face, and what's hiding behind it." In other words, don't place too much trust into appearances that can quickly change without warning.

The proverb "Don't let your mouth write (Don't write) a check that your ass (behind) can't cash" (1966, 174) also presents a bit of a semantic challenge at first glance. This is where the dictionary with its contextual references provides a great service:

> Don't let your mouth write (Don't write) a check that your ass (behind) can't cash. 1966 Charles Portis, *Norwood* (New York: Simon & Schuster) 184: "Watch it now. You're taking liberties. Don't make things worse than they are. Don't let your mouth write a check that your ass can't cash, son." 1980 Edith A. Folb, *Runnin' Down Some Lines: The Language and Culture of Black Teenagers* (Cambridge MA: Harvard UP, 1980), 235: "Don't let your mouth overload your ass; don't let your mouth write a check your ass can't cash" (with the gloss "Don't talk too much, in such a belligerent manner, or there's going to be a fight").

Proverbs following the imperative "Don't ..." pattern have long been popular, often making a proverb out of a proverbial expression that usually predates it. This is the case in the following two examples that first cite the phrase and then the proverb:

> to stick one's neck out.
> Don't stick your neck out. (1937, 177)

> to shoot oneself in the foot.
> Don't shoot yourself in the foot. (1980, 84)

There is no difficulty in comprehending the proverb "Don't ask a barber if you need a haircut" (1972, 13). As an astute businessman he will want to cut the hair, with the proverb trying to argue against asking questions whose answers are obvious. Perhaps the proverb has pretty much fallen out of use because it is too mundane for a society where barbers have become hair stylists and where barber shops have been turned into hair salons. But things are not always so straight forward, as can be seen from two examples that almost make no sense without contexts and explanation. The "chin"-text never gained great currency and was more or less restricted to the world of sports:

> Don't lead with your chin. 1931 *Washington Post* 26 May: "I believe in the silver lining, the rainbow after the storm, ... the infallibility of the slogan 'Never lead with your chin.' ... I believe the worst is over and that it never was as bad as it was advertised." The proverb makes figurative and general a sentence of conventional advice from boxing.

Of special interest is doubtlessly this next proverb about what not to do to an innocent baby with its message of not taking suggestions literally:

> Don't put beans (peas) in the baby's ears (up the baby's nose). 1905 Martin G. Brumbaugh, *The Making of a Teacher* (Philadelphia: Sunday School Times) 295–96: "A very well-disposed mother, but not wise, on leaving her home one day, said to the older children, 'Now be sure to put no beans in the baby's ears.' The children had never thought of such a thing, but when she returned the baby's ears were well filled with beans!" The proverb warns about the power of suggestion.

The proverb "Loose lips sink ships" (1942, 148) makes a lot of sense if one knows that it originated during World War II when that proverbial slogan was literally used to realize that uncontrolled talk might give away secrets to the enemy. Today the proverb can be used in a general way to discourage people from giving away a secret or sensitive information. One also wonders about the proverb "A ring on the finger is worth two on the phone" (1911, 218) that plays off the double meaning of the "ring" as in engagement or wedding ring on the finger and the proverbial phrase "to give someone a ring" on the telephone. In the modern age of cell phones and other electronic ways of communicating with a phone it is hard to imagine that the younger generations would use it any longer. It serves as another example for the fact that proverbs can wear out their usefulness as things change. This particular proverb has been around for a century and is probably on its last leg, as the proverbial expression goes.

Even though America is in love with the automobile, its modern proverbs do not pay particular attention to the car. But there is the delightful proverb "You can't judge a car by its paint (job)" (1908, 33) from the early twentieth century that is modeled on the older proverb "You can't judge a book by its cover." Equally telling is the proverbial claim that "Nobody washes a rental car" (1985, 33). Be that as it may, modern proverbs prefer to zero in on the body and its feet when it comes to mobility that includes the need for rest as well (Senga 1987). The proverbs "It is better to die on your feet than to live on your knees" (1924, 84) and "Never miss a chance to sit down and rest your feet" (1951, 36) contain considerable wisdom for everyday life. Yet a proverb like "Move your feet, lose your seat" (1987, 84) is perhaps not immediately clear. It originated in the unfortunate world of the homeless who lose their resting place if they move for whatever reason. By now it also has the more general meaning of losing one's occupied or claimed space anywhere if moving away temporarily. Of much interest is also the origin and meaning of the very recent proverb "Slow feet don't eat" (2014, S3, in print). As the following references show, it began as a sports metaphor that can now also be applied to the necessity of action in general:

2014 *Telegram & Gazette [Worcester MA]*, 20 Sep.: "Coach ... told me to trust my speed .... It's footwork. Slow feet, don't eat." 2015 *Telegram & Gazette [Worcester MA]*, 25 Sep.: "You must have quick feet .... As they say, 'Slow feet don't eat.'" 2016 Courier-*News [Bridgewater NJ]*, 11 Jul.: "[Football player Andrew] Roberts said he loves two quotes .... The other is, 'Slow feet, don't eat,' as in work hard or you won't succeed." 2017 Solae Dehvine, *Stupid Love 2: Vengeance Is Mine* (Hazelwood MO: Dehvine): "Closed mouths don't get fed and slow feet don't eat son." 2017 *Hawaii Warrior World [Honolulu]*, 11 Apr.: "One of the catchiest phrases in this conditioning cycle is: Slow feet, don't eat." 2018 *Atlanta Journal-Constitution*, 8 Nov.: "Slow feet don't eat in South Florida. And they especially don't return punts." 2018 (name of a company in Essex MD): "Slow Feet Dont [sic] Eat Racing, Inc." 2019 *WM [Worcester MA]*, 7 Aug (quoting football player Dexter McCluster): "You have to have great feet. Slow feet don't eat. If your feet can't keep up with your mind, you're not going to be a great running back." The proverb appears frequently as a motto on the front of T-shirts.

Indeed, moving forward belongs to the American worldview (Dundes 1969), and it is surprising that the proverb "What you haven't in your head, you have in your feet" (1933, 119) was only recorded in the early 1930s in America. It is actually a proverb known in a number of European languages but entered into English only later as a loan translation. It is thus not a homegrown American proverb and serves as an example for those proverbs that became current in the United States by way of immigrants. Of course, today such modern American proverbs as for example "The grass is always greener o the other side of the fence" (1913, 110–111), "One picture is worth a thousand words" (1911, 196), and "It takes two to tango" (1952, 266) have found international distribution in English or as loan translations (Mieder 2019b) by way of the mass media in particular.

And the move goes on, as can be seen from the advice about advancing without being too aggressive about it all: "Keep your head down and your feet moving" (1990, 118). Care must be taken not to be too bullish for "A hard head makes a soft (sore) behind (back, butt, ass, tail)" (1905, 118). But no matter what, people should use their head for good purposes and not rest: "Use your head for something besides a hat rack" (1910, 118). America being a country where religion continues to play a major role has also brought forth the proverb "When you pray, move your feet" (1936, 84–85) that tells practitioners that positive action must accompany praying. And if the prayer seems to no avail, there exists another proverb that warns against blaming God Almighty: "Your arms are too short (not long enough) to box (fight) with God" (1912, 7). The proverb is especially current among African-Americans and is a wonderful somatic message to keep parishioners humble. It would most certainly do them no good to confront God with a proverbial chip on their shoulder since that would be futile behavior and showing no brain as it were. All of this is convincingly expressed in the somatic proverb "A chip on the shoulder is a good indication of wood higher up" (1926, 39). The second part of the proverb is a delightful metaphor for a head with a lack of brain power and as such can be employed in various situations.

In a more concise and direct way the proverb "Big mouth, small brain (mind)" (1958, 173) says something quite similar. And there is even a proverb that warns against rash speaking: "It is better to be thought a fool than to open your mouth and let the world know it" (1907, 83). As has been done with other proverbs as well, this text has been credited to President Abraham Lincoln but no corroborative evidence exists. And yet, silence is not always the best way to deal with life's challenges, as stated by the proverb "A closed mouth does not get fed" (1989, 173) with the meaning that one must speak up in order to be effective or acknowledged. All of this amounts to yet another example for the fact that proverbs can give opposite advice and that the proverb that fits a particular situation will be cited. Finally, it makes a lot of sense that the pecuniary as well as somatic proverb "Put your money where your mouth is" (1913, 170) has been around for a hundred years. In its literal sense it encourages vocal people to give actual money to the political or social cause that they happen to believe in. By now, it can also be employed more generally to get people to make a commitment after having expressed a serious interest in a matter. In this sense it is remindful of the seventeenth-century proverb "Actions speak louder than words" (Mieder, Kingsburg, Harder 1992: 7).

This proverb finds its highly positive modern equivalent in meaning as "Busy hands are happy hands" (1956, 115). The "hand" appears in several new proverbs, including the humane advice "Give a hand up, not a handout" (1938, 115) that started as a slogan to get people involved in effective welfare programs. Doing so by giving money and time, symbolically expressed by flowers, proves the following benevolent proverb true: "Flowers leave fragrance in the hand that bestows them" (1944, 82). The proverb "Two (Both) hands for beginners" (1910, 116), perhaps a bit perplexing on first encounter, is simply solid advice that using both hands is best when first learning to ride a bicycle, drive a car, play basketball, etc. That all makes sense, but one might well wonder what brought about the following two proverbs that probably started as anti-proverbs of the older "You can choose your friends, but you cannot choose your family" (Mieder, Kingsbury, Harder 1992: 240): "You can pick your friends, and you can pick your nose, but you can't pick your friend's nose" (1975, 88) and "You can pick your nose, but you can't pick your family (relatives)" (1997, 179). The motivation for these somewhat crass proverbs was most likely a bit of somatic folk humor to add some expressiveness to it all. In this regard it needs to be pointed out that the proverb "Keep your nose clean" (1903, 179) has nothing to do with picking or blowing one's nose but is merely a somatic metaphor to admonish people to keep things in proper perspective. And there is also that short proverb "Your (The) nose knows" (1905, 179) that does not credit that organ any cerebral anilities but is just a metaphor for assuring people that they can figure things out in due time.

The main thing is that people adhere to the wisdom of the American proverb "Keep your eyes on the prize" that has been traced back to the seventeenth century (Doyle 2017). It was popularized in a "freedom song" during protest marches, sit-ins, freedom rides, and the many demonstrations during the Civil Rights movement of the 1960s with its refrain:

Hold on (hold on), hold on (hold on)
Keep your eyes on the prize, hold on
Hold on (hold on), hold on (hold on)
Keep your eyes on the prize, hold on

Congressman John Lewis, one of the major surviving African-American civil rights leaders, made this sociopolitical slogan his leitmotif during the past five decades, and he remains a most powerful voice in combatting racism and in fostering humaneness and civility in the United States (Mieder 2019: 145–181). The somewhat modern proverb "Keep your eye on the donut and not on the hole" (1908, 71) is a more metaphorical albeit banal restatement, but it too gives the advice to remain focused on the essential matter at hand. The message is to be watchful and involved, as two short proverbs advise as well: "Every shut eye is not asleep" (1900, 70) and "The eyes do not lie" (1986, S3, in print). Regarding the modern computer world, there is now even the proverb "Given enough eyeballs (eyes), all bugs are shallow (Many eyes make all bugs shallow" (1997, S3, in print) where the bugs are certainly not insects! It is a proverb current among technology experts, but it has a chance to become more prevalent in a general sense of saying that "Four eyes see more than two" (Mieder, Kingsbury, Harder 1992: 190) as an older sixteenth-century proverb has it. For now, the *Dictionary of Modern Proverbs* provides a number of references as a welcome introduction for the layperson:

> 1997 John Udall, "Web Project: The Value of Free Software," *Byte* 22, no. 12 (Dec.) 112: "What about Eric Raymond's assertion that all bugs are shallow given enough eyeballs? [Rob] Kolstad counters that it's not the number of eyeballs that matters; it's the quality of the brains behind them." 1998 *Birmingham [UK] Post*, 1 Aug.: "'Given enough eyeballs, all bugs are shallow' is a simple tenet of Open Source software." 1999 *Sydney [Australia] Morning Herald*, 6 Apr.: "It is reassuring to know that just as many eyes ensure all bugs are shallow, many voices ensure the marketplace of ideas is a beautiful one." 2000 Nicholas Thompson, "How Linux and Open-Source Development Could Change the Way We Get Things Done," *Washington Monthly* 32, no. 3 (Mar.) 10: "There is a saying known as 'Linus' law' that 'given enough eyes, all bugs are shallow.' In other words, given enough people working on them, all problems are solvable." 2005 *Salt Lake City Tribune*, 20 Nov.: "Today, the open source movement has realized the effectiveness of leaderless decision making. They have a saying that to many eyes all bugs are shallow ...." 2009 *Weekly Standard [Washington DC]*, 20 Jul.: "When you do computer programming there's an old maxim that to 10,000 eyes all bugs are shallow." 2011 *Guardian [London]*, 2 Mar.: "In the open-source world we have a saying: 'Many eyeballs

make all bugs shallow.'" The origin of the saying is attributable to a paper presented orally (and subsequently published in several versions) by Eric Steven Raymond, "The Cathedral and the Bazaar," at the Linux Kongress, 22 May 1997, in Würzburg, Germany: "Given a large enough beta-tester and co-developer base, almost every problem will be characterized quickly and the fix obvious to someone. Or, less formally, 'Given enough eyeballs, all bugs are shallow.' I dub this: 'Linus's Law.'" (Linus Torvalde was a Finnish graduate student who, about 1991, invented the Linux computer operating system.)

After all of this, how about the "heart" (Gréciano 1998) in modern American proverbs for some final remarks? Recognizing that such large cities as New York, Chicago, Los Angeles, and a few more are actually more the exception and that the United States is covered with small towns and even villages, it makes a lot of sense to have come up with the proverb "Small town, big heart" (1982, S1, 118) to describe the generally pleasant and comfortable life there. And despite the hustle and bustle of modern American lives there is the proverb "The heart has a mind of its own" (1960, 119) acknowledging the importance of emotions and heartfelt love. Yet it is the proverb "You can't measure heart" (1967, 119) that can serve as a final piece of folk wisdom. It can relate to basically anything that people might put their heart into with commitment and conviction. Such professional or philanthropic efforts can well be immeasurable, but their positive results add up to a fair and compassionate society where the golden rule "Do unto others as you would have them do unto you" (Matthew 7:12) is the moral guidepost. Generally speaking, then, the somatic aspects of modern American proverbs help to express an American worldview of fairness, compassion, and also love in its various manifestations. A culture and society that might overcome its ridiculous emphasis on exceptionalism, that is a responsible partner in international concerns regarding the environment and immigration, and that makes this world a better and safer place for all humankind. One thing is for certain, traditional and new American proverbs (Mieder 1989 and 2015) contain wisdom that can offer advice and guidance towards these laudable goals. It would most certainly be a big mistake to think or claim that proverbs have outlived their usefulness in the modern age. While some proverbs have survived for centuries, others have come and gone, but there will always be new ones as well (Mieder 1993). But there is no doubt that the meta-proverb "Proverbs are never out of season" with its claim that proverbs will always be part of human communication will always hold true.

Bibliography

This chapter was first published at the University of Perm, Russia, as "'No Body Is Perfect': Somatic Aspects of Modern American Proverbs." *Evraziiskii gumanitarnyi zhurnal/Eurasian Humanitarian Journal*, no volume given, no. 1 (2020), 4–20.

Aroutunova, Bayara. 1979. "Gesture and Word: A Semiotic Treatment of Russian Phraseologic Expressions and Proverbs." *Folia Slavica*, 3,1–2: 48–79.

Carter, Elena V. 2015. "'With an Open Heart': Somatic Idioms in Nikita Khrushchev's Political Discourse." *Linguo-Cultural Research on Phraseology*. Eds. Joanna Szerszunowicz, Bogusław Nowowiejski, Priscilla Ishida, and Katsumasa Yagi. Białystok: University of Białystok Publishing House. 347–360.

Čermák, František. 1998. "Somatic Idioms Revisited." *Europhras 95: Europäische Phraseologie im Vergleich: Gemeinsames Erbe und kulturelle Vielfalt*. Ed. Wolfgang Eismann. Bochum: Norbert Brockmeyer. 109–119.

Doyle, Charles Clay. 1996. "On 'New' Proverbs and the Conservativeness of Proverb Dictionaries." *Proverbium*, 13: 69–84.

Doyle, Charles Clay. 2017. "'Keep Your Eyes on the Prize': The Background and Evolution of the Proverb." *Proverbium*, 34: 79–89.

Doyle, Charles Clay, and Wolfgang Mieder. 2016. "*The Dictionary of Modern Proverbs*: First Supplement." *Proverbium*, 33: 85–120.

Doyle, Charles Clay, and Wolfgang Mieder. 2018. "*The Dictionary of Modern Proverbs*: Second Supplement." *Proverbium*, 35: 15–44.

Doyle, Charles Clay, and Wolfgang Mieder. 2020. "*The Dictionary of Modern Proverbs*: Third Supplement." *Proverbium*, 37: 53–86.

Doyle, Charles Clay, Wolfgang Mieder, and Fred R. Shapiro. 2012. *The Dictionary of Modern Proverbs*. New Haven, CT: Yale University Press.

Dundes, Alan. 1969. "Thinking Ahead: A Folkloristic Reflection of the Future Orientation in American Worldview." *Anthropological Quarterly*, 42: 53–72.

Dundes, Alan. 1972. "Folk Ideas as Units of Worldview." *Towards New Perspectives in Folklore*. Eds. Américo Paredes and Richard Bauman. Austin, TX: University of Texas Press. 93–103.

Dundes, Alan, and Carl Pagter. 1987. *When You're Up to Your Ass in Alligators … More Urban Folklore from the Paperwork Empire*. Detroit, MI: Wayne State University Press.

Gordy, Mirosława. 2010. *Somaticheskaia frazeologiia sovremennykh russkogo i pol'skogo iazykov*. Szczecin: volumina.pl Daniel Krzanowski.

Gréciano, Gertrud. 1998. "Zur Phraseologie des Herzens." *Europhras 97: Phraseology and Paremiology*. Hrsg. von Peter Ďurčo. Bratislava: Akadémia PZ. 144–150.

Gułowska-Gawkoskwa, Małgorzata. 2013. *Somatische und emotionale Konzepte in der deutschen und polnischen Phraseologie*. Frankfurt am Main: Peter Lang.

Hakamies, Pekka. 2002. "Proverbs and Mentality." *Myth and Mentality: Studies in Folklore and Popular Thought*. Ed. Anna-Leena Siikala. Helsinki: Finnish Literature Society. 222–230.

Litovkina. Anna T., and Wolfgang Mieder. 2006. *Old Proverbs Never Die, They Just Diversify. A Collection of Anti-proverbs*. Burlington, VT: The University of Vermont; Veszprém, Hungary: The Pannonian University of Veszprém.

Ly, Thang Toan. 2015. "Conceptualizing Human Body Parts in Proverbs: A Cross-Linguistic and Cross-Cultural Study." *Proceedings of the Eighth Interdisciplinary Colloquium on Proverbs, 2nd to 9th November 2014, at Tavira, Portugal*. Eds. Rui J.B. Soares and Outi Lauhakangas. Tavira: Tipografia Tavirense. 110–121.

Mellado Blanco, Carmen. 2004. *Phraseologismos somáticos del alemán. Un studio léxico-semántico*. Frankfurt am Main: Peter Lang.

Mieder, Wolfgang. 1989. *American Proverbs: A Study of Texts and Contexts*. Bern: Peter Lang.

Mieder, Wolfgang. 1993. *Proverbs Are Never Out of Season. Popular Wisdom in the Modern Age*. New York: Oxford University Press; reprint New York: Peter Lang, 2012.

Mieder, Wolfgang. 2004. *Proverbs. A Handbook*. Westport, CT: Greenwood Press; reprint New York: Peter Lang, 2012.

Mieder, Wolfgang. 2009a. *International Bibliography of Paremiology and Phraseology*. 2 Bde. Berlin: Walter de Gruyter.

Mieder, Wolfgang. 2009b. *"Yes We Can": Barack Obama's Proverbial Rhetoric*. New York: Peter Lang.

Mieder, Wolfgang. 2010. *"Making a Way out of no Way": Martin Luther King's Sermonic Proverbial Rhetoric*. New York: Peter Lang.

Mieder, Wolfgang. 2011. *International Bibliography of Paremiography. Collections of Proverbs, Proverbial Expressions and Comparison, Quotations, Graffiti, Slang, and Wellerisms*. Burlington, VT: The University of Vermont.

Mieder, Wolfgang. 2014. *Behold the Proverbs of a People. Proverbial Wisdom in Culture, Literature, and Politics*. Jackson, MS: University Press of Mississippi.

Mieder, Wolfgang. 2015. *"Different Strokes for Different Folks". 1250 authentisch amerikan-ische Sprichwörter*. Bochum: Nobert Brockmeyer.

Mieder, Wolfgang. 2017. "Futuristic Paremiography and Paremiology: A Plea for the Collection and Study of Modern Proverbs." *Poslovitsy v frazeologicheskom pole: Kognitivnyi, diskursivnyi, spoostavitel'nyi aspekty*. Ed. T.N. Fedulenkova. Vladimir: Vladimirskii Gosudarstvennyie Universitet. 205–226.

Mieder, Wolfgang. 2018. "'Life Is not a Spectator Sport'. Proverbial Emotions about Modern Life." *Emotsional'naia sfera cheloveka v iazyke i kommunikatsii: Sinkhroniia i diakhroniia*. Ed. E.R. Ioanesian. Moscow: Institut Iazykoznaniia RAN. 7–17.

Mieder, Wolfgang. 2019a. "'Age Is Just a Number'. American Proverbial Wisdom about Age and Aging." *Emotsional'aia sfera cheloveka v iazyke i kommunikatsii: Sinkhroniia i diakhroniia*. Eds. M.L. Kovshova, H.K. Riabtseva, and P.S. Dronov. Moskva: Instiutut Iazykoznaniia RAN. 7–23.

Mieder, Wolfgang. 2019b. " 'Proverbs Are Worth a Thousand Words': The Global Spread of American Proverbs." *Contexts of Folklore. Festschrift for Dan Ben-Amos on His Eighty-Fifth Birthday.* Eds. Simon Bronner and Wolfgang Mieder. New York: Peter Lang. 217–229.

Mieder, Wolfgang. 2019c. *"Right Makes Might": Proverbs and the American Worldview.* Bloomington, IN: Indiana University Press, 2019c.

Mieder, Wolfgang. 2020. " 'Love Is Just a Four-Letter Word'. Sexuality and Scatology in Modern Anglo-American Proverbs." *Proceedings of the 13th Interdisciplinary Colloquium on Proverbs, 3rd to 10th November 2019, at Tavira, Portugal.* Eds. Rui J.B. Soares and Outi Lauhakangas. Tavira: Tipografia Tavirense. in press.

Mieder, Wolfgang, Stewart A. Kingsbury, and Kelsie B. Harder. 1992. *A Dictionary of American Proverbs.* New York: Oxford University Press.

Mokienko, Valerii M. 2003. *Novaia russkaia frazeologiia.* Opole: Uniwersytet Opolski— Instytut Filologii Polskiej.

Niemi, Jussi, Juha Mulli, Marja Nenonen, Sinikka Niemi, Alexandre Nikolaev, and Esa Penttilä. 2010. "Body-Part Idioms across Languages: Lexical Analyses of VP Body-Part Idioms in English, German, Swedish, Russian and Finnish." *Korpora, Web und Datenbanken. Computergestützte Methoden in der modernen Phraseologie und Lexikographie.* Eds. Stefaniya Ptashnyk, Erla Hallsteinsdóttir, and Noah Bubenhofer. Baltmannsweiler: Schneider Verlag Hohengehren. 67–76.

Piirainen, Elisabeth. 2016. "The Human Body." *Lexicon of Common Figurative Units. Widespread Idioms in Europe and Beyond.* Ed. E. Piirainen. New York: Peter Lang. 533–574,

Schipper, Mineke. 2003. *"Never Marry a Woman with Big Feet": Women in Proverbs from Around the World.* New Haven, CT: Yale University Press.

Senga, Anikó N. 1987. "Correspondences between Hungarian and English Somatic Proverbia with 'Leg' and 'Foot'." *Ural-Altaic Yearbook,* 59: 15–33.

Skrypnik, Irina. 2011. "Interpersonal Relationships in Ukrainian and English: Similarities and Discrepancies (on the Material of the Somatic Phraseological Units)." *Linguo-Cultural Competence and Phraseological Motivation.* Eds. Antonio Pamies [Bertrán] and Dmitrij Dobrovol'skij. Baltmannsweiler: Schneider Verlag Hohengehren. 173–178.

Zhu, Kaifu. 1998. *Lexikographische Untersuchung somatischer Phraseologismen im Deutschen und Chinesischen.* Frankfurt am Main: Peter Lang.

Chapter Six

"Time Spent Wishing Is Time Wasted"

Temporal Worldview in Modern American Proverbs

Twenty-five years ago, I had the pleasure and honor to meet Prof. Veronika N. Teliya at an international phraseological conference at Graz, Austria. I still remember her intriguing lecture on "Phraseological Entities as a Language of Culture" that was published three years later in 1998. In the same year appeared her important chapter on "Phraseology as a Language of Culture: Its Role in the Representation of a Collective Mentality" that she wrote together with three colleagues. There is no doubt that her insights into the interrelationship of phraseologisms and culture as well as their significance for the understanding of worldview have been and continue to be of great significance for the study of mentality. Following her lead, Roumyana Petrova looked in considerable detail at "proverbs as cultural texts" (2003: 331), with Pekka Hakamies agreeing that "proverbs provide relevant and interesting data for mentality studies, as long as the many-sided problems involved with their use are taken into account" (2002: 229). Indeed, care must be taken that proverbs are not studied in isolation when looking at them as cultural signs or expressions of a general worldview (Mieder 2008 and 2019b, Nedeva 2014: 105, Profontova 1996: 719,

White 1987: 168). Alan Dundes warned against the danger of over-simplification or over-generalization in interpreting proverbs without context and without knowing the frequency of their use (1969: 55). In fact, in a seminal article on "Folk Ideas as Units of Worldview" (1972) he made the important point that proverbs and other folkloric matters are best looked at as groups of "folk ideas" that collectively might amount to a general worldview. Thus, looking at groups of proverbs of a certain language culture about age, love, or money can lead to a generalized picture of the mentality of a certain people (Mieder 2018 and 2019a). Dundes showed by way of proverbs and other traditional materials that there appears to be something like a "future orientation in American worldview" (1969) and a "lineal worldview in American folk speech" (2004). This does not necessarily have anything to do with "national character" which can too quickly lead to stereotypical and misguided conclusions. Cultural linguistics and folkloristics should refrain from such questionable interpretations.

It should not come as a surprise that the question of how various cultures and societies have interpreted the omnipresent concerns with "time" has led to fascinating studies. John Hassard's *The Sociology of Time* (1990) speaks of the contrast between "social-time vs. clock-time" and "linear-time vs. circular-time" (6–9) and concludes that "increasingly our social life is structured in accordance with 'mechanical'-time: that is, an artificial form [the clock] which is quite independent of the cyclic rhythms of man's organic impulses and needs" (11). Alfred Gell in his book *The Anthropology of Time. Cultural Constructions of Temporal Maps and Images* (1992) quite convincingly concludes that "time is a familiar dimensional property of our experienced surroundings" (315) and argues more specifically that "the time handling expressions in common use in our language reveal the very widespread use of process-related time indicators of a non-metric type. We talk about events and organize ourselves in relation to them by making use of a socially embedded temporal schema" (107). This speaks, albeit indirectly, of proverbs referring to the multifaceted aspects of time and space that can be understood as "ubiquitous components that constitute the perception of the world" (Piirainen 2012: 399). Thus, concerning the proverbial expression "To kill time" that has been identified in 57 European languages, Elisabeth Piirainen points out convincingly that "it illustrates the conceptualization of time as a resource that can be consumed or wasted and, at the same time, shows a metaphorization of time as a living being that can be killed" (2012: 446). This preoccupation with phrasemes about time has led to Heinz-Gerhard Friese's monograph *Zeiterfahrung im Alltagsbewußtsein. Am Beispiel des deutschen Sprichworts der Neuzeit* (1984) as well as two other articles dealing with German „time"-expressions (Cox 1999–2000, Pérennec 2001).

Regarding Anglo-American proverbs about time, the cultural linguist Ali Dabbagh points out that "English proverbs profile schemas which associate time with a valuable entity" and that "nothing is more important in this world than the present moment due to the fact that nothing else is permanent and stationary" (2017: 588). More revealing yet is Kimberly Lau's seminal article on "'It's about Time': The Ten Proverbs Most Frequently Used in Newspapers and Their Relation to American Values" (1996). While it is primarily concerned with the innovative use of the computer for paremiological research, Lau is able to list ten of the most frequently used proverbs in the database, among them three "time"-expressions: "Time will tell", "Time is money", and "Time flies" (for additional texts see Mieder, Kingsbury, Harder 1992: 598–599). This leads her to the conclusion that "time is a driving force in American life" and "without question, time entertains a primary position in American culture and ideology" (139–140). Stan Nusbaum, in his little-known book *American Cultural [and Proverbial] Baggage. How to Recognize and Deal with It* (2005) cites such old stand-by proverbs like "Time is money", "Time flies", "No time like the present", and "Time marches on" to prove that "If Americans are obsessed with anything, that thing is time. The view of time as a scarce, valuable thing affects all of American life" (124) and that "Americans are time-conscious to an extreme" (127). There certainly is some truth in this, and he also might be quite right in claiming that for Americans "Life is a race, a race against time". And yet, the proverb "Time is money" is not of American coinage and has long been loan translated into numerous languages worldwide. Its earliest reference was found in a British journal of 1719 from which Benjamin Franklin, who usually is credited with having coined it, copied it in 1751 (Villers and Mieder 2017). And, of course, the proverb "Time flies" goes even back to antiquity and is current internationally! So, the question arises how valid it is to claim a particular American worldview by way of such texts? But it is true that both proverbs are very popular in American oral and written speech and their frequent use in different contexts makes them at least part of the American worldview.

But here is something that Americans have done with the ancient proverb "Time flies"! In *The Dictionary of Modern Proverbs* (2012; cited throughout with dates of earliest reference found and page numbers in parentheses), edited by Charles Clay Doyle, Wolfgang Mieder, and Fred R. Shapiro, appears the anti-proverb "Time flies when you're having fun" (1939, 259) with its earliest recorded date of 1939. It has long become an American proverb in its own right and it can be interpreted as expressing the "folk idea" of enjoying life to the fullest, somewhat in accord with the classical "carpe diem". But be that as it may, the following deliberations about the American mentality about time are all based on modern proverbs (not older than the year 1900) coined in the United States! They have all been found in numerous contexts of which some are cited in our dictionary and its three supplements. The proverbs under discussion are thus not a "mixed bag" of proverbs from different times and different cultures but rather authentic American proverbs in actual use today (Mieder 2015). As such, they allow a more informed and valid discussion of how Americans in general (!) think about that important commodity of time.

Before looking at these authentic modern American proverbs about temporal matters, the following chronologically arranged list of earlier texts coined in the United states might be of some interest. They can be found in Wolfgang Mieder's annotated collection *"Different Strokes for Different Folks". 1250 authentisch amerikanische Sprichwörter* (2015: 228–231):

> Time and chance happen to all men. (1677)
> Time is an herb that cures all diseases. (1738, coined by Benjamin Franklin)
> Lost time is never found again. (1748, coined by Benjamin Franklin)
> Nothing is more precious than time, yet nothing is less valued. (1775)
> These are the times that try men's souls. (1776, coined by Thomas Paine)
> There is always a first time. (1792)
> Time wasted is time lost. (1865)

These proverbs indicate that their wisdom about time is by no means metrical but rather general in nature. This will also be the case with modern "time"-proverbs to be dealt with in the following paragraphs. In fact, there really are only two modern proverbs dealing with measurable time. There is first of all the interesting proverb "If you are fifteen (ten, etc.) minutes early, you are on time (already five minutes late)" (1963, 167) that somewhat ironically comments on how clock-time governs modern professional life with its stress and frustrations. The other proverb is "A week is a long time in politics" (1961, 274) that at times has been attributed to British Prime Minister Harold Wilson with no record of his use having been found before 1968.

While this proverb clearly relates to the vicissitudes of political life, there are several proverbs that express the American insistence on having fun, that is, having a good time. Since "party life" can go too far, there is the cautionary proverb "Always leave the party (leave, go home, quit) while you're having fun (a good time)" (1953, 191) that circulates in a number of variants. This emphasis on pleasure is also expressed in the proverb "We're here for a good time, not a long time" (1977, S3, 81–82; S1, S2, and S3 refer to Charles Clay Doyle's and Wolfgang Mieder's three supplements to the *Dictionary of Modern Proverbs*). This proverbial wisdom appears to play on the classical opposites of "carpe diem" and "memento mori". But not to worry, there is also the proverb "Time you enjoy wasting is not (always) wasted time" (1912, 259).

More important and certainly in much more frequent use is the titular proverb "Time spent wishing is time wasted" (1922, 259) of this chapter that had its origin in the popular song "Carolina in the Morning" (1922). The first stanza includes the line turned proverb:

Wishing is good time wasted,
Still it's a habit they say,
Wishing for sweets I've tasted,
That's all I do all day.
Maybe there's nothing in wishing,
But, speaking of wishing I'll say,
Nothing could be finer
Than to be in Carolina
In the morning.

No one could be sweeter
Than my sweetie when I meet her
In the morning.

It's a love song of sorts where someone remembers a sweet relationship and wishes that it could be rekindled. But since chances of that happening are slim or even non-existent, such hope might well be a waste of precious time. And yes, the American worldview is clearly that time is too precious to let pass by without a success in whatever that might be.

Already Benjamin Franklin coined the proverb "There will be sleeping enough in the grave" in 1741 as an admonishment against letting time pass by without taking action. The implication of death in this proverb might have been the reason that it is not particularly current in American parlance any longer, but I must admit that I do enjoy citing it to justify my positive obsession with work. In any case, there is a "milder" modern proverb that has taken its place in the middle of the twentieth century: "Life (Time, etc.) is too short (too precious) to waste it sleeping" (1944, 145). This is once again somewhat of a reminiscence of the well-known classical dichotomy of "vita contemplativa" and "vita activa". Not that Americans do not treasure reflection or philosophical pursuits, but the general mentality leans towards an existence of active pursuits since after all life really is but short and must be lived to the fullest. But to return to my personal work ethics, I wonder what my thoughts might be at the end of my life in the service of paremiology. Will I finally agree with the proverb "No one on his deathbed has ever said, 'I wish I'd spent more time at the office (at work, on business)'" (1984, 52)? Benjamin Franklin, to whom we owe the so-called Protestant ethics with its emphasis on constructive work, would surely have disagreed with this mentality (Mieder 1989: 129–142). But times have changed, and while the belief in the value of solid work continues to be part of the American worldview, the pleasure principle is plenty strong as well. That is perfectly expressed in the proverb "Take time to smell the flowers (roses)" (1951, 259) with the meaning of not to hurry or worry but rather to enjoy the beauty of life.

But there is a proverb that good old Franklin doubtlessly would have liked: "The best way to kill time is to work it to death" (1914, 271).

That is a solid dose of pragmatism that obviously is part of the American worldview. But care must be taken that the so-called "Parkinson's Law" does not take over that says proverbially that "Work expands to fill the available (allotted) time" (1955, 281). It originated with C. Northcote Parkinson and basically argues that work should be executed in a very efficient way without wasting unnecessary time. One is reminded of the classical proverb "Nothing is excess is best".

In classical times and in many cultures still today the advice "To take opportunity by the forelock" encouraged people to step up to the plate and make things happen at the right time. Two modern proverbs with animal metaphors express this idea quite convincingly, to wit "The time to shoot (catch) bears is when they are out (around)" (1914, 259) and "The best time to fish is when they are biting" (1921, 80). But there is a third proverbial animal metaphor giving some down-to-earth advice, once again touching on the concern about wasting valuable time: "Never try to teach a pig to sing; it wastes your time, and it annoys the pig" (1973, 197).

With some of these new proverbs one gets the feeling that they are nothing else but reformulations of traditional proverbs. Thus, the Biblical proverb "There is a time for everything" (Ecclesiastes 3:1) seems to be restated as "Nothing happens until it happens (before its time)" (1901, 180). Of special interest is doubtlessly the fascinating rephrasing of the traditional proverb "Time heals all wounds" into the clever anti-proverb "Time wounds all heels" (1938, 259) with its homonymous pun and the allusion to the passing of time becoming an Achilles heel of sorts. Of interest is also the seemingly innocuous proverb "When it's time to go, it's time to go" (1936, 260). It usually refers to the departure from a meeting or a social gathering, but in a more morbid sense it can also imply dying. Humorously stated. it can also imply the necessity of a visit to the toilet, something that can also be expressed with the similar modern proverb "When you've got to go, you've got to go (1937, 100). In both cases the verb "to go" can signify urination or defecation. All of this shows that the essence of modern proverbs just like old proverbs lies in their polyfunctionality, polysituativity, and polysemanticity (Mieder 2004: 9). But in any case, modern American proverbs about time, albeit not a large number of them, appear to express the worldview that time is definitely of the essence and that it must be enjoyed while at the same time condoning good work ethics for a ful-filled and successful life.

Bibliography

Cox, Heinrich L. 1999–2000. "'Morgenstund hat Gold im Mund': Sprichwörter mit einer Zeit-Komponente im Sprichwortschatz Bonner Student(inn)en." *Rheinisches Jahrbuch für Volkskunde*, 33: 81–95.

Dabbagh, Ali. 2017. "Cultural Linguistics as an Investigative Framework for Paremiology: Comparing Time in English and Persian." *International Journal of Applied Linguistics*, 27: 577–595.

Doyle, Charles Clay, and Wolfgang Mieder. 2016. "*The Dictionary of Modern Proverbs*: A Supplement." *Proverbium*, 33: 85–120.

Doyle, Charles Clay, and Wolfgang Mieder. 2018. "*The Dictionary of Modern Proverbs*: Second Supplement." *Proverbium*, 35: 15–44.

Doyle, Charles Clay, and Wolfgang Mieder. 2020. "*The Dictionary of Modern Proverbs*: Third Supplement." *Proverbium*, 37: 53–86.

Doyle, Charles Clay, Wolfgang Mieder, and Fred R. Shapiro (eds.). 2012. *The Dictionary of Modern Proverbs*. New Haven, CT: Yale University Press.

Dundes, Alan. 1969. "Thinking Ahead: A Folkloristic Reflection of the Future Orientation in American Worldview." *Anthropological Quarterly*, 42: 53–72.

Dundes, Alan. 1972. "Folk Ideas as Units of Worldview." *Towards New Perspectives in Folklore*. Eds. Américo Paredes and Richard Bauman. Austin, TX: University of Texas Press. 93–103

Dundes, Alan. 2004. "'As the Crow Flies': A Straightforward Study of Lineal Worldview in American Folk Speech." *"What Goes Around Comes Around": The Circulation of Proverbs in Contemporary Life. Essays in Honor of Wolfgang Mieder*. Eds. Kimberly J. Lau, Peter Tokofsky, and Stephen D. Winick. Logan, UT: Utah State University Press. 171–187.

Friese, Heinz-Gerhard. 1984. *Zeiterfahrung im Alltagsbewußtsein. Am Beispiel des deutschen Sprichworts der Neuzeit*. Frankfurt am Main: Materialis.

Gell, Alfred. 1992. *The Anthropology of Time. Cultural Constructions of Temporal Maps and Images*. Oxford: Berg Publishers.

Hakamies, Pekka. 2002. "Proverbs and Mentality." *Myth and Mentality. Studies in Folklore and Popular Thought*. Ed. Anna-Leena Siikala. Helsinki: Finnish Literature Society. 222–230.

Hassard, John (ed.). 1990. *The Sociology of Time*. New York: St. Martin's Press.

Lau, Kimberly J. 1996. "'It's about Time': The Ten Proverbs Most Frequently Used in Newspapers and Their Relation to American Values." *Proverbium*, 13: 135–159.

Mieder, Wolfgang. 1989. *American Proverbs. A Study of Texts and Contexts*. Bern: Peter Lang.

Mieder, Wolfgang. 2004. *Proverbs. A Handbook*. Westport, CT: Greenwood Press; rpt. New York: Peter Lang, 2012.

Mieder, Wolfgang. 2008. "'Wisdom Is Better Than Wealth'. Proverbs as Expressions of Culture and Folklore." *"Proverbs Speak Louder Than Words". Folk Wisdom in Art, Culture, Folklore, History, Literature, and Mass Media*. Ed. Wolfgang Mieder. New York: Peter Lang. 9–44.

Mieder, Wolfgang. 2015. *"Different Strokes for Different Folks". 1250 authentisch amerikanische Sprichwörter*. Baltmannsweiler: Norbert Brockmeyer.

Mieder, Wolfgang. 2018. "'Life is not a Spectator Sport': Proverbial Emotions about Modern Life." *Emotsional'naia sfera cheloveka v iazyke i kommunikatsii: Sinkhroniia i diakhroniia*. Ed. E.R. Ioanesian. Moscow: Institut Iaazykoznaniia RAN. 7–17.

Mieder, Wolfgang. 2019a. "'Age is Just a Number': American Proverbial Wisdom about Age and Aging." *Emotsional'naia sfera cheloveka v iazyke i kommunikatsii: Sinkhroniia i diakhroniia*. Ed. E.R. Ioanesian. Moscow: Institut Iaazykoznaniia RAN. 7–23.

Mieder, Wolfgang. 2019b. *"Right Makes Might". Proverbs and the American Worldview*. Bloomington, IN: Indiana University Press.

Mieder, Wolfgang, Stewart A. Kingsbury, and Kelsie B. Harder (eds.). 1992. *A Dictionary of American Proverbs*. New York: Oxford University Press.

Nedeva, Svetla. 2014. "Achieving Better Intercultural Communication Through Learning to Interpret Cultural Value of Proverbs in a Language and the Way They Reflect National Character." *Revista Economică*, 66: 105–116.

Nussbaum, Stan. 2005. *American Cultural [and Proverbial] Baggage. How to Recognize and Deal with It*. Maryknoll, New York: Orbis Books.

Pérennec, Marie-Hélène. 2001. "Lexikalisierte Zeitmetaphern und ihre Abwandlungen." *Phraseologiae Amor: Aspekte europäischer Phraseologie. Festschrift für Gertrud Gréciano*. Eds. Annelies Häcki Buhofer, Harald Burger, and Laurent Gautier. Baltmannsweiler: Schneider Verlag Hohengehren. 199–209.

Petrova, Roumyana. 2003. "Comparing Proverbs as Cultural Texts." *Proverbium*, 20: 331–344.

Piirainen, Elisabeth. 2012. *Lexicon of Common Figurative Units. Widespread Idioms in Europe and Beyond*. New York: Peter Lang.

Profantová, Zuzana. 1996. "Worldview, Proverbs, Folk Narrative." *Folk Narrative and World View*. Ed. Leander Petzoldt. 2 vols. Frankfurt am Main: Peter Lang. II, 719–793.

Teliya, Veronika N. 1998. "Phraseological Entities as a Language of Culture (Methodological Aspects)." *Europhras 95: Europäische Phraseologie im Vergleich: Gemeinsames Erbe und kulturelle Vielfalt*. Ed. Wolfgang Eismann. Bochum: Norbert Brockmeyer. 783–794.

Teliya, Veronika N., Natalya Bragina, Elena Oparina, and Irina Sandormirskaya. 1998. "Phraseology as a Language of Culture: Its Role in the Representation of Cultural Mentality." *Phraseology: Theory, Analysis, and Applications*. Ed. A.P. Cowie. Oxford: Oxford University Press. 55–75.

Villers, Damien, and Wolfgang Mieder. 2017. " 'Time is Money'. Benjamin Franklin and the Vexing Problem of Proverb Origins." *Proverbium*, 34: 391–404.

White, Geoffrey M. 1987. "Proverbs and Cultural Models. An American Psychology of Problem Solving." *Cultural Models in Language and Thought*. Eds. Dorothy Holland and Naomi Quinn. Cambridge: Cambridge University Press. 152–172.

Chapter Seven

"Money Makes the World Go 'Round"

The Pecuniary Worldview of Modern American Proverbs

There is a sixteenth-century English proverb whose basic idea is well exemplified by an old nursery rhyme that shows that money makes things possible:

Will you lend me your mare to ride a mile?
—No, she is lame leaping over a stile.
—Alack! and I must go to the fair!
I'll give you good money for lending your mare.
—Oh, oh! say you so?
Money will make the mare to go.

The proverb "Money makes the mare go" (Mieder, Kingsbury, Harder 1992: 417) might well have been the structural and semantic background for the much younger and very popular American proverb "Money makes the world go 'round" (1871) with the pervasive message that money belongs to the fundamental ingredients to make essential things in life happen. This is well expressed by Fred Ebb's song "Money, Money" (1966) that was popularized in Bob Fosse's musical drama film *Cabaret* (1972) starring Liza Minnelli and Michael York:

Money makes the world go around
The world go around
The world go around
Money makes the world go around
It makes the world go 'round

A mark, a yen, a buck, or a pound
A buck or a pound
A buck or a pound
Is all that makes the world go around
That clinking clanking sound
Can make the world go 'round

No matter in what currency, money rules personal and commercial commerce to a remarkable degree, and it is not surprising that international proverb collections contain a plethora of examples from antiquity to the modern age (Cordry 1997: 178–180, Mieder 1986: 329–334). Not surprisingly, the same is true for the many national collections, to wit for example the rich treasure of pecuniary Anglo-American proverbs (Cheales 1874: 98–102, Hood 1885: 398–406, Loomis 1964, Mieder, Kingsbury, Harder 1992: 415–418, Speake 2015: 210–203). The concept of "money" is, of course, but a collective term for other mercantile aspects, such as business, poverty, prosperity, purchase, sale, stocks, wealth, etc. There exist several major quotation dictionaries for all of this that include some proverbs as well, the largest of which is Ted Goodman's *The Forbes Book of Business Quotations. 14,173 Thoughts on the Business of Life* (1997: 52–64, 106–120, and 582–594; see also Braude 1965: 37–42, Forbes 1984, Thomsett 1990: 96–97, White 1986: 32–50 and 66–86).

With all of this textual information, albeit usually without any historical or contextual information, it is tempting to draw certain national or worse, stereotypical conclusions about the worldview or mentality of certain cultures or groups. A multitude of studies exist, notably about proverbs depicting so-called national characters or anti-feminist attitudes, for example (Schipper 2003, Nedeva 2014). Usually such ahistorical studies take proverbs at their face value without asking whether they are still in use today and with what frequency. To a certain degree this is also true for some investigations of cultural or more specifically economic attitudes expressed in proverbs, to wit Dimitri Shimkin and Pedro Sanjuan, "Culture and World View: A Method of Analysis Applied to Rural Russia" (1953), Alpha Chiang, "Religion, Proverbs, and Economic Mentality [in Chinese Proverbs]" (1961), Abdel-Malek Mortad, "Economic Relations among Social Classes in Algerian Proverbs" (1991), Ğorğ Mifsud-Chircop, "Proverbiality and Worldview in Maltese and Arabic Proverbs" (2001), Tok Thompson, "Getting Ahead in Ethiopia: Amharic Proverbs about Wealth" (2009), Dhubra Gautam, "Business Practices and Paradoxical Proverbs in Nepal" (2013), and Xiangyang Zhang, "Language as a Reflection of Culture: On the Cultural Characteristics of Chinese and English Proverbs" (2016). Without wanting to discredit these investigations, it needs to be remembered that conclusions about worldview or national character by way of proverbs must take other important indicators into consideration so that they do not lead to overgeneralizations. The following caveat must be kept in mind: "Care must be taken when looking at proverbs as expressing aspects of a certain worldview or mentality of a people that no stereotypical conclusions and a so-called 'national character' are drawn" (Mieder 2008: 22). Pekka Hakamies, in his enlightening article on "Proverbs and Mentality" (2002) echoes this warning: "Even if proverbs can reveal an aspect of the user's way of thinking, this hardly means that proverbs are always the most reliable key" (224) for mentality conclusions.

Basing such studies on historical and comparative footings and enhancing them by social and psychological findings, proverbs can be of value in drawing some general attitudinal conclusions. Even if there is such a concept as a general worldview pertaining to a certain culture, it must be kept in mind that "a worldview is like a stage set on which each human being is a character seeing himself, speaking his lines, and viewing everything else. [...] Worldviews do differ with cultures" (Naugle 2002: 246). In other words, when looking at national worldviews, it is important to keep in mind that such a construct is indeed very complex, with such communal character having to leave space for the deviating character traits of individuals (Potter 1954: 8–9). From a folkloristic point of view, it can be said that individual "human thought and action are affected [to a degree] by worldview perception and interpretation" (Naugle 2002: 299). Zuzana Profantová is correct in stressing in her short yet insightful article "Worldview, Proverbs, Folk Narrative" (1996) that certain general worldview traits can be ascertained from particularly often-used proverbs as socially sanctioned "signs communicating tradition, the past and the presence" (723). In his equally revealing article on "Proverbs and Cultural Models" (1987), Geoffrey White reaches similar conclusions: "The fact that certain proverbs are frequently used suggests that they express key understandings about everyday life. If so, proverbs may provide a source of insight into cultural models in particular areas of common experience" (152–153). Indeed, proverbs "appeal to common-sense reasoning based on cultural models of experience" (168), and they reveal "folk ideas", a term for worldview/mentality favored by the American folklorist/anthropologist Alan Dundes in his article on "Folk Ideas as Units of Worldview" (1971).

Before discussing what folk ideas, worldview, or mentality can be extrapolated from authentic American (not British) proverbs about financial matters, a few more general comments about the American worldview, if indeed there is such a thing, are in order. John Tierney begins his scholarly study *Conceived in Liberty. The American Worldview in Theory and Practice* (2016) with the fitting statement that "A deep and enduring characteristic of the American worldview stems from the unique nature of US society as being a 'melting pot' or, as the late President John Kennedy put it in his own book, 'A nation of immigrants'" (1–2). True enough, but his introductory statement "Having been spared the traumas of periodic and systemic revolutions, modern America has thrived on political stability and a singular worldview. […] The validity of liberty as the fundamental American worldview" (xviii) is a bit too general. The proverbial idea of "life, liberty, and the pursuit of happiness" and the proverb that "All men are created equal" from the famed *Declaration of Independence* (1776) are indeed almost sacred cornerstones of American democracy, but care must be taken that these noble concepts are not transfigured into a worldview of hubristic exceptionalism. And yet, the idea of individual and political freedom is part of the psyche of the entire highly diverse American population. The quintessential modern American proverb "Different strokes for different folks" from about 1945 is a liberating piece of folk wisdom that quite naturally was coined in the United States (Mieder 1989: 317–332).

Realizing that folk ideas (mentalities or worldview) can change over time, Jim Norwine and Jonathan Smith entitled their edited volume as *Worldview Flux. Perplexed Values among Postmodern Peoples* (2000). In one of the article on "Values in Flux", the authors rightfully add pragmatism to liberty/freedom as a basic element of the American worldview: " 'Value that which works, discard that which does not' is such a fundamental and defining American sensibility that *pragmatism* has been referred to as our most 'homegrown' intellectual tradition" (Norwine et al, 2000: 29). David Potter in his earlier book with the befitting title *People of Plenty. Economic Abundance and the American Character* (1954) decided that "in America 'liberty,' meaning 'freedom to grasp opportunity,' and 'equality,' also meaning 'freedom to grasp opportunity,' have become almost synonymous. In short, equality came to mean, in a major sense, parity in competition" (92). And yes, the embracing of "mobility" (97) became part of the American society of abundance in considerable difference towards attitudes of changing places for the sake of better employment opportunities in other countries. Of course, the emphasis on competition also has led to "American life being geared to success rather than to status. That is, the American measures his own worth by the distance which he progressed from his point of departure rather than by the position which he occupies; he esteems high current income more than the possession of long-accumulated wealth" (Potter 1954: 48). This brings to mind the American ideal of the achievements of the "self-made" person, best expressed by Puritan ethics and the proverbial expression "from rags to riches" (Dundes 1971: 99).

Competition, success, and wealth led Alan Dundes in his seminal article on "Folk Ideas as Units of Worldview" (1971) to the justified conclusion that there exists in the American society "a materialistic, capitalistic view of the world" that can best be summarized as the folk idea of "the principle of unlimited good [abundance]" (1971: 96; see Mullen 1978: 209–212) to which can be added "the future orientation in American worldview" (98). Drawing on various folkloric materials, including numerous proverbs and proverbial expressions, Dundes showed the seeming American obsession with the future in two seminal studies: "Thinking Ahead: A Folkloristic Reflection of the Future Orientation in American Worldview" (1969, and " 'As the Crow Flies'. A Straightforward Study of Lineal Worldview in American Folk Speech" (2004). What distinguishes Alan Dundes's three articles about American folk ideas is that he amasses much folkloric and particularly proverbial material to back up his convincing claims that Americans in general are grounded in capitalist beliefs, that they are future oriented, and that they have progressive ideas about moving forward. Americans look from the present to the future and at times tend to ignore the lessons of history. Dundes would be quick to point out that his findings are generalizations, but they are to a considerable degree founded on the folk ideas, worldview or mentality as expressed in American folklore of today. Other folk ideas and beliefs, notably aspects of independence, individualism, ingenuity, freedom, and unlimited opportunities in the sociopolitical American life are described and analyzed in Wolfgang Mieder's book *"Right Makes Might"*. *Proverbs and the American Worldview* (2019b).

With this having been said, it is time to move on to what worldview, at least to some degree, American proverbs about monetary matters express. First of all, here is a short chronologically arranged list of such authentic American proverbs as established by historical research based on multiple contextualized references from literary works and the mass media. They are part of Wolfgang Mieder's annotated collection *"Different Strokes for Different Folks"*. *1250 authentisch amerikanische Sprichwörter* (2015). Each proverb is listed together with the date of its first registered occurrence in a printed source in parentheses:

Money is the sinews of trade. (1731)
Money is power. (1741)
He that will increase in riches, must not hoe corn in silk breeches. (1750)
Taxation without representation is tyranny. (1761, attributed to James Otis; also as revolutionary slogan as "No taxation without representation")
The longest [fullest] purse will prevail. (1764)
Money works miracles. (1766)
A bad penny is sure to return. (1766, coined by Abigail Adams)

Despair never pays any debts. (1767)

Money once gone never returns. (1771)

Discount is good pay. (1780)

There is no friendship in trade. (1784, coined by Samuel Adams)

The world will do its own business. (1800)

Competition is the life of trade. (1816)

Never spend your money before you have it. (1817)

Promises cost little. (1836)

Courtesy costs nothing. (1837, coined by Ralph Waldo Emerson)

Cheapest is the dearest labor. (1841, coined by Ralph Waldo Emerson)

Don't mix business with pleasure. (1847)

Banks have no heart. (1853)

When you die, you can't take it with you. (1855)

Money can't buy happiness. (1856)

Health is a call loan. (1858, coined by Josh Billings)

A dollar saved is a dollar earned. (1859, based on the older English proverb "A penny saved is a penny earned")

There are some things that money can't buy. (1864)

It pays to advertise. (1868)

Equal pay for equal work. (1869, coined by the feminist Susan B. Anthony)

Money isn't everything. (1870)

Money makes the world go around. (1871)

From shirtsleeves to shirtsleeves in three generations. (1874, attributed to Andrew Carnegie)

The best things in life are free. (1881)

Buy low, sell high. (1895)

As can be seen, these proverbs include plenty of wisdom about business, money, finances, prosperity, trade, and much more. Most of them are quite positive in their stress of abundance, competition, and advancement, but there are also proverbs that show that money cannot do everything, to wit the proverbs "Money can't buy happiness" and "Money isn't everything". But there is also the proverb that very positively states that "Money works miracles". Of mixed blessing is the proverb that "Money is power" that unfortunately can be observed in present-day America! Regarding this proverb, it is befitting to cite a short statement from Edward Bulwer Lytton's essay "On the Management of Money" (1864): "Money is character—money is also power. I have power not in proportion to the money I spend on myself, but in proportion to the money I can, if I please, give away to another. We feel this as we advance in years" (Lytton 1864: 97–98). One might wish that more wealthy people would feel philanthropically inclined in this way, thus changing the rather aggressive proverb "Money is power" to the more humane anti-proverb "Money is character". In any case, even this short list of earlier proverbs includes already much economic sense that is still most appropriate for the modern age, as can be seen from just these few examples: "Money is the sinews of trade", "Competition is the life of trade", " It pays to advertise", and "Equal pay for equal work", Susan B. Anthony's early feminist slogan for equal treatment in work compensation between the sexes.

By now the question quite naturally has arisen where the proverb "Time is money" enters into all of this with its international dissemination in many languages. After all, any Google or other data search as well as a check in most quotation and proverb dictionaries will reveal that Benjamin Franklin, the renowned American printer, publisher, inventor, scientist, businessman, and diplomat—also one of the founding fathers of the United States—coined this by now ubiquitous proverb. He did in fact cite it in his essay "Advice to a Young Tradesman" (1748):

> Remember that Time is Money. He that can earn Ten Shillings a Day by his Labour, and goes abroad, or sits idle one half of that Day, tho' he spends but Sixpence during his Diversion or Idleness, ought not to reckon That the only Expence; he has really spent or rather thrown away Five Shillings besides. (Labaree 1961: III, 306)

He included it again in the 1751 issue of his *Poor Richard's Almanack*, an annual publication for the early colonies that he edited and published for twenty-five years between 1733 and 1758 in about 10,000 copies each year:

> And he that is prodigal of his Hours, is, in effect, a Squanderer of Money. I remember a notable Woman, who was fully sensible of the intrinsic Value of *Time*. Her Husband was a Shoemaker, and an excellent Craftsman, but never minded how the Minutes passed. In vain did she inculcate to him *That Time is Money*. He had too much Wit to apprehend her, and it prov'd his Ruin. (Labaree 1961: IV, 86–87)

But, and here lies a truly revolutionary discovery by Damien Villers and Wolfgang Mieder, who, in their recent article *"Time is Money*: Benjamin Franklin and the Vexing Problem of Proverb Origins" (2017), were able to show that Franklin copied this reference verbatim from a small statement in the British journal *Free Thinker* of May 18, 1719 (vol. 3, no. 121, p. 128). The proverb is thus, as far as the record stands today, of British origin. Consequently, it cannot be considered as an authentic American proverb, even though it is utterly fair that to say Americans to this day have accepted it into their pecuniary worldview by usually claiming Franklin as its originator.

To be sure, Benjamin Franklin included 1044 proverbs in the 25 issues of his almanac, that is about 40 proverbs each year, of which most were copies from earlier English proverb collections (Barbour 1974). However—credit where credit is due—he also coined a few proverbs himself that became current among his compatriots and are still known today, among them "Three removes is (are) as bad as a fire", "Laziness travels so slowly that poverty soon overtakes it", and "There will be sleeping enough in the grave" (Gallacher 1949, Gallagher 1973). But with his keen interest in business and knowledge of finances, he also created the following proverbs to educate his fellow colonists in the finer points of commerce and trade:

> Necessity never made a good bargain. (1735)
> Industry pays debts, while despair increases them. (1742)
> If you would be wealthy, think of saving more than of getting. (1743)
> If you would have your business done, go; if not, send. (1743)
> Drive thy business, or it will drive thee. (1744)
> He who multiplies riches multiplies cares. (1744)
> Wealth and content [satisfaction] are not always bed-fellows. (1749)
> Spare and have is better than spend and crave. (1758)

There is also "Nothing can be said to be certain, except death and taxes" from Franklin's letter of 1789 to Jean Baptiste Le Roy that remains popular to this day. However, the English dramatist Christopher Bullock had it quite similarly already in his comedy *The Cobbler of Preston* (1716) as " 'Tis impossible to be sure of any thing but Death and Taxes."

Be that as it may, of utmost importance is the fact that Franklin selected 105 proverbs from his almanacs and assembled them in a classic essay that he gave the appropriate name of "The Way to Wealth" (1758). It became a universally accepted and followed "hit"—today one would say that it went viral, being translated into several languages—instructing his fellow subjects (still British at that time) and later American generations about virtue, prosperity, prudence, and above all economic common sense. The essay contains the so-called Puritan ethics with its emphasis on achievement and striving (McClelland 1961: 46–49) expressed in proverbs that without any doubt helped to shape the worldview of the young American nation. This magisterial *tour-de-force* proverbial treatise thus became a secular Bible of sorts, spreading social and economic wisdom in the form of folk wisdom to thousands of eager followers. Doubtlessly "The Way to Wealth" is one of the truly significant documents in the long history of proverbs, even if, as Franklin admitted in 1758 at the end of his essay, "not a tenth part of the wisdom was my own" (Mieder 2004: 216–224, Mieder 2007: 213–218); Sparks 1840: II,94–103; these sources contain the text of the entire essay).

Regarding the incredible influence of this essay, the proverb "Time is money", and other proverbs expressing aspects of the American psyche, the sociologist David Norman Smith has made the following valuable observation in his lengthy treatise on "'Time is Money': Commodity Fetishism and Common Sense" (2006):

> Proverbs and popular sayings express hegemonic worldviews. Yet in capitalist society, even hegemonic ideas are riven with deep contradictions. Cultural fissures at the level of ideas bisect structural fractures at the level of economy. The consequence is that, for many people, ambivalence has become the norm, with respect to many of the most common everyday phenomena—time and money, work and profit, war and peace, sex and ethics. And yet there is also a kind of universality in this fractured world. Capital has become a common denominator, the source and inspiration of a global common sense. People everywhere know the ads and logos, the jingles and ring-tones of the new corporate order. Rural sayings blend into the sound bites of the global city. Hegemony and money entwine. Common sense vibrates with the energy

of commodity culture. (Smith 2006: xix; for global economics education see Girardi 2010)

Dean Wolfe Manders, whose book *The Hegemony of Common Sense. Wisdom and Mystification in Everyday Life* (2006) is based to a degree on communist ideology informed by Karl Marx and Antonio Gramsci, takes an even dimmer view of proverbial common sense that to him encapsulates a "capitalist ideological hegemony and the popular philosophy of American pragmatism" (Manders 2006: 97). He consequently presents a very negative view of Franklin's proverbial wisdom summarized in the by now world-proverb "Time is money":

> Franklin's statement. "time is money," an American common sense phrase of great, enduring popularity, expresses in full, the lived meaning of capitalist time. For to equate *time* with the capitalist commodity of *"divine power"*—i.e., "the almighty dollar" [Forrest 1940; earliest reference thus far from 1836]—*money*, bespeaks the commodification of experienced time. (Manders 2006: 148)

Not surprisingly, he finishes his attack on American capitalism informed in part on common-sense proverbs with this somewhat one-sided generalization: "American capital is constitutive of American everyday lived experience. Systematic and hegemonic features of American capital—alienation. fetishization, mystification, etc.—are constituent elements within collective and individual praxis of American daily life" (Manders 2006: 165). While this extreme viewpoint has some legitimacy, it would indeed be better to speak of "hegemonic worldviews" that characterize the modern American culture that is much more complex than the proverb "Time is money" might suggest. Thus Stan Nussbaum acknowledges that "Americans are very time-conscious and very money-conscious" (2005: 20), but he does not go so far as Dean Manders in seeing it as proverbial wisdom used by capitalism to manipulate or control people. The American worldview or better worldviews are much more fragmented than to be reduced to just one element. As Steven Shapin observed a few years earlier in a more balanced article on "Proverbial Economies" (2001): "Many learned condemnations of proverbs are not merely wrong but interestingly misdirected and misconceived. They tell us little about what proverbs are or about how proverbs work in naturally occurring settings, and they set up a contrast with learned knowledge that makes it hard to understand what *that* knowledge is in *its* naturally occurring settings" (734).

Pursuant to Shapin's observation, it is important that polysituativity, polyfunctionality, and polysemanticity (Mieder 2004: 9 and 132) are brought to bear on the investigation of the worldviews, mentalities or folk ideas expressed in proverbs. This means that proverbs under investigation should be in actual use at a given time and that they need to be interpreted in oral or written context. Without wanting to automatically discredit earlier studies of worldview, it must be stated that most of them ignore these matters and also the important matter whether the proverbs under investigation are part of the paremiological minimum, that is that they are known and in use (Lau 1996, Mieder 2004: 127–131). Be that as it may, considering modern times, there is no doubt that the pecuniary element is clearly part and parcel of proverbs in American life just as such dominant matters as age, friend, God, life, love, success, time, etc. are quite dominant. (Mieder 2018 and 2019a). In order to make the following remarks more timely and revealing, some one hundred authentically American proverbs coined after the year 1900 will be discussed, with all of them having been registered in actual contexts of which due to space restrictions but a few can be included here. Since they are in fact "homegrown" and "modern", a few careful conclusions can in fact be drawn from them about the role of financial matters in American proverbial wisdom. The proverbs are all registered with dates and contexts in *The Dictionary of Modern Proverbs* (2012; cited throughout with dates and page numbers in parentheses) edited by Charles Clay Doyle, Wolfgang Mieder, and Fred R. Shapiro, and in three supplements subsequently edited by Doyle and Mieder (2016, 2018, 2020; abbreviated as S1, S2, and S3 plus date and page number). These publications contain 1617 (1422 in the dictionary and 195 in the supplements) modern proverbs, of which 110 or 6.8% are concerned with such financial issues as business, cost, money, price, etc. This is perhaps not a large percentage, but this group of proverbs most assuredly makes up a significant part of American folk ideas. And yes, as already mentioned, the pecuniary worldview contains contradictions, just as proverbs are contradictory and not universal truths (Mieder 2004: 133–134)

The folklorist Simon J. Bronner has rightfully observed that among other components "Capitalism—particularly in the United States, which has been called 'the capitalist country par excellence'—depends on the institutionalization of private property, accumulation of wealth as profits from enterprises, agencies for credit functions such as banks, and investments to enlarge markets and improve production" (Bronner 2019: 210). Without doubt America is a consumer culture with somewhat of a unified vision or worldview. And this very emphasis on the accumulation of wealth that started in the late nineteenth-century "led Americans to a new age of ease and abundance. In short, wealth in America promised the flowering of a sprawling, glorious American civilization" (Bronner 1989: 13). Little wonder, that President Calvin Coolidge summarized the evolution of the United States into a major economic power with the befitting declaration that "After all, the chief business of the American people is business." By August 28, 1928 it appeared in the *New York Times* somewhat shorted as "The business of America is business" (1928: 30) that has long become a popular proverb. A considerably earlier proverb states "Business goes where it is invited and stays where it is well treated" (1910, 30), and Irving Berlin's famous song "There's no business like show business" (1946, 30) connected the world of the theater with that of business. There are also quite straight-forward modern proverbs that deal with the basic business aspects of bargains. loans, and mortgages. It is interesting to note that a number of these proverbs and other examples to be cited are anti-proverbs of older texts that have become proverbs in their own right (Litovkina and Mieder 2006, Mandziuk 2017: 8–13):

> Home is where the mortgage is. (1904, 123)
>> The proverb originated as an anti-proverb based on the old expression "Home is where the heart is."
> New goods are better than bargains. (1919, 109)
> A bargain is something you don't need at a price you can't resist. (1964, 13)
>> There exist other proverbial warnings about "bargains," some of them older than the twentieth century: "A bargain is usually worth no more

than you pay for it"; "A bargain usually costs more in the end"; "On a good bargain think twice."

Don't let your mouth write (Don't write) a check that your ass (behind) can't cash. (1966, 174)

What you don't owe won't hurt you. (1968, 186)

> The proverb originated as an anti-proverb based on "What you don't know won't hurt you."

Always be closing. (1971, 41)

> The close is the goal of all salespeople, the point when the customer agrees to part with the money.

A rolling loan gathers no loss. (1984, 149)

> The proverb originated as an anti-proverb based on "A rolling stone gathers no moss."

It will come as no surprise that the verb "to sell" is part of the world of business proverbs that includes personal sales as well as such insights that "Sex sells", showing that two-word proverbs like the older "Time flies" or "Money talks" (Olbrys 2005) continue to be created:

> Sex sells. (1926, 226)
> Never give anything away that you can sell. (1953, 98)
> Pile it high, sell it cheap. (1955, 198)
> Offense sells tickets, defense wins games. (1976, 183)
> The proverb can apply to football, basketball, soccer, hockey, and other sports.

There are, of course, also proverbs that reflect an opposing view of selling, to wit the proverb "Less is the new more" (2001, 138). The proverb asserts the trendiness of "minimalism"—in economic behavior, environmental stewardship, sartorial fashion, etc. It is based on the older paradoxical proverb "Less is more." The pattern "X is the new Y" is productive: "Gray is the new black," "Small is the new large," "Fifty is the new thirty," etc. Very negative is the proverb "Everything is (It's all) a racket" (1928, 213), basically saying that all these money deals are a questionable scheme. There is also the proverb "No one ever went broke (went bankrupt, get poor, etc.) underestimating the intelligence of the American people" (1926, 129) that H.L. Mencken coined somewhat sarcastically depicting Americans as being susceptible to scams. But the business world has also brought forth the proverb "He profits most who serves best" (1909, 207) with its ethical approach to business that in 1910 became the unofficial and in 1950 the official motto of Rotary International.

Profit surely will be enhanced if businesspeople treat their customers fairly and politely. Not surprisingly the proverb "The customer is always right" (1905, 48; see Taylor 1958) had an early start with the proverb "The customer gets what the customer wants" (2001, 48) being a more modern claim whose earliest found reference is from the *Irish Times* of October 2, 2001. Of course, the consumer also faces the proverbial truth that "You have to spend to get" (1904, 238) while following that modern slogan turned proverb "Shop till you drop" (1984, 229) that started with an advertisement for a Volkswagen dealership at Los Angeles of October 21, 1984: "Shop till you drop / You can't beat our deals." As Anand Sw. Prahlad has pointed out so befittingly: "American advertising operates as a system of signs reflecting what can be called the 'religion of capitalism'" (2004: 128). These matters naturally lead to a series of pragmatic proverbs that contain the verb "to buy" as a clear reference point:

> You can buy anything except day and night. (1900, 51)
> The most important consideration for buying (selling) a home are location, location, and location. (1926, 43)
> You break it, you buy it. (1957, 27)
> > Sometimes, in recent years, the proverb is called "the Pottery Barn rule."
> > There is also the older proverb (and legal maxim) "He who breaks pays."
> Buy the best and you only cry once. (1959, 19)
> Buy land, they don't make it anymore. (1968, 137)
> You buy the ticket, you see the show (take the ride). (1977, 257)
> > The proverb asserts that one must accept the consequences of decisions.
> You can't win the raffle if you don't buy a ticket. (1983, 213)

There is also the fascinating proverb "Never argue (quarrel) with a man (someone) who buys ink by the barrel (gallon)" (1931, 160) that refers to the ink of the free press that will print whatever it wants no matter how much one might argue against the coverage. In contrast the proverb "If you want a friend, get (buy) a dog" (1941, 86) is more benign but also quite depressing in its message about human relationships. It alludes to the old saying "A dog is man's best friend" and usually suggests that, in some particularly hostile or competitive setting a dog will be the only friend that a person can hope to find—and that (human) friendship itself is a quality not only improbable but even undesirable.

Buying involves paying, and there are a number of telling proverbs based on the verb "to pay". It should be noted, however, that in some of the following examples its meaning is not so much pecuniary but rather that something is "worthwhile". But these proverbs nevertheless show the monetary inclination in American folk speech with the modern proverb "Live now, pay later" (1946, 148) representing an Epicurean worldview without much concern for financial consequences. As expected, there is also the proverbial warning "You pay now (You can pay now) or you pay later (with interest)" (1974, 192):

> It pays to pay attention. (1902, 10)
> It pays to look well (good). (1902, 192)
> Worry is interest paid on trouble before it is due. (1909, 282)
> Courtesy pays dividends (compound interest). (1922, 46)
>> The proverb originated as an anti-proverb elaborating on the proverb "Courtesy pays."
> A baby's smile pays the bill. (1936, 11)
>> The proverb might have originated from a reported reminiscence from c. 1916: One afternoon, visiting in Columbia, South Carolina, Woodrow Wilson "became thirsty and stopped at a drugstore. When the party had been served and the President prepared to pay the bill, the clerk serving him said, 'One smile pays the bill.' The smile was forthcoming."
> If you're going to play, you have to pay (You have to pay to play). (1955, 200)
>> The proverb had its start from the song "If You Play, You Must Pay," written and performed by "Enyatta Holta" (Laverne Holt).
> Play big (You have to play big) to win big. (1978, 201)
>> The "play big" can refer to money being spent betting at a casino, races, etc.
> Fast pay (payment) makes (for) fast friends. (1980, 85)

Special note might be taken of the proverb "Crime doesn't pay and neither does farming" (1975, 46) that originated as an anti-proverb based on "Crime doesn't pay" (1874) and first appeared on a sign referring to the plight of farmers, who were demanding parity prices for their products. Their financial lot has become more serious yet, especially for small farms. And this leads to the proverb "Payback is a bitch" (1970, 192) referring to financial or personal debts that have to be repaid. It might have originated as an anti-proverb of the older modern proverb "Life is a bitch" (1940).

With all this paying, the question arises what the folk thinks about "free" commodities in the United States. After all, the basic idea of "freedom" is definitely part of the American worldview, accepted by its citizens and immigrants alike. Little wonder that the following two proverbs originated in the 1940s during the Second World War and the reestablishment of free societies:

Freedom is not free. (1943, 85)
Freedom is not for sale. (1949, 85)

Today, with various internet resources, the proverb "Information wants to be free" (1984, 128) has become the battle-cry that their materials should be free from censorship and also free from any cost so that everybody has access to this flood of information. The proverb "Nothing ain't worth nothing, but it's free (1969, 180) also tells an interesting story in that it stresses the fact that things of little value might be a good bargain after all since they are free. It might be regarded as a modern incarnation of the traditional proverb "Nothing comes from nothing" or as an anti-proverb responding to a version of that saying. This brings to mind the proverb "When you have nothing, you have nothing to lose" (1965, 182) that was included in the same year of its earliest reference in Bob Dylan's song "Like a Rolling Stone" (1965) as "When you got nothing, you got nothing to lose."

With this a very popular modern American proverb has been reached that is older than one might have expected (including myself making frequent use of it). Its structure "There is no such thing as ..." has yielded such proverbs as "There is no such thing as a definitive study" (1936, 252–253), "There is no such thing as bad publicity" (1941, 253), "There is no such thing as a little pregnant" (1942, 253), "There is no such thing as bad sex" (1971, 253–254), and "There is no such thing as bad weather, only the wrong clothes" (1979, 254). But here then is the quintessential proverb of this type with its economic message:

> There is no such thing as a free lunch. (1917, 253)
>> Applied figuratively, the proverb appears as the "punch line" of a fable: A king asks his counselors to summarize economics in a brief and simple way. They respond with 87 volumes, more than 600 pages each, drawing the king's wrath and incurring executions. Further demands and more executions encourage ever-briefer summations until, finally, the last economist, "a man of profound wisdom," speaks: "Sire, in eight words I will reveal to you all the wisdom that I have distilled through all these years from all the writings of all the economists who once practiced their science in your kingdom. Here is my text: 'There ain't no such thing as free lunch.'" (see also Kauffman 1990: 21–22; Levy and Peart 2004: 422).

It comes as no surprise that in the country of the automobile the proverb "There is no such thing as a free ride (Nobody rides for free)" (1949, 253) with its similar message came into being. But there is yet another, but crasser proverb that has appeared as bumper stickers on cars: "Gas, grass, or ass: Nobody rides for free" (1978, 94). In other words, if someone wants to hitch a free automobile ride, money for gas, marijuana (grass) or sexual favors (ass) have to be provided. This proverb is clearly capitalism at its worst as it takes advantage of a person in need.

This brings to mind the older American proverb "Everything has its price" (1829) that originated with the transcendentalist Ralph Waldo Emerson (Mieder, Kingsbury, Harder 1992: 185). The noun "price" appears in several modern proverbs, notably in such short texts based on the structure "X has a (its) price". These proverbs do not necessarily imply a monetary value but rather effort, sacrifice, or resources necessary to obtain a desired goal:

> Glory has a price. (1917, 98)
> Fame has a price. (1932, 74)
> Silence has a price. (1943, 231)
>> The proverb can have a range of applications: blackmail, the frustration of keeping a secret, and the luxury of quiet living, for example.
> Power has its price. (1966, 205)

Two additional proverbs with a similar structure, "Grief is the price we pay for love (loving)" (1912, 111) and "Pain is the price of glory (2005, 188) also do not deal with money as such. This is also the case with the proverb "Age is a high price to pay for maturity" (1969, 3), but in the following three modern proverbs "price" clearly is dealing with pecuniary matters:

> If you have to ask the price (the cost, how much it costs), you can't afford it. (1926, 207)
> The (only) difference between men and boys is the price of their toys. (1963, 55)
> The risk is the price you pay for opportunity. (1981, 218)

The last proverb in its normal use refers to investment risks, but it does have other meaning possibilities depending on the risks that are taken.

With this emphasis on financial concerns it is no wonder that American folk ideas also concern themselves with the dichotomy of rich and poor. Unfortunately, the schism between the two socio-economic states is getting ever more extreme. Regarding the rich, the following four proverbs emphasize their difference, in part most likely from the viewpoint of not so well-to-do Americans:

> If you're so smart, why aren't you rich? (1909, 234)
> The rich are different. (1926, 217)
>> The proverb probably originated as a misquotation from F. Scott Fitzgerald's story "The Rich Boy" (1926): "Let me tell you about the very rich. They are different from you and me."
> Rich people (folks) have mean (hateful) ways. (1924, S2, 35)
> You can't be too rich or too thin (too thin or too rich). (1974, S1, 113)

No wonder that poor people have come up with the proverb "It's hell being (to be) poor" (1904, 120) as they often face the unfortunate situation of losing their jobs because of the employment rule "Last hired, first fired" (1918, 121). For them the American worldview of going from the proverbial "rags to riches" holds true, well expressed in the modern proverb "The road to Easy Street goes (runs) through the dump (sewer)" (1970, 219). The dream that with hard work and some luck "Prosperity is always just around the corner" (1936, 208) also plays into this. In its origins, the saying mocked the Hooverite slogan applied to the Great Depression, "Prosperity is just around the corner," from 1931. However, today it summarizes the forward-looking American worldview that things will work out and that financial success can be achieved. Of course, there is also the disturbing proverb "White folks got the money and black folks got the signs" (1934, 83). The *signs* are superstitious beliefs that falsely promise prosperity or success, something that to this very day has not happened to many black families in this country.

Also of unsettling importance is the nineteenth-century American proverb "The rich get richer and the poor get poorer" dealing with the growing gap between the rich and the poor that is destroying the solid middle class. It expresses in a concise and oppositional way that America is splitting itself into two extreme halves. The proverb is of relatively young origin, with the earliest reference found thus far appearing in a short untitled "jotting" by the author and journalist Nathaniel Parker Willis in *The New Mirror* of August 5, 1843. It was popularized by way of its appearance in the song "Ain't We Got Fun" (1920):

> There's nothing surer,
> The rich get richer and the poor get poorer,
> In the meantime, in between time,
> Ain't we got fun.

The song also includes the anti-proverb "The rich get richer and the poor get (have) children" (1920, 217) as a humorous variant that has gained currency, but certainly not always as a light-hearted comment on social issues (Mieder, Kingsbury, Harder 1992: 508). As a two-time presidential candidate, Bernie Sanders, US Senator from Vermont, has made the original proverb his political *leitmotif* by citing it numerous times in his speeches and books (Mieder 2019: 235–240). As a democratic socialist with a strong socio-economic agenda, he paints his attacks on the wealthy with a very wide brush and borders on being somewhat unfair to those wealthy people who are not driven by greed alone and who are responsible citizens committed to social improvements by word and deed. Sanders knows that, and he usually singles the billionaires Warren Buffet and Bill Gates out as representatives of philanthropically-minded rich people. But no matter what, there is this modern American proverbial wisdom: "Rich or poor, it's good to have money" (1949, 170).

Speaking of money, here are a few American proverbs referring to pennies (Ross1978), dollars, and gold as they give financial advice for modern consumers ready to do some serious shopping, hopefully mindful of the older proverb "It costs nothing to look" as well as its anti-proverb turned modern proverb "It costs nothing to dream" (1920, 44):

> A penny spent is a penny earned (A penny saved is a penny lost). (1901, 193)
>> The proverb originated as an anti-proverb to the earlier "A penny saved is a penny earned (got)."
>
> A dollar in the bank is worth two in the hand. (1904, 59)
>> The proverb originated as an anti-proverb based on "A bird in the hand is worth two in the bush."
>
> Another day, another dollar. (1907, 50)
> Don't take wooden nickels. (1912, 178)
>> Since there are no such five-cent wooden coins, the proverb advises against gullibility or credulity.
>
> You can only spend a dollar (spend money, spend earning) once. (1913, 60)
> No dough, no go. (1952, 61)
>> "Dough" is slang for money.
>
> Go for the gold. (1963, 106)
> He who has the gold makes the rules. (1967, 106)
>> Often the proverb includes the satirical designation "The Golden Rule" (Matthew 7:12) that has a much more humane message as "Do unto others as you would have them do unto you".
>
> If you sift through enough dirt (mud, crap), you may find gold (a diamond). (1997, 56)

Speaking of gold conjures up the dream of "rags to riches" from the fairy-tale world and there are indeed "many modern financial success stories that correspond to this sequential structure" (McDowall 2013: 253–254). The famed Stock Market might just make such movement to personal wealth possible, and it is important to remember that investing in stocks and bonds is by no means reserved to well-off Americans. There are many small-time investors looking to make some money without being greedy. But they, as well as investors in general, look for advice and patterns that might lead them to some financial advancement. To assist them, Michael Maiello has put together his book *Buy the Rumor, Sell the*

Fact. 85 Maxims of Investing and What They Really Mean (2004) and Jason Zweig published a "Wall Street's Platitude Poem" (2018) with about the same number of modern investment proverbs that include—quite expectedly—contradictory statements. After all, investments are not governed by absolute truths that predict certain positive outcomes for every stock purchase. Some of these texts do not qualify as proverbs, but Wall Street certainly has produced some modern proverbs that give valuable investment advice. What is of importance is that they serve large portions of the American population, since stock and bond investments are somewhat of a "folk sport" in this capitalist society. Most of them in the following list are self-explanatory as sound advice, but where necessary, a short explanatory comment is added. The second text, even though its earliest written reference is from Australia, is included since it is such a fundamental investment insight:

No one ever went bankrupt (went broke, lost money) taking (making) a profit. (1902, 208)
> The proverb is often attributed to the financier J. P. Morgan.

If you don't speculate, you can't accumulate. (1903, 238)

You can (either) eat well or sleep well (sleep well or eat well). (1912, S3, 59–60)
> The proverb advises against overextension in unsure investments.

Never sell America short. (1922, 5)
> The proverb refers to the idea of selling a stock short (at a loss), meaning that America should be held in high esteem.

Scared money can't make money (Scared money is dead money). (1935, S1. 109)

Sell in May and (then) go away. (1938, 164)
> The proverb is based on the usual underperformance of some stocks in the summery six-month period beginning in May and ending in October.

As California goes, so goes the nation. (1940, 32)
> The proverb does not only refer to the financial influence of this large state but also to electoral politics, fashions, and fads of various kinds. It is modelled on the older "As Maine goes, so goes the nation."

What is good for General Motors is good for America (the country). (1953, 95)
> The proverb originated as a misquotation from U.S. Senate testimony of Charles E. Wilson (former president of General Motors): "For years I thought what was good for our country was good for General Motors, and vice versa. The difference did not exist." The proverb most often satirizes the concept that the well-being of giant corporations including their

stocks (!) is inextricably and benevolently connected with the welfare of
the nation and its populace.

Look before you leave. (1958, 150)
>   Originating as an anti-proverb based on "Look before you leap," the
>   proverb has had a wide range of applications, urging caution about with-
>   drawing one's money from an investment, about ascertaining that no
>   body lies on the bottom of a private swimming pool, about ensuring that
>   no children or pets are left locked in a car, etc.

When the United States (U.S., America, Wall Street, etc.) sneezes, the world
catches (a) cold (pneumonia). (1977, S3, 84)

The trend is your friend (Trend is friend). (1983, 263)
>   The advice is to follow the developing market.

Don't marry (fall in love with) a stock. (1969, S3, 80)

As can be seen from these texts, they often exist in variants, as do traditional proverbs as well. It does take time until a standard form crys-
talizes and gains general acceptance (Mieder 2004: 9). In the case of
the proverb "What's good for Wall Street is good for Main Street (If
it's good for Wall Street, it's good for Main Street" (1995, S1,118) it is of
great paremiological interest that its reversal, that is that Main Street
is the first element, developed in the same year as the independent
proverb "What's good for Main Street is good for Wall Street" (1995, S1,
107). President Barack Obama used both proverbs repeatedly to stress
the interdependence of big and small business in the United States
(Mieder 2009: 259 and 334–335). But there is no doubt that the Stock
Market on Wall Street is the driving engine of capitalist America where
earning and spending money is part of the national worldview.

   This having been said, it is finally time to look at those proverbs
that refer to "money" in particular. Some of them deal with human relationships, as for example "Those who marry for money earn it" (1903,
170) and the somewhat related proverb that had a British start: "Never
(Don't) marry for money; it's cheaper to borrow it (you can borrow
it cheaper) (1927, 170). But speaking of relations, American proverbial
wisdom has changed the old proverb "Blood is thicker than water" into
the pecuniary anti-proverb "Money is thicker than blood" (1904, S1,
109), emphasizing the capitalist preoccupation with money. Things can
get quite brutal, if a loan shark states the proverb "You can't get money
from a dead man" (1964, 171) to explain why the ruined borrower is

kept alive. Speaking of criminal matters, there is the well-known modern proverb "Follow the money (1974, 168), claiming that when all is well and done the best way to catch a criminal is by way of money trails.

As one would expect, modern proverbs also give good advice, to wit "The best way to make money is to save it (is not to lose it) (1922, 272). Following the pattern of "The best way to X is to Y" brings to mind the quite recent proverb "The best way to rob a bank is to own one" (1986, 272) that seems to argue that people should take matters in their own hands to succeed financially. In any case, the proverb "Put your money where your mouth is" (1913, 170) has been a solid piece of advice since the early twentieth century, arguing that financial promises must be followed by action. That money does count in human relationships is also clearly expressed by the more recent proverb "My money, my rules (Your money, your rules)" (1975, 169). The structural pattern "My X, my rules" has become quite productive in recent years, to wit "My game, my rules (Your game, your rules)" (1963, 93) and "My house, my rules (Your house, your rules)" (1983, 126). Certain proverbial structures most certainly are involved in the creation of new monetary proverbs. For example, the pattern "X is wasted on Y" of the proverb "Youth is wasted on the young" (1931, 284) formed the basis of the more recent proverb "Money (Wealth) is wasted on the rich (wealthy) (1981, S2, 32), a rather flippant comment possible only in a society where money plays a dominant role. This is also in the background of the proverb "A billion (million) here and a billion (million) there—pretty soon it adds up (begins to add up) to real money" (1938, 21) that had its start as a satirical comment on the ever increasing federal budget of the United States.

The following last group of five rather short proverbs about money can well represent the concluding comments of this survey about the American pecuniary worldview. They certainly depict the positive and negative power of money and wealth, as it is found in abundance among Americans of all walks of life:

Money has no morality. (1905, 169)
  In its ambiguous wording, the proverb can mean either that money itself
  is amoral or that it—or the greed it represents—is immoral.

Money never sleeps. (1907, 169)
> The proverb has two (related) meanings: the value of money that is merely hoarded can slip away, and the value of money that is prudently invested will grow relentlessly.

Money talks, bullshit walks. (1969, 169)
> "Bullshit" refers to worthless matters. The proverb probably originated as an anti-proverb based on "Money talks."

Money talks, wealth whispers. (1989, S1, 109)
> Also based on the traditional proverb "Money talks", this proverb emphasizes that true wealth is discreet and in no need to brag.

Money has no memory. (1991, 169)
> This proverb basically states that money is a commodity without any concern of its (il)legitimate use.

What all of this shows is, of course, that the proverb "Money makes the world go 'round" contains much truth, both in its positive and negative aspects. This can be found in the proverb repertoire of other cultures and languages, but there can be no doubt that money and wealth in all of their iterations are a dominant part of the American capitalist worldview. There are numerous other components to the image of a general American mentality, but business and finance are certainly part of it all. The main point to keep in mind here is not to vilify money and wealth themselves. It is people who pervert them or put them to good use that benefits the American society in general. Adding the forward-looking aspect of the American psyche to this, there is always hope that the emphasis on capitalism might develop into a more balanced social-democratic pecuniary society without such an extreme difference between rich and poor. With good will and a belief in the golden rule, this might well happen someday.

Bibliography

Barbour, Frances M. 1974. *A Concordance to the Sayings in Franklin's Poor Richard*. Detroit, MI: Gale Research Company.

Braude, Jacob M. 1965. *Complete Speaker's and Toastmaster's Library*. 8 vols. Englewood Cliffs, NJ: Prentice-Hall. II: *Business and Professional Pointmakers*.

Bronner, Simon J. 1989. "Reading Consumer Culture." In S.J. Bronner (ed.), *Consuming Visions. Accumulation and Display of Goods in America 1880–1920*. New York: W.W. Norton. 13–53.

Bronner, Simon J. 2019. "From Farm to … Farmers' Markets. Amish Folk Society in the Age of Fast Capitalism." In S.J. Bronner (ed.), *The Practice of Folklore. Essays toward a Theory of Tradition*. Jackson, MS: University Press of Mississippi. 201–237.

Cheales, Alan B. 1874. "Money Maxim." In A.B. Cheales (ed.), *Proverbial Folk-Lore*. London: Simpkin, Marshall & Co.; rpt. Folcroft, PA: Folcroft Library Editions, 1976. 98–102.

Chiang, Alpha C. 1961. "Religion, Proverbs, and Economic Mentality." *American Journal of Economics*, 20: 253–264.

Cordry, Harold V. 1997. *The Multicultural Dictionary of Proverbs. Over 20.000 Adages from More Than 120 Languages and Ethnic Groups*. Jefferson, NC: McFarland.

Doyle, Charles Clay, and Wolfgang Mieder. 2016. "*The Dictionary of Modern Proverbs*: A Supplement." *Proverbium*, 33: 85–120.

Doyle, Charles Clay, and Wolfgang Mieder. 2018. "*The Dictionary of Modern Proverbs*: Second Supplement." *Proverbium*, 35: 15–44.

Doyle, Charles Clay, and Wolfgang Mieder. 2020. "*The Dictionary of Modern Proverbs*: Third Supplement." *Proverbium*, 37: 53–86.

Doyle, Charles Clay, Wolfgang Mieder, and Fred R. Shapiro (eds.). 2012. *The Dictionary of Modern Proverbs*. New Haven, CT: Yale University Press.

Dundes, Alan. 1969. "Thinking Ahead: A Folkloristic Reflection of the Future Orientation in American Worldview." *Anthropological Quarterly*, 42: 53–72.

Dundes, Alan. 1971. "Folk Ideas as Units of Worldview." *Journal of American Folklore*, 84: 93–103. Also in *The Meaning of Folklore. The Analytical Essays of Alan Dundes*. Ed. Simon J. Bronner. Logan, UT: Utah State University Press, 2007. 179–195 (with Bronner's introduction and Dundes's postscript).

Dundes, Alan. 2004. "'As the Crow Flies'. A Straightforward Study of Lineal Worldview in American Folk Speech." In Kimberly J. Lau, Peter Tokofsky, and Stephen D. Winick (eds.), *"What Goes Around Comes Around": The Circulation of Proverbs in Contemporary Life. Essays in Honor of Wolfgang Mieder*. Logan, UT: Utah State University Press. 171–187. Also in Simon J. Bronner (ed.), *The Meaning of Folklore. The Analytical Essays of Alan Dundes*. Logan, UT: Utah State University Press, 2007. 196–210 (with Bronner's introduction). Again in Alan Dundes, Wolfgang Mieder (ed.), *"The Kushmaker" and Other Essays on Folk Speech and Folk Humor*. Burlington, VT: The University of Vermont, 2008. 93–108.

Forbes, Malcolm S. (ed.). 1984. *The Forbes Scrapbook of Thoughts on the Business of Life*. New York: B.C. Forbes & Sons.

Forrest, Rex. 1940. "Irving and 'The Almighty Dollar'." *American Speech*, 15: 443–444.

Gallacher, Stuart A. 1949. "Franklin's *Way to Wealth*: A Florilegium of Proverbs and Wise Sayings." *Journal of English and Germanic Philology*, 48: 229–251.

Gallagher, Edward J. 1973. "The Rhetorical Strategy of Franklin's *Way to Wealth*." *Eighteenth Century Studies*, 6: 475–485.

Gautam, Dhruba Kumar. 2013. "Business Practices and Paradoxical Proverbs in Nepal: A Case of NABIL Bank." *International Journal of Nepalese Academy of Management*, 1: 109–119.

Girardi, Gherardo. 2010. "Transformative Economics Education: Using Proverbs from Around the World in the Classroom." *Investigations in University Teaching and Learning*, 6: 119–124.

Goodman, Ted (ed.). 1997. *The Forbes Book of Business Quotations. 14,173 Thoughts on the Business of Life*. New York: Black Dog & Leventhal.

Hakamies, Pekka. 2002. "Proverbs and Mentality." In Anna-Leena Siikala (ed.), *Myth and Mentality. Studies in Folklore and Popular Thought*. Helsinki: Finnish Literature Society. 222–230.

Hood, Edwin Paxton. 1885. "Concerning Money." In E.P. Hood (ed.), *The World of Proverb and Parable. With Illustrations from History, Biography, and the Anecdotal Table-Talk of All Ages*. London: Hodder and Stoughton. 398–406.

Kauffman, Draper. 1990. "System Proverbs." *ETC. A Review of General Semantics*, 47: 20–29.

Labaree, Leonard W. (ed.). 1961. *The Papers of Benjamin Franklin*. 43 vols. New Haven, CT: Yale University Press.

Lau, Kimberly J. 1996. "'It's about Time': The Ten Proverbs Most Frequently Used in Newspapers and Their Relation to American Values." *Proverbium*, 13: 135–159. Also in Wolfgang Mieder (ed.), *Cognition, Comprehension, and Communication: A Decade of North American Proverb Studies (1990–2000)*. Baltmannsweiler: Schneider Verlag Hohengehren, 2003. 231–254.

Levy, David M., and Sandra J. Peart. 2004. "Analytical Egalitarianism, Anecdotal Evidence and Information Aggregation via Proverbial Wisdom." *Journal of Economic Methodology*, 11: 411–435.

Litovkina, Anna T., and Wolfgang Mieder. 2006. *Old Proverbs Never Die, They Just Diversify. A Collection of Anti-proverbs*. Burlington, VT: The University of Vermont; Veszprém, Hungary: The Pannonian University of Veszprém.

Loomis, C. Grant. 1964. "Proverbs in Business." *Western Folklore*, 23: 91–94.

Lytton, Edward Bulwer. 1864. "On the Management of Money." In E.B. Lytton (ed.), *Caxtonia. A Series of Essays on Life, Literature, and Manners*. 2 vols. Leipzig: Tauschnitz. 81–106.

Maiello, Michael. 2004. *Buy the Rumor, Sell the Fact. 85 Maxims of Investing and What They Really Mean*. New York: McGraw-Hill.

Manders, Dean Wolfe. 2006. *The Hegemony of Common Sense. Wisdom and Mystification in Everyday Life*. New York: Peter Lang.

Mandziuk, Justyna. 2017. "Why Money Cannot Buy Happiness. The Painful Truth about Traditional Proverbs and Their Modifications." *New Horizons in English Studies*, 2: 4–16.

McClelland, David C. 1961. *The Achieving [American] Society*. New York: Nostrand.

McDowall, Robert. 2013. "The Folklore of Finance." *Folklore* (London), 124: 253–264.

Mieder, Wolfgang. 1986. *Encyclopedia of World Proverbs*. Englewood Cliffs, NJ: Prentice-Hall.

Mieder, Wolfgang. 1989. *American Proverbs. A Study of Texts and Contexts*. Bern: Peter Lang.

Mieder, Wolfgang. 2004. *Proverbs. A Handbook*. Westport, CT: Greenwood Press; rpt. New York: Peter Lang, 2012.

Mieder, Wolfgang. 2007. "Yankee Wisdom: American Proverbs and the Worldview of New England." In Paul Skandera (ed.), *Phraseology and Culture in English*. Berlin: Walter de Gruyter. 205–234.

Mieder, Wolfgang. 2008. "'Wisdom Is Better Than Wealth'. Proverbs as Expressions of Culture and Folklore." In Wolfgang Mieder (ed.), *"Proverbs Speak Louder Than Words". Folk Wisdom in Art, Culture, Folklore, History, Literature, and Mass Media*. New York: Peter Lang. 9–44.

Mieder, Wolfgang. 2009. *"Yes We Can". Barack Obama's Proverbial Rhetoric*. New York: Peter Lang.

Mieder, Wolfgang. 2015. *"Different Strokes for Different Folks". 1250 authentisch amerikanische Sprichwörter*. Baltmannsweiler: Norbert Brockmeyer.

Mieder, Wolfgang. 2018. "'Life is not a Spectator Sport': Proverbial Emotions about Modern Life." In E.R. Ioanesian (ed.), *Emotsional'naia sfera cheloveka v iazyke i kommunikatsii: Sinkhroniia i diakhroniia*. Moscow: Institut Iaazykoznaniia RAN. 7–17.

Mieder, Wolfgang. 2019a. "'Age is Just a Number': American Proverbial Wisdom about Age and Aging." In E.R. Ioanesian (ed.), *Emotsional'naia sfera cheloveka v iazyke i kommunikatsii: Sinkhroniia i diakhroniia*. Moscow: Institut Iaazykoznaniia RAN. 7–23.

Mieder, Wolfgang. 2019b. *"Right Makes Might". Proverbs and the American Worldview*. Bloomington, IN: Indiana University Press.

Mieder, Wolfgang, Stewart A. Kingsbury, and Kelsie B. Harder (eds.). 1992. *A Dictionary of American Proverbs*. New York: Oxford University Press.

Mifsud-Chircop, Ġorġ. 2001. "Proverbiality and Worldview in Maltese and Arabic Proverbs." *Proverbium*, 18: 247–255.

Mortad, Abdel-Malek. 1991. "Economic Relations among Social Classes in Algerian Proverbs." In Eric Savid and Nicolas Gavrielides (eds.), *Statecraft in the Middle East*. Miami, FL: Florida International University Press. 228–247.

Mullen, Patrick. 1978. "The Folk Idea of Unlimited Good in American Buried Treasure Legends." *Journal of the Folklore Institute*, 15: 209–220.

Naugle, David K. 2002. *Worldview. The History of a Concept*. Grand Rapids, MI: William B. Erdmans.

Nedeva, Svetla. 2014. "Achieving Better Intercultural Communication Through Learning to Interpret Cultural Value of Proverbs in a Language and the Way They Reflect National Character." *Revista Economică*, 66: 105–116.

Norwine, Jim, Michael Bruner, Allen Ketcham, and Michael Preda. 2000. "'I Love You, Man': Values in Flux." In Jim Norwine and Jonathan M. Smith (eds.), *Worldview Flux. Perplexed Values among Postmodern Peoples*. Lanham, MD: Lexington Books. 20–61.

Nussbaum, Stan. 2005. *American Cultural [and Proverbial] Baggage. How to Recognize and Deal with It*. Maryknoll, NY: Orbis Books.

Olbrys, Stephen Gencarella. 2005. "Money Talks: Folklore in the Public Sphere." *Folklore* (London), 116: 292–310.

Potter, David M. 1954. *People of Plenty. Economic Abundance and the American Character*. Chicago: University of Chicago Press.

Prahlad, Sw. Anand (Dennis Folly). 2004. "The Proverb and Fetishism in American Advertisements." In Kimberly J. Lau, Peter Tokofsky, and Stephen D. Winick (eds), *"What Goes Around Comes Around": The Circulation of Proverbs in Contemporary Life. Essays in Honor of Wolfgang Mieder*. Logan, UT: Utah State University Press. 127–151.

Profantová, Zuzana. 1996. "Worldview, Proverbs, Folk Narrative." In Leander Petzoldt (ed.), *Folk Narrative and World View. Vorträge des 10. Kongresses der Internationalen Gesellschaft für Volkserzählforschung (ISFNR), Innsbruck 1992*. 2 vols. Frankfurt am Main: Peter Lang. II, 719–793.

Ross, David J.A. 1978. " 'Not Worth a Penny'." *Reading Medieval Studies*, 4: 69–87.

Schipper, Mineke. 20003. *"Never Marry a Woman with Big Feet". Women in Proverbs from Around the World*. New Haven, CT: Yale University Press.

Shapin, Steven. 2001. "Proverbial Economics: How an Understanding of Some Linguistic and Social Features of Common Sense Can Throw Light on More Prestigious Bodies of Knowledge, Science for Example." *Social Studies of Science*, 31: 731–769.

Shimkin, Dimitri, and Pedro Sanjuan. 1953. "Culture and World View: A Method of Analysis Applied to Rural Russia." *American Anthropologist*, 55: 329–348.

Smith, David Norman. 2006. " 'Time is Money': Commodity Fetishism and Common Sense." In Dean Wolfe Manders (ed.), *The Hegemony of Common Sense. Wisdom and Mystification in Everyday Life*. New York: Peter Lang. xix-xci (introduction).

Sparks, Jared (ed.). 1840. *The Works of Benjamin Franklin*. 10 vols. Philadelphia, PA: Childs & Peterson.

Speake, Jennifer (ed.). 2015. *Oxford Dictionary of Proverbs*. 6th ed. Oxford: Oxford University Press.

Taylor, Archer. 1958. " 'The Customer Is Always Right'." *Western Folklore*, 17: 54–55.

Thompson, Tok. 2009. "Getting Ahead in Ethiopia: Amharic Proverbs about Wealth." *Proverbium*, 26: 367–386.

Thomsett, Michael C. 1990. *A Treasury of Business Quotations*. New York: Ballantine Books.

Tierney, John J. 2016. *Conceived in Liberty. The American Worldview in Theory and Practice*. New Brunswick, NJ: Transaction Publishers.

Villers, Damien, and Wolfgang Mieder. 2017. " 'Time is Money'. Benjamin Franklin and the Vexing Problem of Proverb Origins." *Proverbium*, 34: 391–404.

White, Geoffrey M. 1987. "Proverbs and Cultural Models. An American Psychology of Problem Solving." In Dorothy Holland and Naomi Quinn (eds), *Cultural Models in Language and Thought*. Cambridge: Cambridge University Press. 152–172.

White, Rolf B. (ed.). 1986. *The Great Business Quotations*. Secaucus, NJ: Lyle Stuart.

Zhang, Xiangyang. 2016. "Language as a Reflection of Culture: On the Cultural Characteristics of Chinese and English Proverbs." *Intercultural Communication Studies*, 25: 275–291.

Zweig, Jason. 2018. "I Found Wall Street's Platitude Poem." https://blogs.wsj.com/moneybeat/2018/07/06/i-found-wall-streets-platitude-poem/ 3 pp. I owe this reference to my nephew David Busker of Bronxville, New York.

Chapter Eight

"Dogs Don't Bark at Parked Cars"

Zoological Messages in Modern Anglo-American Proverbs

More than a hundred years ago Carl Sylvio Köhler published his philological study about *Das Tierleben im Sprichwort der Griechen und Römer. Nach Quellen und Stellen in Parallele mit dem deutschen Sprichwort* (1881), whose reprint in 1967 might have contributed somewhat to the fact that paremiologists and phraseologists have occupied themselves more intensively with animal proverbs. Linguo-cultural and folkloric studies about individual proverbs, proverbial expressions, and proverbial comparisons based on animals have been undertaken for a long time (Mieder 2009a), but large collections of them with explanations started to appear only since the 1960s. The largest English language collection of animal proverbs from around the world is Rachid Lyazidi's *Animal Proverbs and Quotes Kingdom. Domestic Animals* (2012), but there are also smaller collections with important commentaries for British and American animal proverbs, to wit Robert Hendrickson, *Animal Crackers. A Bestial Lexicon* (1983), Darryl Lyman, *The Animal Things We Say* (1983) and *Dictionary of Animal Words and Phrases* (1994), G.F. Lamb, *Animal Quotations* (1985), Wolfgang Mieder, *Howl Like a Wolf: Animal Proverbs* (1993), Michael Macrone, *Animalogies. "A Fine Kettle of Fish" and 150 Other Animal Expressions* (1995), Robert Palmatier, *Speaking of Animals: A Dictionary of Animal Metaphors* (1995), Udo Steuck, *One Thousand and More Animal Proverbs* (1997), and Martha Barnette, *Dog Days and Dandelions. A Lively Guide to the Animal Meanings Behind Everyday Words* (2003). Large proverb collections of the English language quite naturally also include numerous animal proverbs dealing especially with such animals as the bear, cat, chicken, dog, donkey, fox, horse, mouse, ox, pig, rabbit, sheep, wolf, etc. (Mieder, Kingsbury, Harder 1992, Speake 2015; see also Ward 1987, Krikmann 2001: 11–12, Mussner 2012: 115–116).

With such a prevailing dominance of animal proverbs it should not come as a surprise that an impressive amount of secondary literature has appeared during the past few decades. There have been a number of comparative studies between animal proverbs of two or more languages and cultures: German-Dutch (Jarosińska 1991), German-Spanish (Thiele 1997, Piñel López 1999), Spanish-German (Alonso Ímaz 2003), German-Finnish (Aakko (2003), German-Japanese (Ueda 2004), German-Latin (Schnoor 2007), Portuguese-French-Spanish-Dutch (Augusto 2008), English-Bulgarian (Holandi 2011), German-Polish (Biadún-Grabarek 2012), German-French-Italian (Mussner 2012 und 2013), German-Slavic (Bock 2013), English-Chinese (Liu 2013), English-Kazakh (Mazhitaeva 2013), Japanese-Brazilian (Pinheiro Pereira 2013), Persian-English (Rashidi and Ghaedi 2013), German-Polish (Stypa 2014), Cuban-Spanish (Pacheco Carpio, Cabrera Albert, and Cabrera 2015), and German-Russian-Tatar (Yusupova und Kuzmina 2015). These compilations together with the analysis of similarities and differences in animal metaphors are clear indications how much people throughout the world have relied om proverbs describing animal behavior that often are generalized metaphors for human behavior as well. Little wonder that animal fables have frequently been reduced to proverbial wisdom about human nature couched in animal imagery (Carnes 1988, Bodi 2015).

As one would expect with such a predominance of animal proverbs, there have also been studies that have looked at these proverbs in only a specific language and culture, as for example English (Čermák 2012), Galician (Martinez Blanco and Veiga Alonso 2010), German

(Preußer 2003, Abdulrahman 2016), Persian (Estaji and Nakhavali 2011), Portuguese (Cristea 2016), Russian (Velasco Menéndez 2008), and Spanish (Domínguez 1974, Nuessel 2010, Santiago Álvarez 2014, Suárez 2015). Of great importance is Arvo Krikmann's semantic, structural, and typological study "Proverbs on Animal Identity: Typological Memoirs" (2001), which by way of numerous examples from various languages established somewhat of a systematization for this rich proverbial material. And yet, it comes as somewhat of a surprise that he had to start his thorough overview with the observation that animal proverbs despite of their large numbers had not received the proper attention by scholars from various fields: "The number of publications on animal proverbs and zoo-metaphors in proverbs is undeservedly small, considering that the semantic field of animals must be the most productive one in proverbial metaphors" (Krikmann 2001: 11). This picture has changed during the past two decades, as the bibliography at the end of these deliberations shows rather convincingly.

With direct reference to Krikmann's work Antonio Pamies Bertrán has by now published his valuable comparative study of "Zoo-Symbolism and Metaphoric Competence" (2011) that shows that a considerable amount of linguo-cultural knowledge is necessary in order to understand various animal proverbs of different languages and cultures. Of course, there are internationally disseminated animal proverbs that go back to classical times, the Bible, and animal fables (Abdulrahman 2016: 123–130, Carnes 1988). But there are also culturally specific expressions for which there are no exact equivalents in other languages. But animal proverbs most certainly exist in all languages based on the one hand on the observation of the animal world and in a figurative way on "die augenfällige Übereinstimmung menschlichen und tierischen Verhaltens (the obvious correspondence of human and animal behavior)" (Meisser 1969: 871). This can be seen in myths, legends, fairy tales, and fables that show, "daß die Grenzen zwischen Mensch und Tier nicht so scharf zu ziehen sind, wie es uns manche Philosophen der Neuzeit (z.B. R. Descartes) einreden wollen (that the borders between man and animal should not be drawn as sharply as some philosophers of modern times want to convince us)" (Cherubim 2008: 113). Thus, Dmitrij Dobrovol'skij and Elisabeth

Piirainen have included a long chapter on "Tiere als Symbole (Animals as Symbols)" in their important book on *Symbole in Sprache und Kultur. Studien zur Phraseologie aus kultursemiotischer Perspektive* (1996) that shows, "daß Tiere wie Bär, Eule, Fuchs, Hase, Hund, Schlange und Wolf einen Symbolcharakter in Tierphraseologismen annehmen kön-nen, der über die bloße Metaphorik der Übertragung aus dem Tierreich auf Verhaltens—oder Handlungsweisen des Menschen hinausgeht (that such animals as bear, owl, fox, rabbit, dog, snake, and wolf can take on a symbolic character in animal proverbs that goes beyond the mere metaphor of the transfer from the animal world on the behavior and acting of human beings)" (Dobrovol'skij und Piirainen 1996: 158–159). Thus the dog can, for example, be a symbol for inferiority, malice/aggression, faithfulness or quarrelsomeness, as can be seen from such phrases as "to go to the dogs", "let sleeping dogs lie", "faithful like a dog", and "to live like cat and dog". But whether animal metaphor or animal symbol, proverbs from the animal world get their expressive-ness not solely from their texts but also from their different functions in various contexts.

All of this makes a lot of sense, and the many examples cited in the numerous publications on animal proverbs provide ample proof that they can be seen as generalizations about animal behavior as such or as metaphorical or symbolic statements of human interaction as social beings. But there is one aspect that is missing in collections and studies of animal proverbs, namely the important fact that there are new or modern proverbs that differ considerably in language and metaphor/symbol from some of the traditional texts. But as will be shown by the following 117 (7.2%) proverbs from *The Dictionary of Modern Proverbs* (2012) and its three supplements (identified as S1, S2, and S3) with a total of 1617 (1422 in the dictionary and 195 in the supplements) proverbs edited by Charles Clay Doyle, Wolfgang Mieder, and Fred R. Shapiro, these newly identified and recorded animal proverbs with references to their earliest appearance in print also contain in usually indirect (metaphorical, symbolic) language the all-too-human behavior of people.

Interestingly enough there is only one proverb that contains the generic noun "animal", and it started as a literary quotation from

George Orwell's famous novel *Animal Farm* (1945): "All animals are created equal, but some are more equal than others (1945, 6; all proverbs will be cited with their year of first appearance in print followed by the page number of its registration in *The Dictionary of Modern Proverbs* and the supplements). It started as an anti-proverb to the well-known proverb "All men are created equal" from the American "Declaration of Independence" (1776; see Mieder 2015a, Mieder, Kingsbury, Harder 1992: 398) that had been expanded to "All men and women are created equal" by the early American feminist Elizabeth Cady Stanton in 1848 (Mieder 2014a: 65–74). Orwell's statement has long taken on a proverbial ring, and its satirical tone in a way sets the tone for many of the following modern animal proverbs of which most are of American origin. What this new proverb expresses is, of course, that in the animal world and by extension the human world, nobody is really equal with some having more opportunities and a better life than others. This new proverb is thus a correct summation of modern existence with its unfair social inequalities.

There are a few proverbs that basically begin with a reference to "man" or "woman" and then bring into focus a certain relationship to an animal that is obviously not meant to be complimentary:

A man is no better than his horse. (1905, 158)
A man who kicks his dog (hound) will beat his wife. (1952, 159)
A man is not a camel. (1911, 158)

The third text is perhaps in need of some explanation, as is so often the case with proverbs in general. In any case, nowadays the proverb jocularly justifies a need for the frequent slaking of human thirst, especially with alcoholic decoctions.

But then there is also the following proverb that indicates in a positive way how much men need women:

A man without a woman is like a fish without a tail. (1909, 159)

The proverb may represent a collapsing of two lines in the old song "A Man without a Woman": "An Association without an object / Is like a ship without a sail, / A boat without a rudder, / Or a fish without a tail."

But following that basic structure and reversing "man" and "woman", a new proverb was created that became a feminist slogan known in a number of foreign languages (Mieder 2015b: 247):

> A woman without a man is like a fish without a bicycle. (1976, 279)

It is also known in its variant form of "A woman needs a man like a fish needs a bicycle". The proverb perhaps originated as an anti-proverb patterned after "A woman without a man is like a handle without a pan" (or other old similes suggesting uselessness or absurdity). The feminist Gloria Steinem disclaimed credit for originating the feminist expression, and it has now been established that Irina Dunn, a distinguished Australian educator, journalist and politician, coined the phrase back in 1970. The image of a fish without (or not needing) a bicycle has had a life of its own.

> A man without a woman is like a fish without a bicycle. (1983, 159)
> A man without faith (religion, God) is like a fish without a bicycle. (1958, 160)

With such preoccupation with the ridiculous imagery of a fish riding a bicycle, it comes as no surprise that Jack Prelutsky came up with his humorous poem "My Fish Can Ride a Bicycle" (1990):

> My fish can ride a bicycle,
> my fish can climb a tree,
> my fish enjoys a glass of milk,
> my fish takes naps with me.
>
> My fish can play the clarinet,
> my fish can bounce a ball,
> my fish is not like other fish,
> my fish can't swim at all.
> (Prelutsky 1990: 146)

And here is yet another variant that has gained enough currency and distribution to be considered a proverb in its own right. Of course, this proverb emphasizes the freedom of emancipated modern women who are perfectly capable of handling their affairs without men:

A woman without a man is like a fish without a net (A woman needs a man like a fish needs a net. (1993, 280)

Clearly the proverb derives from "A woman without a man is like a fish without a bicycle" but now with the meaning of a man being not just an absurd irrelevancy to a woman but an actual impediment to her success or happiness, even a danger to her.

To a certain extent these proverbs are based on somewhat of a wordplay since one does not normally talk about fish and bicycles in the same sentence. In the following proverb man is equated with animal to which is added an allusion to the animal proverb "There is more than one way to skin a cat", resulting in a fascinating wordplay about the vulnerability of modern humankind in an inhumane world:

Man is the only animal that can be skinned more than once. (1920, S2, 31)

There is also this next proverb based on a playful folk etymology uncovering the problems with unfounded assumptions:

Assume makes an ass of you and me. (1975, 9)

Speaking of an ass (donkey, jackass) in the folk meaning of "stupid", here is another wordplay based on the absurd image of an unintelligent person:

There are more horses' asses than horses (in the world). (1957, 125)

This type of crude or absurd wordplay leads to so-called proverbial interrogatives with plenty of wisdom being hidden in the seemingly simple question. The best example is the following proverb that was first recorded in Joseph Stein's *Fiddler on the Roof* (1964):

A bird may love a fish, but where would they live (build a home, build a nest)? (1964, 21)

As can be seen, the proverb has become current in a number of variants, but it is usually cited as a comment about two socially or ethnically unmatched persons wanting to build a good relationship or to get married (Mahoney 2009).

Here is another proverbial interrogative that in its longer variant ends with a question mark and most likely had its origin in Rose Fitzgerald Kennedy's *Times to Remember* (1974): "Birds sing after a storm; why shouldn't people feel as free to delight in whatever sunlight remains to them?":

> Birds sing after a storm (so why shouldn't we?) (1974, 21)

The next proverbial question comes from the corporate world and had its origin in the claim that large multi-national corporations (gorillas) can do whatever they wish:

> Where does a five-hundred-pound (eight hundred-pound, etc.) gorilla sit? (1976, 109)

The obvious answer is "Anywhere it wants!" Regarding the next proverbial interrogative, it can be observed that it is truly nothing but a rhetorical question. Clearly it does not make a difference how a cat looks like in order for it to be a good mouser:

> Who cares if a cat is black or white as long as it catches mice? (1968, 35)

But things are not so simple or innocuous with the next proverbial question once one becomes aware of the fact that the "cow" stands for a woman, revealing the proverb as an anti-feministic statement:

> Why buy milk when a cow is so cheap (when you've got a cow at home)? (1957, 166)

In fact, the proverb probably originated as an anti-proverb responding to the anti-marriage saying "Why buy the cow when you can get milk for free?"

One is inclined to say, "Don't use this ridiculous and slanderous proverb", but unfortunately it has gained currency among male chauvinists. But speaking of not doing certain things, there are several modern proverbs that follow the long-established structural formula of "Don't ..." as a solid piece of advice for proper behavior or action. It should be noted that there exist variants that indicate that some of these modern proverbs have not yet reached a standardized form:

> Don't use a sledgehammer (hammer, hatchet) to kill a fly (gnat, mosquito) (Don't try to kill a fly with a sledgehammer). (1910, S1, 114)
> Don't try to swallow an elephant whole (It is possible to swallow [You can eat] an elephant—one bite at a time. (1921, 67)
> Don't fatten frogs for snakes. (1922, 88)
> Don't let the (same) dog bite you twice. (1932, 58)
> Don't let the same bee sting you twice. (1911, 18)

The last two proverbs obviously advise against getting into the same bind twice. They have the same meaning but use different animal metaphors. Regarding the last text, it might be of interest to cite the song "Don't Let the Same Bee Sting You Twice" (2012) by the British rock band The Veils where the proverb is employed as a leitmotif to deal with a problematic love relationship. Proverbs appearing in songs is nothing new, of course, and there is a long tradition of proverbs in various types of songs, including such modern artists as The Beatles, Bob Dylan, Bruce Springsteen, and others (Mieder 1989: 195–221):

> I left a message to myself
> That girl ain't no good for your health
> Unhooked my brother's telephone
> Pretended nobody was home
> Your love weren't nothing but trouble—
>
> I guess I'm only now paying the price
> Don't let the same bee sting you twice
> Don't let the same bee sting you twice
> Climbing up your mama's stairs
> Oblivious to your affairs
> But really how could I have known?
> Your lies were seeds carefully sewn
> But now I know I should always have listened

to dear daddy's advice
Don't let the same bee sting you twice
Don't let the same bee sting you twice
Well now ain't you meant to die after one sting, honey?
But you just keep on coming back for more
And I've been losing my mind over this and ain't it funny
I've still got no idea what it is you're looking for?
Oh, and here she comes again—
And now you're standing at my door
Just too damn pretty to ignore
And I think that maybe I've gone mad
And your love really weren't so bad
And then you claim it was a case of neurotic perception

and I say "Maybe, well that sounds about right"
And then I let the same bee sting me twice
Yeah I let the same bee sting me twice

(www.theveils.com >trouble-of-the-brain)

Just like with older traditional proverbs, there are also modern proverbs that follow the pattern of "Never ...", a formulaic way of giving advice against doing a questionable thing. The drastic or ridiculous imagery of these texts is meant to be humorous or satirical, and they certainly bring the message across that a certain action should definitely not be undertaken:

> Never get in a pissing contest (match) with a skunk. (1943, 198)
> Never wrestle (wallow with) a pig; you will both get dirty, and the pig likes it. (1946, 197)
> Never try to teach a pig to sing; it wastes your time, and it annoys the pig. (1973, 197; see Dundes and Pagter 1991)
> Never play leapfrog with a unicorn. (1977, 137)

Talking about wanting to do ridiculous things, there are also modern proverbs that express this idea by couching their animal metaphors into the structural pattern of "You can't ..." It should be noted that once again some of these proverbs are current in variants:

> You can't rise with the lark if you've been on one the night before. (1908, 136)
> Based on the wordplay with "lark" as a bird or as a frivolous undertaking.

You can't catch a fish without baiting a hook (putting the line in the water, etc.). (1921, 79)

You can't get all your coons up one tree. (1937, 43)

> That is, you can't gain all the advantages through one act, stroke or operation.

You can't make chicken salad out of chicken shit (chicken feathers). (1949, S1, 91)

You cannot herd cats. (1992, 35)

> As a simile betokening difficulty or impossibility ["like trying to herd cats," "as easy as herding cats"], the image or conceit of herding cats is probably older; certainly, the motif of herding hares, rabbits, grasshoppers, etc. is.

All of these animal proverbs this far place a human being into a situation that is exemplified by way of animals. This is also true for such modern animal proverbs that are based on the common structural pattern of "If you … you …" (Mieder 2004: 6–7). This is clearly a matter of cause and effect, and the messages of the proverbs are primarily to give advice or direction for future action:

If you're going to be a bear, be a grizzly. (1908, 88)

If you can't ride two horses at once, you shouldn't be in the circus. (1935, 125)

> The proverb may derive from "No one can ride two horses except in a circus," itself an anti-proverb based on "You can't ride two horses at once."

If you want a friend, get (buy) a dog. (1941, 86)

> The proverb alludes to the old saying "A dog is man's best friend." It usually suggests that, in some particularly hostile or competitive setting (Hollywood, Washington DC, Wall Street), a dog will be the *only* friend that a person can hope to find—and that (human) friendship itself is a quality not only improbable but even undesirable.

If you pay peanuts, you get monkeys (Only monkeys work for peanuts). (1953, 171)

If you are looking for (hunting) elephants, go to elephant country (go where elephants are). (1954, 67)

If you hoot with the owls at night, you can't soar with the eagles in the morning (If you wish to soar with the eagles in the morning, you can't hoot with the owls at night. (1961, S2, 34)

If you aren't the lead dog, the scenery (view) never changes. (1980, 58)

If you can't run with the big dogs, stay on (under) the porch. (1985, 58)

If you're going to swallow (have to swallow) a frog, don't look at it (don't think about it) too long. (1986, 88)
The common attribution to Mark Twain appears to be spurious.

There remains but one dominant pattern to be considered, namely "Sometimes you're ..., and sometimes you're ..." that results in modern proverbs that express the arbitrariness of life's situations. Once again, these proverbs exist in a number of variants:

Sometimes (Some days) you're the windshield and sometimes you're the bug (bird)
    (Sometimes you're the bird (bug), and sometimes you're the windshield).
    (1981, 277)
Sometimes (Some days) you're the dog, and sometimes (some days) you're the fireplug
    (Sometimes you're the fireplug (fire hydrant), and sometimes you're the dog). (1989, 59)
Sometimes (Some days) you're the pigeon, and some (other) days you're the statue. (1993, 198)
Sometimes (Some days) you get the bear, sometimes the bear gets you. (1970, 16)

It does not take much imagination to understand some of the unpleasant happenings that can occur at times. Such realia as windshields and hydrants together with the animals are indicators of the modernity of these proverbs that once again show how human beings can be exposed or confronted with animals that bring unexpected and negative consequences. Modern life has its pitfalls to be sure!

With this being said, these comments can turn to an alphabetically arranged review of various animals as they appear in modern proverbs. Once again it should be noted that many of the modern proverbs exist in variants, as for example in the following two texts with the keyword of "bear". The first proverb expresses the old proverbial idea of "to take time by the forelock" that is not in much use today any longer:

The time to shoot (catch) bears is when they are out (around). (1914, 259)
We killed a (the) bear (, but Papa (Brother, etc.) shot it. (1939, 16)

This second text is an indirect statement to silence a braggart boasting about his feats. It is not so much a proverb giving advice but rather a sarcastic comment that confronts someone with a needed reality check.

Things are considerably different with the proverb "The bee that gets the honey doesn't hang around the hive" (1906, 18) that had its start with the chorus of Ed Rose's song that also carries the proverb as its title:

> The bee that gets the honey
> doesn't hang around the hive
> and the man that makes the money
> 's got to work and strive.
> You can't get no honey buzzin
> 's round dis room
> unless you flop your wings your'e
> gwine to get stung soon.
> The bee that gets the honey
> doesn't hang around the hive.
> https://digital.gonzaga.edu/digital/collection/p15486coll3/d/4029

Numerous modern proverbs come from popular songs like this, while others are attached to famous people even though they might not have originated it. This is the case with the proverb "Float like a butter-fly, sting like a bee" (1964, 31) that is usually attributed to the boxer Muhammed Ali (Cassius Clay), even though it has been established that it actually was Drew Brown, Clay's spiritual adviser and assistant trainer, who coined it in February of 1964.

Things are considerably easier with the following two proverbs from the world of birds, both of which use an animal metaphor to comment about some very basic human concerns:

> A robin's song is not pretty to the worm. (1938, 219)
> A bird never flies so far that his tail doesn't follow. (1969, 21)

Things are not much different with the first two of three "cat" proverbs, but the third text needs an explanatory comment to be understood:

Sleeping cats catch no mice. (1903, 35)

Cats look down on you, dogs look up at you, pigs look as you as equals. (1937, 35)

> The saying has sometimes been attributed to Sir Winston Churchill.

Even a dead cat will bounce. (1987, 35)

> This is a metaphor that alludes to the stock market bouncing back after a loss.

Two modern proverbs based on a chicken or rooster are easily understood since they basically express the thought that a person might be alive and well one day and reduced to bits and pieces the next day:

A rooster one day, a feather duster the next. (1907, 219)

Chicken today, feathers tomorrow. (1958, 37)

In the following group of three "cow" proverbs the first two are once again perfectly clear but the third text does need a bit of an explanation since it does seem to relate to journalism in particular. This is an indication that some modern proverbs deal with matters that might not be known generally:

Better a good cow than a cow of a good kind. (1922, 46)

Salt (Feed, Pet, Court, Woo, Buy) the cow to get the calf. (1949, 46)

Sacred cows make great (good, the best, gourmet) hamburgers (burgers). (1965, 46)

> Proverbial wisdom from journalism where exposing famous people or important issues make great news stories.

With this the large group of modern proverbs that deals with the most popular pet has been reached. The proverb "A dog is man's best friend" from the middle of the nineteenth-century is universally acknowledged, and since dogs are ever present in modern society, new proverbs continue to be coined even though there are so many in existence already (Mieder, Kingsbury, Harder 1992: 157–163). Two of these proverbs deal with insights concerning the ownership and the training of a dog:

A dog is for life, not just for Christmas. (1978, 58)

> The saying entered oral tradition as a proverb from a slogan introduced by the UK's National Canine Defence League to discourage the giving of

puppies as Christmas presents. It as well as its allusive adaptations can
refer metaphorically to concerns other than the disposition of puppies.
There are no bad dogs, only bad owners. (1949, 59)

This last proverb is based on the structural pattern of "There are no
bad Xs, only bad Ys" on which the modern proverbs "There are no bad
children, only bad parents" (1910, 38) and "There are no bad students,
only bad teachers" (1958, 242) are based as well.

The next four proverbs, while addressing the behavior of dogs,
clearly have human beings and their behavior in mind:

It's not the size of the dog in the fight that matters; it's the size of the fight in
the dog. (1911, 232)
It's a poor dog that won't wag its own tail. (1922, 59)
It's a dog-eat-dog world. (1935, 282)
    The proverb probably alludes to the proverb "Dog does not eat dog."
It's a foolish dog that barks at a flying bird. (1975, 59)
    The proverb first occurs in the song "Jah Live" (1975) by Bob Marley
    and Lee Perry that is comprised of a pastiche of proverbs and other say-
    ings: "The truth is an offence / And not a sin, / And he who laughs last /
    Is he who wins, / It's a foolish dog / Barks at a flying bird." The proverb
    refers to any futility or pointless hostility.

This leaves the relatively recent proverb "Dogs don't bark at parked
cars" (1993, 58) which, in its literal meaning, makes sense as can be
observed in the natural world of dogs surrounded by parked cars. But
what then is its figurative meaning? It refers to changes in socio-political
structures that will doubtlessly result in some expected opposition.
Leaving things alone (parked), would bring no opposition (dogs) but
also no progress.

It is perhaps somewhat surprising that the "duck" is represented
several times among these modern proverbs. Their meaning is rather
self-evident, with the duck of the first three proverbs representing a
person so to speak. The last text, however, is referring to the idea of
getting one's affairs or things in order

Go hunting where the ducks are. (1930, 64)
It is better to be a big duck in a little puddle (pond) than a little duck in a big
puddle (pond). (1934, 64)

> Nothing ruins a duck but (like) its bill (A wise duck takes care of its bill).
> (1955, 181)
>   The proverb warns against excessive or injudicious talking.
> Get your ducks in a row. (1956, 63)

There is yet one more "duck" proverb that was registered in *The New York Times* as early as in 1948. For quite some time it did not appear with much frequency orally or in print, but it has become rather popular in more recent times. Why might this be? Probably because of the absurd image of a duck waddling and quacking along as well as its message that someone or something is exactly what it appears to be: "If it looks like a duck, walks like a duck, and quacks like a duck, it's a duck" (1948, 64).

In comparison to ducks, eagles are majestic birds of prey at the very top of the hierarchy of birds. Turkeys, on the other hand, are considered to be rather clumsy and stupid birds. In fact, "turkey" in its slang sense refers to a foolish, inept, or socially awkward person. Little wonder that metaphorically speaking eagles and turkeys are placed in opposition to each other in the following two proverbs:

> In any group (flock) of eagles, there will be at least one turkey. (1979, 111)
> It is hard to soar with the eagles when you are surrounded by (scratching with, running with, etc.) turkeys. (1980, 65)

Turning to "fish" proverbs, it should first of all be noticed that two of them state nothing else but two of the "duck" proverbs cited above, albeit this time relating the proverbial message by way of a "fish" metaphor:

> Fish where the fish are. (1901, 79)
> Better a big fish in a little pond (puddle, pool) than a little fish in a big pond (mighty ocean). (1903, 78)

Since both of these proverbs are considerably older than the "duck" equivalents, it could well be that they served as models for the "fish" texts. They are all well-known today, and people simply choose one or the other depending on their personal preference or on a particular context. In any case, the next six texts contain clear-cut messages:

A fish doesn't know it is in water (it is wet) (A fish doesn't know it is in water
until it is taken out; A fish doesn't see water). (1909, S1, 96)
The bigger the bait, the bigger the fish. (1913, S1, 87)
A fish wouldn't get caught if it kept its mouth shut. (1921, 79)
You've got to fish while they are biting. (1921, 80)
Smart fish don't bite (don't get caught, keep their mouth shut). (1935, 79)
Only dead fish go with the flow.(1989, 79)
    Contradicting the proverb "Go with the flow."

Two additional modern "fish" proverbs deserve a short comment. The
obvious truth that "Half a fish is better than none (at all)" (1905, 114) is
clearly nothing else but a restatement of the much older proverb "Half
a loaf is better than none" with the identical meaning. And the same
is true for the proverb "A fish in the net (creel) is worth two in the
water (sea, river)" (1902, 78) that is a reformulation of the very popular proverb "A bird in the hand is worth two in the bush" (Mieder,
Kingsbury, Harder 1992: 51) with the same structure. This British proverb from the fifteenth century brings to mind the short poem "Which is
Best? (1865) by the American poet Emily Dickenson which most surely
is one of the most challenging proverb poems of the rich tradition of
proverbial verse:

Which is best? Heaven—
Or only Heaven to come
With that old Codicil of Doubt?
I cannot help esteem
The "Bird within the Hand"
Superior to the one
The "Bush" may yield me
Or may not
Too late to choose again.
(Sobieski and Mieder 2005: 52)

While this poem contains an existentialistic depth, there is also the
poem "Bird Watcher" (1993) that its author R.J. Owens wrote while
he was a student at the University of Vermont. Here the old proverb
serves to express the sadness of a lost love:

A bird in the hand,
Beats two in the bushes.
This is what they say.
But the bird, in my hand, has left.
One sunny afternoon, she flew away,
And now my hand is empty, vacant.
Like that of a young child,
Open, wanting to be filled.

So now I am a Bird Watcher,
Once again, Seeking to embrace.
Not birds, but a Single one.
In my hand, A magnificent bird.
Forever, So I can watch no more.
(Mieder and Sobieski 2005: 179)

Just as there are many traditional proverbs about birds, horses have also appeared in proverbs for centuries as a domestic animal of much use to humankind. Some of the modern "horse" proverbs don't seem particularly innovative in their insights, and one might wonder why the following three proverbs are of a relatively recent origin:

There was never a horse that couldn't be ridden. (1921, 125)
When you fall off a horse (bicycle), you have to get (right) back on. (1962, 125)
Always ride the (your) horse in the direction it's going (it wants to go). (1975, 124)

While these texts in their literal sense deal with the world of horses, they relate in their figurative way to their human riders and the challenges they face. That is not the case with the proverb "The horse is (already) out of the barn" (1961, S3, 66) that may be related to the much older proverbial phrase about the futility of "locking the (stable) door after the horse is stolen." The idea of something having been completed already has resulted in two somewhat later equivalents with different images but the same meaning: ""The train has (already) left the station (1976, S3, 82) and "The ship has (already) sailed (1978, S3, 77).

While these proverbs can be used in various situations due to their general metaphor and meaning, this is quite different with the modern proverb "When you hear hoofbeats, think horses, not zebras (When you hear hoofbeats, don't look for zebras)" (1969, 123). It is a piece of advice given to medical students in the United States, telling them that they should look for simple answers when checking patients (Dundes, Streiff, Dundes 1999). In other words, they might merely have a simple cold (horses) and not a severe or obscure disease (zebras). This proverb does not necessarily have any wider application than the one in medical schools, but it is a perfect example for showing that there are many proverbs known primarily to a particular folk group. This also shows that proverbs might not necessarily be understood by those who do not belong to a certain section of the population. There is no doubt that the meaning of proverbs can be allusive, as is the case with the following proverbs and its variants, for which Charles Clay Doyle, Wolfgang Mieder, and Fred R. Shapiro present the attached references and explanation in their *Dictionary of Modern Proverbs* (2012):

> There is (There must be, There just has to be, I know there is) a pony (in) there somewhere. (1958, 203)
>> 1958 H. K. Beecher, "Relation of Drugs to Reaction Components in Subjective Responses," in *Psychopharmacology*, edited by Harry H. Pennes (New York: Hoeber-Harper) 353 (relating a story, which "many of you have heard," by way of illustrating the hypothesis "that whether one is optimistic or pessimistic is a matter of inborn temperament"): "The optimistic child was similarly locked in a room, containing only a large pile of manure. At the end, the child emerged covered with manure and smiles. 'I could not find it, but there must be a pony somewhere!'" 1960 James Kirkwood, *There Must Be a Pony! A Novel* (Boston: Little, Brown). 1966 Marvin J. Gersh, *How to Raise Children at Home in Your Spare Time* (New York: Stein & Day) 104: "… When he came out they asked him what he was so happy about. 'Of course I'm happy,' he said. 'With all that manure in there, there must be a pony somewhere.'" The allusive proverb satirically cautions against credulity or excessive optimism.

Of interest are also two proverbs with monkeys appearing as substitutes for people who by their questionable behavior bring about disruptions of one type or another:

> One monkey don't stop no show. (1961, 171)
> Not my circus, not my monkeys. (2014, S1, 91)

The second text with its earliest reference found thus far from 2014 is a perfect example for proverbs still being coined in the very modern age (Honeck and Welge 1997, Mieder 2015c: 38–44). Using the images of a circus and monkeys, it brings across the idea that someone is not responsible for or concerned with certain problems.

Speaking of problems, for most people mice in the house would be an unpleasant intrusion to be dealt with by way of handy mousetraps. Since catching mice is a rather common phenomenon, it is no wonder that there are two modern proverbs of relatively recent coinage. One might have thought that they would actually be a little older:

> There's always free cheese in a mousetrap. (1962, 37)
> The second mouse gets the cheese. (1997, 173; probably of Australian origin)
>> 1997 *Sydney [Australia] Morning Herald* 13 Sep.: "Thought for the week-end, culled by Greg Cocks, of Brooklyn, from the Internet: The early bird may get the worm, but the second mouse gets the cheese." The proverb might be thought of as an anti-proverb responding to "The early bird gets the worm"; often (as in the quotation) it appears in conjunction with the older proverb.

But speaking of "second", here is a proverb that plays on the supposed stupidity of mules and the even greater ignorance of someone who gets kicked by it another time. And as indicated by an additional proverb, mules do not adhere to normal behavior in any case:

> There is no (little) education (wisdom) in the second kick of a mule. (1966, S1, 94)
> Mules don't kick according to rules. (1968, 175)

Just like the mules actually stand for contrite people, pigs can also be equated with human beings, notably men, as is rather directly expressed in the first proverb of the following group:

> Men (All men) are pigs. (1910, 158)
> Pigs smell their own smells first. (1966, 197)
> Pigs get fat; hogs get slaughtered (killed, butchered). (1967, 197)
>> Usually referring to management getting the money while labor is deprived.
> You have to throw (put, pant) the corn where the hogs can get it. (1990, 44)

> You can put lipstick on a pig but it's still a pig (A pig wearing lipstick is still a pig). (1985, 148)
>> The *lipstick-on-a-pig* version is the predominant modern form of older expressions that assert the futility of dressing or decorating pigs or other animals.

The last proverb gained considerable notoriety during one of President Barack Obama's campaign events on September 9, 2008, at Lebanon, Virginia, that was blown way out of proportion by the Republicans and by especially the mass media. As it were, Barack Obama was commenting spontaneously on Senator John McCain's economic plan, peppering his remarks with the by now famous "lipstick" proverb while adding a second colloquially expressed thought based on a similar structure to it:

> John McCain says he's about change too, and so I guess his whole angle is, "Watch out George Bush—except for economic policy, health care policy, tax policy, education policy, foreign policy and Karl Rove-style politics—we're really going to shake things up in Washington." That's not change. That's just calling something [that's] the same thing something different. You know you can put lipstick on a pig, but it's still a pig. You know you can wrap an old fish in a piece of paper called change, it's still going to stink after eight years. We've had enough of the same old thing.

As can be seen, this statement definitely was directed at John McCain and not at his vice-presidential running mate Governor Sarah Palin from Alaska. However, in light of the fact that Palin had spoken of lipstick, hockey moms, and pit bulls in her speech of September 3, 2008, at the Republican Convention in Minneapolis ("I was just your average hockey mom. I love those hockey moms, you know, they say, what is the difference between a hockey mom and a pit bull? Lipstick."), it was easy to attack Obama's colorful remarks as being directed at Sarah Palin as an ill-chosen sexist remark. Even though this claim was utterly absurd, this accusation in the heat of the vigorous campaign gave Obama and his staff a few days of anxiety, to be sure. Luckily there were a number of journalists who very quickly helped to set the record straight by proving that the proverb or parts of it has a solid standing in American politics. Using paremiographical tools, they pointed out that the "lipstick" proverb has a sixteenth-century precursor in the form of "You can't make a silk purse from a sow's ear." Similar proverbs are "A hog in armor [a person of strange appearance] is still a hog" (eighteenth century) and "A hog in a silk waistcoat is still a hog" (nineteenth century). From the twentieth century there are also such variants as "A pig in a palace is still a pig", "A pig with feathers behind its ears is still a pig", "The pig may have a tuxedo on, but he is still a pig", "A pig painted gold is still a pig", and "A pig in a parlor is still a pig." Since the word "lipstick" dates only from about 1880, its appearance in proverbial language also had to wait until more recent times. In fact, the earliest reference found thus far is from November 16, 1985, in the *Washington Post* (for all of this and more see Mieder 2009b: 83–85).

Things are not always that complex, as can be seen from the following animal proverbs arranged alphabetically according to the animal named in them. For some of them other proverbs have already been cited as examples for certain repeated structures above:

cockroach
There is never just one cockroach (in the kitchen). (1991, S3, 58)

elephant
Women and elephants never forget. (1904, 279)
> The proverb probably originated as an anti-proverb, an ironic extension of the old saying (or belief), "Elephants never forget."

frog
If frogs had wings, they wouldn't bump their tails (butt, etc.) on rocks (logs, the ground, etc.) (If frogs had wings, they could fly). (1914, 88)

lion
Until the lions have their own historians, the stories will glorify the hunters. (1971, 147)

rabbit
Little rabbits have big ears. (1935, 213)
> The proverb is an analog of the older "Little pitchers have big ears" with both proverbs referring to children listening to adult talk.

skunk

There is nothing in the middle of the road but yellow stripes and dead skunks (armadillos, possums, etc.). (1967, 181)

snake

He who has been bitten by a snake fears even a rope. (1901, 235)

squirrel

Even a blind squirrel can sometimes find a nut (an acorn). (1928, 238)

The proverb seems to be the prevalent modern version of "Even a blind hog can occasionally find an acorn."

wolf

The caribou and the wolf are one; for the caribou feeds the wolf, but it is the wolf who keeps the caribou strong. (1963, 34)

With this said, these comments can turn to such modern proverbs that belong to the realms of sexuality, obscenity, and scatology. Looking at earlier proverb collections, one might well get the impression that the folk has no so-called "dirty" or offensive proverbs. But they have always existed, of course, with earlier paremiographers for the most part having been reluctant or kept from including them in their collections (Mieder 2012: 181–186). As will be seen by these examples of modern animal proverbs, they at times exist in clean and dirty variants for speakers to choose from:

If the dog hadn't stopped to shit (rest, etc.), he would have caught the rabbit. (1919, 58)

The proverb usually means that excuses or explanations do not avail. It may have originated as a translation of the German "Wenn der Hund nicht geschissen hätte, hätte er den Hasen gefangen."

Dead birds don't fall out of nests. (1952, 21)

The "bird" here is a euphemism for penis, and the proverb goes back to an anecdote about Winston Churchill caught at some function with his fly-buttons undone. When his attention was tactfully drawn to this, he supposedly said, "A dead bird won't fall out of the nest."

Take (Grab) the bull (life, the world) by the balls. (1954, 28)

The proverb may have originated as an anti-proverb based on the older "Take the bull by the horns." In a literal sense, grasping a bull by the horns will allow a certain measure of control that would be absent in the grabbing of a bull by the balls (i.e., testicles)!

If you lie down with pigs, you get up smelling bad (covered with shit, etc.). (1966, 197)

The proverb parallels to the older "If you lie down with dogs, you get up with fleas."

Play (Mess, Fuck) with a bull and you will get the horns. (1967, 28)

When you're up to your ass in alligators, it's hard to remember you're there to drain the swamp (it's too late to start figuring out how to drain the swamp. (1971, 8; see Dundes and Pagter 1987)

The sun doesn't shine on (up) the same dog's ass every day. (1976, 246)

Old rats like cheese too. (1977, 214)

The proverb refers to an old person's (usually a man's) sexual desire.

You can't run with the (big) dogs if you pee like a pup. (1986, 59)

When the chips are down, the buffalo (cow) is empty. (1997, 39)

The proverb plays punningly on the idiom (from poker) "the chips are down" (in other contexts, *chips* is a slang euphemism for "feces").

These proverbs are not particularly vulgar, and as can be seen, proverbs like "Old rats like cheese too" hide their sexual content quite well with this animal metaphor. Of course, they are also certainly not like "fairy tales" to which at least a couple of modern animal proverbs allude. But to be sure, the proverb "Every beauty needs her beast" (1973, 17) is a rather sexist statement even though it alludes to the common title or plot of the international folktale cycle "Beauty and the Beast." And then there is the popular proverb "You have to kiss a lot of frogs (toads) to find a prince" (1976, 89) that has gained considerable currency in English and in loan translations in many languages. It is not, as one might suspect, a reduction of the well-known fairy tale "The Frog King (Prince)" but at best an allusion to it (Mieder 2014b). Nevertheless, it is a splendid piece of folk wisdom couched in an animal metaphor to describe the difficulty of finding the right partner in the modern world with the variant image of an unattractive toad making the task even more problematic. With the world of fairy tales or legends being put into question, it should come as no surprise that even the traditional hero in shining armor will not be able to defeat the monstrous dragon—whatever or whoever it is—any longer. This is expressed in the proverbial negation of the supposedly positive outcome of the struggle with dragons:

Sometimes the dragon wins. (1981, 62)

Regarding this innovative proverb the folklorist and paremiologist Alan Dundes has stated that "Despite the 'never give up' philosophy of life, sometimes the opposing forces prevail and even heroes are defeated. Certainly in the heroic sagas of the golden past, the hero always slays the dragon. [...] Modern counterculture with its cynical view of the past prefers a more realistic assessment of the hero's chances for success" (Dundes and Pagter 1996: 58–50). This type of realism can be seen in quite a few of the animal proverbs that have been discussed here, especially if they are interpreted literally. However, the modern animal proverbs with their metaphors continue to play the same role as the traditional proverbs have done for centuries. They are proof positive that the time of making new proverbs is definitely not over and they will continue to be used as verbal tools of indirection to express in a figurative way generalizations and observations about animal and human existence alike.

Bibliography

This chapter has appeared in Madrid, Spain as "'Dogs Don't Bark at Parked Cars': Zoological Messages in Modern American Proverbs." *Paremia*, 29 (2019), 93–112.

Major English Collections

Barnette, Martha. 2003. *Dog Days and Dandelions. A Lively Guide to the Animal Meanings Behind Everyday Words*. New York: St. Martin's Press.

Doyle, Charles Clay, and Wolfgang Mieder. 2016. "*The Dictionary of Modern Proverbs*: A Supplement." *Proverbium*, 33: 85–120.

Doyle, Charles Clay, and Wolfgang Mieder. 2018. "*The Dictionary of Modern Proverbs*: Second Supplement." *Proverbium*, 35: 15–44.

Doyle, Charles Clay, and Wolfgang Mieder. 2020. "*The Dictionary of Modern Proverbs*: Third Supplement." *Proverbium*, 37: 53–86.

Doyle, Charles Clay, Wolfgang Mieder, and Fred R. Shapiro (eds.). 2012. *The Dictionary of Modern Proverbs*. New Haven, CT: Yale University Press.

Hendrickson, Robert. 1983. *Animal Crackers. A Bestial Lexicon*. New York: Penguin Books.

Lamb, G.F. 1985. *Animal Quotations*. Illustrations by William Rushton. Harlow, Essex: Longman Group.

Lyazidi, Rashid. 2012. *Animal Proverbs and Quotes Kingdom. Domestic Animals*. Parker, CO: Outskirts Press.

Lyman, Darryl. 1983. *The Animal Things We Say*. Middle Village, NY: Jonathan David.

Lyman, Darryl. 1994. *Dictionary of Animal Words and Phrases*. Middle Village, NY: Jonathan David.

Macrone, Michael. 1995. *Animalogies. "A Fine Kettle of Fish" and 150 Other Animal Expressions*. Illustrations by Thorina Rose. New York: Doubleday.

Mieder, Wolfgang. 1993. *Howl Like a Wolf: Animal Proverbs*. Illustrations by Chris Cart. Shelburne, VT: The New England Press.

Mieder, Wolfgang, Stewart A. Kingsbury, and Kelsie B. Harder (eds.). 1992. *A Dictionary of American Proverbs*. New York: Oxford University Press.

Palmatier, Robert A. 1995. *Speaking of Animals: A Dictionary of Animal Metaphors*. Westport, CT: Greenwood Press.

Speake, Jennifer. 2015. *Oxford Dictionary of Proverbs*. 6th ed. Oxford: Oxford University Press.

Steuck, Udo. 1997. *One Thousand and More Animal Proverbs*. London: Minerva Press.

Secondary Literature

Aakko, Arto. 2003. *Tierbezeichnungen in der deutschen und finnischen Phraseologie. Am Beispiel der Komponenten Bär/Karhu, Hund/Koira und Pferd/Hevonen*. M.A. Thesis University of Helsinki.

Abdulrahman, Abdulhamid. 2016. *Tiermetaphorik in unterschiedlichen Diskurstraditionen*. Berlin: Peter Lang.

Alonso Ímaz, María del Carmen. 2003. "Estudio contrastivo de paremias españolas y alemanas relativos a los animales." *Paremia*, 12: 85–96.

Augusto, Maria Celeste. 2008. "O elemento zoomórfico na paremiologia: uma abordagem léxico-semântica contrastiva." *Fixed Expressions in Cross-Linguistic Perspective. A Multilingual and Multidisciplinary Approach*. Ed. María Álvarez de la Granja Hamburg: Kovač, 193–210.

Biadún-Grabarek, Hanna. 2012. "Einige Aspekte der Wiedergabe deutscher Sprichwörter im Polnischen am Beispiel ausgewählter Sprichwörter mit dem Tiernamen Esel." *Fragen der Phraseologie, Lexikologie und Syntax*. Ed. Hanna Biadún-Grabarek. Frankfurt am Main: Peter Lang, 33–51.

Bock, Bettina. 2013. "'Tierische Menschen.' Übertragungen vom Tier auf den Menschen im Deutschen und in benachbarten slavischen Sprachen." *Studia Scandinavica et Germanica. Vom Sprachlaut zur Sprachgeschichte*. Eds. Józef Jarosz, Stephan

Michael Schröder, and Janusz Stopyra. Wrocław: Wydawnictwo Uniwersytetu Wrocławskiego, 63–72.

Bodi, Daniel. 2015. "Cross-Cultural Transformation of Animal Proverbs (Sumer, Mari, Hebrew Bible, Aramaic Ahiqar and Aesop's Fables)." *Concepts éthiques et moraux: approches multiculturelles et interdisciplinaires. Sémantique des énoncés parémiques.* Eds. Marie-Sol Ortola, and Guy Achard-Bayle. Nancy: Éditions Universitaires de Lorraine, 61–112.

Carnes Pack (ed.). 1988. *Proverbia in Fabula. Essays on the Relationship of the Fable and the Proverb.* Bern: Peter Lang.

Čermák, František. 2012. "Animal Phraseology: The Case of Dog and Cat (A Corpus-based Study)." *Phraseology and Discourse: Cross Linguistic and Corpus-based Approaches.* Eds. Antonio Pamies, José Manuel Pazos Bretaña, and Lucía Luque Nadal. Baltmannsweiler: Schneider Verlag Hohengehren, 55–65.

Cherubim, Dieter. 2008. "Mensch und Tier im Spiegel der Sprache." *Interdisziplinäre Germanistik im Schnittpunkt der Kulturen. Festschrift für Dagmar Neuendorff.* Eds. Michael Szurawitzki and Christopher M. Schmidt. Würzburg: Königshausen & Neumann, 111–128.

Cristea, Simion Doru. 2016. "Os animals nos provérbios / Animals in Proverbs." *Proceedings of the Ninth Interdisciplinary Colloquium on Proverbs, 1st to 8th November 2015, at Tavira, Portugal.* Eds. Rui J.B. Soares and Outi Lauhakangas. Tavira: Tipografia Tavirense, 173–188.

Dobrovol'skij, Dmitrij, and Elisabeth Piirainen. 1996. *Symbole in Sprache und Kultur: Studien zur Phraseologie aus kultursemiotischer Perspektive.* Bochum: Norbert Brockmeyer.

Dobrovol'skij, Dmitrij, and Elisabeth Piirainen. 1999. "'Keep the Wolf from the Door': Animal Symbolism in Language and Culture." *Proverbium*, 16: 61–93.

Domínguez, José M. 1974. "Los animales en la fraseología española." *Yelmo*, 16: 23–25.

Dundes, Alan, and Carl R. Pagter. 1987. *When You're Up to Your Ass in Alligators … More Urban Folklore from the Paperwork Empire.* Detroit, MI: Wayne State University Press.

Dundes, Alan, and Carl R. Pagter. 1991. *Never Try to Teach a Pig to Sing: Still More Urban Folklore from the Paperwork Empire.* Detroit, MI: Wayne State University Press.

Dundes, Alan, and Carl R. Pagter. 1996. *Sometimes the Dragon Wins: Yet More Urban Folklore form the Paperwork Empire.* Syracuse, NY: Syracuse University Press.

Dundes, Lauren, Michael B. Streiff, and Alan Dundes. 1999. "'When You Hear Hoofbeats, Think Horses, Not Zebras': A Folk Medical Diagnostic Proverb." *Proverbium*, 16: 95–103.

Estajl, Azam, and Fakhteh Nakhavali. 2011. "Semantic Derogation in Persian Animal Proverbs." *Theory and Practice in Language Studies*, 1, no. 9: 1213–1217.

Holandi, Rayna. 2011. "Language Symbolism in Animalistic Phraseology (a Contrastive Study on English and Bulgarian)." *Linguo-Cultural Competence and Phraseological Motivation.* Eds. Antonio Pamies [Bertrán] and Dmitrij Dobrovol'skij. Baltmannsweiler: Schneider Verlag Hohengehren, 255–270.

Honeck, Richard P., and Jeffrey Welge. 1997. "Creation of Proverbial Wisdom in the Laboratory." *Journal of Psycholinguistic Research*, 26: 605–629.

Köhler, Carl Sylvio. 1881. *Das Tierleben im Sprichwort der Griechen und Römer. Nach Quellen und Stellen in Parallele mit dem deutschen Sprichwort herausgegeben.* Leipzig: Fernau. Rpt. Hildesheim: Georg Olms, 1967.

Krikmann, Arvo. 2001. "Proverbs on Animal Identity: Typological Memoirs." *Folklore* (Tartu), 17: 7–84.

Liu, Jianwen. 2013. "A Comparative Study of English and Chinese Animal Proverbs— From the Perspective of Metaphors." *Theory and Practice in Language Studies*, 3, no. 10: 1844–1849.

Mahoney, Dennis F. 2009. "'The Bird and the Fish Can Fall in Love ...': Proverbs and Anti-Proverbs as Variations on the Theme of Racial and Cultural Intermingling." *The Proverbial "Pied Piper." A Festschrift Volume of Essays in Honor of Wolfgang Mieder on the Occasion of His Sixty-Fifth Birthday* Ed. Kevin J. McKenna. New York: Peter Lang, 245–256.

Martinez Blanco, Xulián, and Serxio Veiga Alonso. 2010. "Fraseoloxía galega de peixes e outros animals mariños." *Cadernos de fraseoloxía galega*, 12: 155–173.

Mazhitaeva, Shara, and Zhanar Omasheva. 2013. "Polysemantics of Zoomorphic Images in Proverbs and Sayings of the English and Kazakh Languages." *European Researcher*, 58, no. 9: 2247–2251. (In Russian.)

Meisser, Ulrich M. 1969. "Tiersprichwörter und Verhaltensforschung. Zur gegen- seitigen Erhellung von didactischer Literatur und Naturwissenschaft." *Studium Generale*, 22: 861–889.

Mieder, Wolfgang. 1989. *American Proverbs. A Study of Texts and Contexts.* Bern: Peter Lang.

Mieder, Wolfgang. 2004. *Proverbs. A Handbook.* Westport, CT: Greenwood Press.

Mieder, Wolfgang. 2009a. *International Bibliography of Paremiology and Phraseology.* 2 vols. Berlin: Walter de Gruyter.

Mieder, Wolfgang. 2009b. *"Yes We Can". Barack Obama's Proverbial Rhetoric.* New York: Peter Lang.

Mieder, Wolfgang. 2012. "'Thinking Outside the Box': Origin, Nature, and Meaning of Modern Anglo-American Proverbs." *Proverbium*, 29: 137–196.

Mieder, Wolfgang. 2014a.*"All Men and Women Are Created Equal". Elizabeth Cady Stanton's and Susan B. Anthony's Proverbial Rhetoric Promoting Women's Rights.* New York: Peter Lang.

Mieder, Wolfgang. 2014b. "'You Have to Kiss a Lot of Frogs (Toads) Before You Meet Your Handsome Prince': From Fairy-Tale Motif to Modern Proverb." *Marvels & Tales: Journal of Fairy-Tale Studies*, 28: 104–126.

Mieder, Wolfgang. 2015a. "'All Men Are Created Equal'. From Democratic Claim to Proverbial Game." *Scientific Newsletter. Series: Modern Linguistic and Methodical-and- Didactic Researches (Voronezh State University of Architecture and Civil Engineering, Voronezh, Russia*, no volume given, no. 1: 10–37.

Mieder, Wolfgang. 2015b. *"Different Strokes for Different Folks". 1250 authentisch ameri- kanische Sprichwörter.* Bochum: Nobert Brockmeyer.

Mieder, Wolfgang. 2015c. "Origin of Proverbs." *Introduction to Paremiology. A Comprehensive Guide to Proverb Studies*. Eds.Hrisztalina Hrisztova-Gotthardt and Melita Aleksa Varga. Berlin: Walter de Gruyter, 28–48.

Mieder, Wolfgang, Stewart A. Kingsbury, and Kelsie B. Harder. 1992. *A Dictionary of American Proverbs*. New York: Oxford University Press.

Mussner, Marlene. 2012. *Jedem Tierchen sein Pläsierchen. Phraseme mit Tierbezeichnungen im Komponentenbestand im Vergleich zwischen den Sprachen Deutsch, Französisch und Italienisch*. Frankfurt am Main: Peter Lang.

Mussner, Marlene. 2013. "Sprichwörter mit Tierbezeichnungen im Komponentenbestand im Vergleich zwischen den Sprachen Deutsch, Französisch und Italienisch und im Vergleich zu anderen satzwertigen Phraseologismen." *Parémiologie. Proverbes et formes voisines*. Eds. Jean-Michel Benayoun, Natalie Kübler, and Jean-Philippe Zouogbo. Sainte Gemme: Presses Universitaires de Sainte Gemme, III, 65–80.

Nuessel, Frank. 2010. "Animals in Spanish Proverbial Language." *Proverbium*, 27: 221–244.

Pacheco Carpio, Carmen Rosa, Juan Silvio Cabrera Albert, and Rafael Cabrera Cabrera, 2015. "La representación de los animales en el sistema fraseológico de la variedad cubana del español." *Paremia*, 24: 191–200.

Pamies Bertrán, Antonio. 2011. "Zoo-Symbolism and Metaphoric Competence." *Focal Issues of Phraseological Studies*. Ed. Joanna Szerszunowicz et al. Białystok: University of Białystok Publishing House, 291–314.

Piñel López, Rosa María. 1999. "El animal en el refrán, reflejo de una cultura: Estudio contrastivo alemán-español." *Paremia*, 8: 411–416.

Pinheiro Pereira, Fausto. 2013. "The Good and Bad Animals in Japanese and Brazilian Proverbs." *Research on Phraseology Across Continents*. Ed. Joanna Szerszunowicz et al. Białystok: University of Białystok Publishing House, 278–290.

Prelutsky, Jack. 1990. *Something Big Has Been Here. Poems*. New York: Greenwillow Books.

Preußer, Ulrike. 2003. *"Warum die Hündin die Hosen an und Mutter Luchs alle Pfoten voll zu tun hat": Vorkommen und Verwendung von Phraseologismen in der populärwissenschaftlichen Literatur am Beispiel der Verhaltensforschung*. Baltmannsweiler: Schneider Verlag Hohengehren.

Rashidi, Nasser, and Hadis Ghaedi. 2013. "Contrastive Discourse Analysis of Persian and English Animal Proverbs." *Babel*, 59: 1–24.

Santiago Álvarez, Cándido. 2014. "La presencia de animales invertebrados en las paremias españolas." *Paremia*, 23: 121–133.

Schnoor, Franziska. 2007. "Octopuses, Foxes and Hares: Animals in Early Modern Latin and German Proverbs." *Early Modern Zoology. The Construction of Animals in Science, Literature and the Visual Arts*. Eds. Karl A.E. Enenkel and Paul J. Smith. Leiden: Brill, 529–545.

Sobieski, Janet, and Wolfgang Mieder (eds.). 2005. *"So Many Heads, So Many Wits". An Anthology of English Proverb Poetry*. Burlington, VT: The University of Vermont.

Suárez, Adriana Yamile. 2015. "Algunas metáforas de animales en el habla bogotana." *Paremia*, 24: 221–228.

Stypa, Hanna. 2014. *Zoologismen im Deutschen und ihre polnischen Entsprechungen.* Bydgoszcz: Wydawnictwo Uniwersytetu Kazimierza Wielkiego Bydgoszcz.

Szreiber, Marta. 2012. "Tiernamen als Komponenten der Bildlichkeit im Deutschen und Polnischen. Phraseologismen bei der Übermittlung von Gedanken und Gefühlen." *Fragen der Phraseologie, Lexikologie und Syntax.* Ed. Hanna Biaduń-Grabarek. Frankfurt am Main: Peter Lang, 109–120.

Thiele, Johannes. 1997. " 'Buey viejo, surco derecho'—'Alte Esel wissen viel' oder: Die Rollenverteilung in der Tiersymbolik in Redensarten und Sprichwörtern." *Über Texte: Festschrift für Karl-Ludwig Selig.* Eds. Peter-Eckhard Knabe and J. Thiele. Tübingen: Stauffenberg, 255–261.

Velasco Menéndez, Josefina. 2008. "Clasificación léxico-gramatical de las unidades fraseológicas deanimalísticas de la lengua rusa." *Colocaciones y fraseología en los diccionarios.* Ed. Carmen Mellado Blanco. Frankfurt am Main: Peter Lang, 181–192.

Ward, Donald. 1987. "The Wolf: Proverbial Ambivalence." *Proverbium,* 4, 211–224.

Chapter Nine

"Love Is Just a Four-Letter Word"

Sexuality and Scatology in Modern American Proverbs

Looking at hundreds of proverb collections, one might well get the impression that the folk has no so-called "dirty" proverbs belonging to the realms of obscenity, sexuality, and scatology. Even though diligent paremiographers usually have included at least some such proverbs, they have in general been reluctant to collect them or their publishers refused to put them into print. And yet, some specialized collections were published separately from standard proverb dictionaries. Thus Ignaz Bernstein in Poland followed his voluminous collection *Jüdische Sprichwörter und Redensarten* (1908) up with a much smaller compendium of *Proverbia Judaeorum Erotica et Turpia. Jüdische Sprichwörter erotischen und rustikalen Inhalts* (1918). And Edwin Miller Fogel in the United States augmented his valuable dialect collection *Proverbs of the Pennsylvania Germans* (1929) with a privately distributed *Supplement to Proverbs o the Pennsylvania Germans* (1929) which I included in my new edition of this significant work in 1995. Other smaller collections of obscene proverbs, proverbial expressions, and wellerisms have appeared in books, journals (Broek 2002, Keller 1910, McKenzie 1992, Richter 1993, Schmidt 1967), and above all in three serial publications dedicated to taboo folkloric texts, namely ten volumes of *Anthropophyteia* (1904–1913), 12 volumes of *Kryptadia* (1883–1911), and thirteen volumes of *Maledicta: The International Journal of Verbal Aggression* (1977–2004, Aman 1996). Naturally, scholars have also occupied themselves with these elusive proverbial materials, as can be seen from a number of studies about African, Arabic, English, German, Jewish, Slavic, and Spanish proverbs (Englisch 1928, Garcia de Mesa 1999, Grzybek 1999, Krauss 1909, Mieder 1982, Peek 1995, Rudeck 1905, Webster 1982).

In any case, when Charles Clay Doyle, Fred R. Shapiro, and I started our work together on the first *Dictionary of Modern Proverbs* (2012), we made a conscious decision to include suggestive or obscene proverbs of which some are rather explicit while others are metaphorical and figurative to the point that many native speakers might have difficulty understanding their sexual and frequently anti-feminist and down-right aggressive messages (Doyle 1996). But the fact remains that such proverbs have always existed and that new ones continue to be created. In fact, our collection of modern proverbs, that is proverbs coined after the year 1900, includes about 110 sexual and scatological proverbs or about 6.8% of the total of 1617 registered proverbs (1422 in the dictionary and 195 in the three supplements [S1, S2, S3] edited by Doyle and Mieder in 2016, 2018, and 2020). Whether we like it or not, these proverbs are part and parcel of the proverbial speech, even if many of them are not necessarily uttered in polite speech and serious literature. These proverbs are part of the world of colloquial language, slang, graffiti, latrinalia, and the so-called "vulgar tongue" (Dundes 1966, Reisner 1971, Nierenberg 1983), with Francis Grose's *Classical Dictionary of the Vulgar Tongue* (1785) in the eighteenth century having set the stage for an impressive tradition of compendia dealing with obscenities of the underworld and "upperworld". Proverbs deal with all aspects of life, and they certainly have always commented on erotic or vulgar matters. It should then not be surprising that in the modern age with its much greater openness towards and awareness of sexuality in particular (Tóthné Litovkina 1999b), new proverbs with at times rather offensive and vulgar content have gained currency. These proverbs, whether as literal or figurative texts, are observations and generalizations about modern existence couched in sexual or scatological language (Mieder 2012: 182–186).

To be sure, proverbs have never been particularly saccharine or romantic, but there are at least a few modern proverbs that deal with beauty and love without any sexual implications (Tóthné Litovkina and Csábi 2002). At times the new proverbs have their start as anti-proverbs as is the case with "Beauty does not buy happiness" (1989, 16; two such numbers refer to the first recorded reference of the proverb and the page of its appearance in the *Dictionary of Modern Proverbs*) that is based on such older proverbs as "Money can't buy happiness" and "Money can't buy love" with the latter having been reborn so to speak by way of the Beatles song "Can't Buy Me Love" (1964) with its refrain "For money can't buy me love". In a similar way, the insightful proverb "Beauty is only skin" (1963, 17) with the meaning that being a good person is more important than looks, is an anti-proverb of the seventeenth-century proverb "Beauty is only skin deep". In any case, there is a price to pay for outside beauty, for "No beauty without pain" (1987, 17). The same observation was expressed ten years earlier in the similar three-word proverb "Beauty is pain" (1978, 17). Despite its conciseness or perhaps because of it, the proverb has two different meanings. On the one hand it expresses the sense that the acquisition and maintenance of physical (especially feminine) beauty requires the endurance of (or obliviousness to) pain. But in other contexts it can mean that a person's beauty—beauty of a more general "esthetic" kind—imparts pain to someone else. And here is yet another quite recent "beauty"-proverb that might well be an enlarged anti-proverb to "Beauty opens unlocked doors", namely "Beauty may open doors but only virtue enters" (2000, 17). Its message is a bit surprising in that it is rather didactic if not puritan in nature, something that is not necessarily prevalent in modern proverbs.

In this regard the proverb "Every beauty needs her beast" (1973, 17) with its allusion to the common title or plot of the international folktale cycle "Beauty and the Beast" is considerably more suggestive since it brings erotic encounters into play. Also alluding to this folk narrative cycle is the proverb "You have to kiss a lot of frogs before you find a prince" (1976, 89) that is not a short reduction of the fairy tale, as has repeatedly been suggested (Mieder 2014). Speaking of kisses, there is also the proverb "A kiss is just a kiss" (1931, 133) that has its origin, as many other modern proverbs do, in a popular song. In this case it started with the lyrics of the song "As Time Goes By" (1931) by Herman Hupfeld (in the musical *Everybody's Welcome*) that contains the lines "A kiss is still a kiss, / A sigh is just a sigh". They entered oral tradition in the conflated form of "A kiss is just a kiss" that became even more popular as the theme song of the BBC television series *As Time Goes By* (1992–2005) starring Judi Dench and Geoffrey Palmer.

Unfortunately finding the right partner is as difficult today as it has always been, even though the proverb "Everyone finds someone" (1943, 77) wants to put a positive spin on this. And since there are proverbs for every human predicament, there is also the proverb "All the good ones are (already) taken (married)" (1935, 248) to express the situation when no available partner can be found. Most often the proverb expresses the perceived difficulty of a person's—usually a woman's—finding a suitable companion or spouse. All of this gets even more complex when the two possible partners are not of the same religious or ethnic background. This is metaphorically expressed in the interrogative proverb "A bird may love a fish, but where would they live?" (1964, 21) that had its start in Joseph Stein's play *Fiddler on the Roof* (1964): "As the good book says, 'Each shall seek his own kind.' Which, translated, means, 'A bird may love a fish, but where would they build a home together?'" (Mahoney 2009).

As is the case with traditional proverbs in various languages and cultures (Mieder 1986, Mieder, Kingsbury, and Harder, 1992, Speake 2015), modern proverbs also contain plenty of wisdom about love as such. Of special interest are the 1967 lyrics of the song "All You Need Is Love" by John Lennon of the Beatles that do not necessarily speak of love between two people but more generally about the love for what life presents in various ways:

> There's nothing you can do that can't be done
> Nothing you can sing that can't be sung
> Nothing you can say, but you can learn how to play the game
> It's easy

Nothing you can make that can't be made
No one you can save that can't be saved
Nothing you can do, but you can learn how to be you in time
It's easy
    All you need is love
    All you need is love
    All you need is love, love
    Love is all you need

A good piece of advice is also "If you love something, let it go; if it comes back to you, it is yours" (1972, 151) that argues against being overly possessive of an object and by extension perhaps also of a person. Equally uplifting is the somewhat older "It takes a lot (heap) of living (loving) to make a house a home" (1916, 151) that originated with Edgar A. Guest's poem "Home" (1916) and that is today usually cited in the variant with "loving". The shorter proverb "Love is where you find it" (1938, 152) that might well be an anti-proverb of the older "Gold is where you find it" expresses a similar thought. But then there is also "Love it or leave it" (1901, 152) that originally meant that one should like one's job or leave it. More recently, the proverb usually occurs as a jingoistic slogan, especially by somewhat chauvinistic Americans. Speaking of slogans, the proverb "Make love, not war" (1965, 152) comes to mind as a powerful anti-war statement. Of more recent coinage is "Love trumps hate" (1996, S2, 30–31), a proverb which, with the election of Donald Trump as President of the United States in 2016, has acquired a special, satiric application.

Here are three more "love"-proverbs that actually speak of love between two people, albeit not in a very romantic way. Thus the proverb "Love is but a four-letter word" (1937, 151) is over eighty years old, but it gained special currency through Bob Dylan's 1967 song with that title and refrain (famously recorded by Joan Baez):

Seems like only yesterday
I left my mind behind
Down in the Gypsy Cafe
With a friend of a friend of mine
She sat with a baby heavy on her knee
Yet spoke of life most free from slavery

With eyes that showed no trace of misery
A phrase in connection first with she [her] I heard
That love is just a four-letter word

Obviously, this relationship did not work out as expressed in stating that "love" is just a word with four letters and not much meaning. This brings to mind a proverbial line out of Erich Segal's best-selling novel *Love Story* (1970): "Love means never having to say you're sorry" (1970, 152). Once its motion picture was released in the same year, this statement became incredibly popular as positive advice for a humane relationship. Finally, there is yet another Beatles song by John Lennon and Paul McCartney with the appropriate title "The End" (1969)

Oh yeah, all right
Are you going to be in my dreams
Tonight?

And in the end
The love you take
Is equal to the love you make
        Love you, love you

The proverb "The love you take is equal to the love you make" (1969, 152) clearly calls for an equal give and take or mutual, respectful, and yes, romantic love.

However, life together, particularly in a marriage, is unfortunately not always in accord with this wisdom. In capitalistic societies with the emphasis on wealth and materialistic possessions it is no surprise that cautionary proverbs warn against marrying for money. It is of interest to note that in the following two proverbs there is no gender differentiation, indicating that there will most likely be problems in "money"-marriages for both men and women:

Those who marry for money earn it. (1903, 170)
Never marry for money; it's cheaper to borrow it. (1927, 170)

Regarding marriage in general, it should be noted that the wise proverb "Marriage is a journey, not a destination" (1943, 163) follows the prevalent structure "X is a journey, not a destination" of such slightly older proverbs as "Success is a journey, not a destination" (1933, 244), "Happiness is a journey, not a destination" (1937, 116), and "Life is a journey, not a destination" (1941, 142; Mieder 2018). This shows that modern proverbs too are based on existing or new structures that help to spread them as easily recallable truths. Yet while this proverb remains value-neutral about marriage by simply implying that this institution is ever evolving, other "marriage"-proverbs have a more cynical view in light of the fact that the grass often looks greener on the other side of the fence, to wit "Just because you're married doesn't mean you're blind" (1961, 163). The proverb "Absence makes the heart go wander" (1908, 1), basically an anti-proverb of the positive "Absence makes the heart grow fonder" from the eighteenth century, expresses a similar thought, and the Bible proverb "Love thy neighbor as thyself" (Gal. 5:14) has mutated into the anti-proverb "Love thy neighbor, but don't get caught" (1967, 177) to comment ironically on extra-marital relationships that have increased in more promiscuous times (Litovkina 2011).

There is even this upsetting but most likely true proverb "The wife is (always) the last to know (hear, find out)" (1901, 275). It is conceivable that this proverb derived from the complementary (and considerably older) "The husband (cuckold) is always the last to know," but the "wife" form seems to occur more prevalently in recent decades. This is bad enough, but there are two despicable proverbs that, while actually stating that a husband is faithful to his wife, use metaphors that somehow reduce her to an animal or a piece of meat:

> Why buy milk when a cow is so cheap (when you've got a cow at home)? (1957, 166)
>> The proverb probably originated as an anti-proverb responding to the anti-marriage saying "Why buy the cow when you can get milk for free?"
> Why go out for hamburger, when you can get steak at home? (1971, 114)
>> Often, in many variants, it is attributed to the actor Paul Newman, explaining his long and faithful marriage to Joanne Woodward.

Even if Paul Newman uttered these words with complimentary humor, they caught on and as a proverb are clearly demeaning and insulting to women.

Little wonder that early in the twentieth century two related proverbs came into existence by way of the song "A Man without a Woman" that put such chauvinistic men into their place by metaphorically declaring that men really can't function without women: "A man without a woman is like a ship without a sail" (1909, 160) and "A man without a woman is like a fish without a tail" (1909, 159). Building on the same proverbial structure, the Australian journalist, educator, and politician Irina Dunn and not the American feminist Gloria Steinem, as has so often been asserted, in 1970 came up with the ridiculous but liberating proverb "A woman without a man is like a fish without a bicycle" (1976, 279). Perhaps it was based on the two "man" proverbs just mentioned, but it might also be an anti-proverb patterned after the much older proverb "A woman without a man is like a handle without a pan" (or other old similes suggesting uselessness or absurdity). And the beat goes on, for by now both men and women have created new anti-proverbs to these formulations that have become proverbial, to wit "A man without a woman is like a fish without a bicycle" (1983, 159) and "A woman without a man is like a fish without a net (A woman needs a man like a fish needs a net" (1993, 280). This last proverb wins the price from a feminist point of view. Clearly, it is based on "A woman without a man is like a fish without a bicycle", but here the man is not just an absurd irrelevancy to a woman but an actual impediment to her success or happiness, even a danger to her. Of course, it was also feminism that came up with an anti-proverb to the seventeenth-century proverb "A miss is as good as a mile", as can be seen in the *Chicago Daily Tribune* of May 25, 1942: "Now that women are to be inducted into the army we may revise the old saying to read, 'A miss is as good as a male'" (1942, 175). Once the term "ms." was invented in the United State to refer to an adult unmarried or married woman, yet another new proverb was created in 1973: "A ms. is as good as a male"—a truly amazing claim of gender equality (Tóthné Litovkina 1999a).

Unfortunately, sexism continues to exist in modern proverbs as can be seen from the anti-feminist proverb "A woman should be (kept) barefoot and pregnant (barefoot, pregnant, and in the kitchen)" (1947, 279). To combat such offensive statements, women have come up with proverbs that touch males where it hurts, that is, questioning their masculinity and ability to do much of anything well: "Men are only good for one thing" (1954, 157). It barely requires Sigmund Freud to realize that men are at least good enough for the sexual act as far as women are concerned. But hold your proverbial horses, since a relatively recent anti-proverb has been coined that is directed against men's very own sexual abilities: "Men are only good for one thing— and sometimes they aren't even good for that" (1994, 157). That is indeed a great example for proverbial indirection where the issue at hand is not really mentioned but everybody knows what is being said. This proverb is most likely used by women among women ridiculing men and having some good sexually implied fun with it. This can be seen in this reference from *The Age [Melbourne, Australia]* of August 29, 1994: "'You know girls, men are only good for one thing,' said Sandy 'Pepa' Denton. (Much whooping from the crowd.) 'And sometimes they're not even good for that'."

Be that as it may, this type of talk will conjure up thoughts or comments about the penis. While the male organ has not been prevalent in traditional western proverb collections, it as well as testicles and the vagina appear in African proverbs, for example, quite naturally (Amali 2001, Ezeh 2013, Nwachukwu-Agbada 1988, Ojoade 1983, Owomoyela 1972). Many English-speaking people will not even think of testicles in the following proverb that uses the slang term "balls" instead: "Grab them (If you've got them) by the balls, their hearts and minds will follow" (1967, 12). The proverb has been attributed to former President Lyndon Johnson, who was known for using crass language, and it came into being during the Vietnam War when it was hoped that the sign of force would win the hearts and minds of the Vietnamese. The proverb in its entirety is not employed very frequently, but the proverbial phrase "to grab someone by the balls" with the meaning of taking solid control of someone, is often heard in colloquial use.

Regarding the penis, there are two rather obscene proverbs used by men primarily to put down other men by questioning their penis size, that is, their masculinity and sexual prowess: "Big car, small dick" (1991, 33) and "Big mouth, small pecker (dick, prick)" (1993, 173). These proverbs and their variants are studies in the slang terms for "penis", and they serve as aggressive verbal put-downs of other men. The penis can even be termed a "pen" as in the proverb "Don't dip your pen in the company ink (inkwell)" (1979, 193). Sure, the proverb can simply imply that one should not let personal matters interfere with one's professional work, but a little bit of Freudian psychology will show that it can also mean that it is best not to let sexual affairs take place at work. This type of indirection will be seen in many of the proverbs to be discussed now that doubtlessly deal with sexual matters.

Continuing with the discussion of the prevalence of the penis in sexually oriented modern proverbs, it must be pointed out that the word "penis" itself is not necessarily stated but certainly implied by various slang expressions, to wit the "meat" designation in the proverb "Don't let your meat loaf" (1969, 164). The proverb advises against sexual inactivity and there is an additional pun involved in that "meat loaf" is actually a dish of ground meat mixed with such ingredients as bread and seasonings and molded in the shape of a loaf of bread. The proverb is usually cited in a humorous way as a parting statement by one male to another, as for example "I'll be seeing you, take it easy, but don't let your meat loaf either." But there is also the proverb "It's not the meat, it's the motion" (1951, 165) that states metaphorically that when it comes to sexual satisfaction, penis size doesn't matter, but intercourse technique does. The proverb "It's not what you've got, it's what you do with it" (1934, 96) states the same idea without actually referring to the penis. And the proverb "It's not the size of the boat (ship) but the motion of the ocean (that matters)" (1968, 232) clearly also belongs to this group with its implicit metaphor commenting on the male proficiency in satisfying a woman even with a somewhat "underendowed" penis.

This leads to the proverb "Size doesn't matter (it's what you do with it, it's how you use it)" (1903, 233) that has been recorded as early as 1903 in a medical journal. It is a clear indication that penis size is of interest and concern, as the following references from our *Dictionary of Modern Proverbs* illustrate:

> 1903 J. L. Sammons, "Sexual Sense" (letter to the editor), *Medical World* 21: 21: "... [A]s for the sexual act, the size of the penis has not much to do with it; the pleasure derived from the act does not depend on the size. I know

a family of a father and three sons, and there is not a penis in the lot that will pass for more than three inches during erection; and they and their wives seem to be happy, and each has a large family." 1952 Frank S. Caprio, *The Adequate Male* (New York: Medical Research) 52: "He [a patient] was told that a woman's gratification is not entirely dependent upon the size of the penis, but rather on the technique of lovemaking." 1963 Maxine Davis, *Sexual Responsibility in Marriage* (New York: Dial) 129: "The size of the penis has nothing whatever to do with a husband's ability to satisfy his wife." 1964 Phyllis Kronhausen and Eberhard Kronhausen, *The Sexually Responsive Woman* (New York: Grove) 75 (quoting a therapy client): "Someone said the *size* doesn't matter, but it certainly seems to matter to *me*. The times I came nearest to orgasm were all with men who were rather well endowed" (italics as shown). 1979 Lorna J. Sarrel and Philip M. Sarrel, *Sexual Unfolding* (Boston: Little, Brown) 197–98: "Until they are examined, some men can say to themselves, 'They may say penis size doesn't matter, but they haven't seen how small mine is!'" 1980 Jerry Rubin and Mimi Leonard, *War between the Sheets* (New York: Richard Marek) 110: "Many other women sincerely do not care about penis size. They have done market research and concluded, in the words of a woman from Santa Barbara, 'Size doesn't matter.'" 1983 Cynthia Heimel, *Sex Tips for Girls* (New York: Simon & Schuster) 187: "Stop any girl on the street and ask her if she cares if a man is well hung, and she will look at you aghast. 'Of course not,' she'll say." 1998 Terry Kelley, *Don't Put Socks on the Hippopotamus* (Brookfield VT: Gower) 145: "Rules of business life no. 50 / Size doesn't matter—it's how you use it that counts." 1999 Tess Gerritsen, *Gravity* (New York: Simon & Schuster) 306: "He gazed at the rocket, a snub-nosed blip on the horizon. 'From this far away, she's [!] not much to look at, is she? So small.' ... 'Well, you know what they say, Mr. Rashad. It's not the size that matters. It's what you do with it.'" *YBQ* Modern Proverbs (86). Of course, the locution "Size doesn't matter" has had older and other uses, but as a current proverb, it most often refers to—or at least glances jokingly at—the concept that penis size is irrelevant *per se* to female sexual gratification. Nowadays, commonly, the use of the expression in other connections will evoke snickers on account of its perceived sexual allusiveness—intended or not. (Doyle, Mieder, and Shapiro 2012: 233)

And yet, as one would expect and as expressed in one of the references cited above, there is now also the emphatic counter-proverb "Size does matter" (1964, 232), arguing that penis size can be relevant when it comes to sexual satisfaction. Be that as it may, what is of importance with these proverbs around the penis is that people have crystallized these sexual matters into proverbs that allow by way of indirection to comment on such matters without using sexually explicit vocabulary.

If one senses a certain preoccupation with "penis" matters, it will come as no surprise that various aspects of "sex" play a major role in modern proverbs. The modern age seems obsessed with sexual talk and information in all modes of communication, notably in the printed mass media, films, advertising, the internet, etc. No wonder that the two-word slogan turned proverb "Sex sells" (1926, 226) turned up almost a hundred years ago. Many years later, about a decade ago, the proverb "If it exists, there is porn of it" (2008, 204) appeared in the media and the internet as a clear indication that this obsession with sex also leads to the spread of pornography. It seems as if everybody talks or writes about sex or sexual experiences with the latter at times being somewhat exaggerated, thus the proverb "Everybody lies about sex" (1973, 226). Of course, the proverb usually refers to boasts about one's own sexual experience or prowess, not to misinformation such as might be conveyed to children by parents or peers. It obviously also does not apply to the medical profession or professional therapists.

What then does the common folk think about sexual activities? The following proverbs have been coined during the past fifty years, indicating that there is much more openness about this matter. One proverb with two variants clearly states that "Bad sex is better than no sex (Any sex is better than no sex, The only bad sex is no sex)" (1969, 226). But there is also the anti-proverb "No sex is better than bad sex" (1984, 226) that has been attributed to the Australian feminist Germaine Greer and which might be interpreted as woman's response to the (presumably) male "Bad sex is better than no sex". Of course, there is also the proverb declaring that "There is no such thing as (You can't have) too much sex" (1961, 254) patterned after the older proverb "There's no such thing as too much money" and other proverbs following the proverbial structure of "There is no such thing as ..." And sure enough, there is a second sex-related proverb espousing that "There is no such thing as bad sex (a bad fuck, a bad piece)" (1971, 253). In one of the variants the word "piece" is used in the slang sense of "woman considered sexually" or "sex act". It is crude enough, and that is most certainly also the case with the "fuck" variant.

With this these deliberations reach a number of modern proverbs that should not but unfortunately do exist despite their obvious disrespectful, aggressive, and violent nature. As one would expect, the word "fuck" with its ever wider currency in colloquial language is prevalent in these texts (Sheidlower 1995):

> Close (Shut) your eyes and think of England (the Empire, the queen, Old Glory, etc.) Put a flag over her head (face) and fuck for Old Glory. (1943, 70)
>> The proverb itself is used by women while the variant is employed by men. Both express the situation of intercourse with an undesirable partner.
> You don't fuck the face. (1984, 72)
>> Used by men about a woman with a good shape but an unattractive face.
> Fuck them and forget them. (1922, 89)
>> Referring to sex without any emotional involvement.

The proverb "Won't tell, won't swell, grateful as hell" (1953, 251) is employed by men who prefer women over forty because they will not talk about casual sex, they will not get pregnant, and they are glad to have sex at all. It is another telling example of men treating women as sex objects in a despicable and disrespectful way (Arora 1993, Samper 1997). This is also true for an innovative version of the modern proverb "There is no such thing as a free ride" (1949, 253) that first appeared as a bumper sticker as "Gas, grass, or ass: Nobody rides for free" (1978, 94). This seems to be a message for female hitch-hikers who, if they want to get a ride in a car, will have to pay for gas, provide some dope, or a "piece of ass", that is, engage in an act of sexual intercourse. Things are not quite as straight-forward with the proverb "Relax (You might as well relax, You might as well lie back) and enjoy it" (1926). In its short form of "Relax and enjoy it" it is an innocuous statement telling someone to have a good time. However, its slightly longer variants can, unfortunately, be used as inhumane advice to a woman being raped. It all depends in what context and with what function and meaning this proverb is employed. Here then is a convincing example of the polysituativity, polyfunctionality, and polysemanticity of proverbs that are by no means sacrosanct bits of folk wisdom (Mieder 2004: 9).

Some modern sexual proverbs regrettably make a joke out of such serious matters as rape (Assefa 2015, Possa-Mogoera 2019, Yusuf 1998).

This is the case with the proverb "A woman (girl) with her skirt (dress) up can run faster than a man with his pants down" (1955, S2, 43). The proverb's message is the ludicrous claim that rape is impossible if the woman or girl just runs away or, as is implied, refuse. And as is well known, not even their use of the proverb "No means 'no'" (1980, 179) towards a male aggressor will save them from possible rape. Since about 1980 this proverb refers to the definitiveness of a woman's rebuff of sexual overtures, while the clause is older in other uses (for example, as something a parent might say to a recalcitrant child).

Sexual predators do not stop with attacking mature women but also pursue young inexperienced girls. They have coined proverbs that serve the purpose of justifying their aggressive acts that approach or reach the state of rape. It could be that at times these proverbs are cited as part of sexual humor, but matters are way too serious to condone these proverbial messages. But they exist with enough references found that they had to be included in our *Dictionary of Modern Proverbs* in order to present a complete picture of the Anglo-American proverbs of modernity:

> When they are big enough, they are old enough. (1932, 20)
>> That is, when girls are more or less grown up, they are ready for sexual intercourse.
> Old enough to bleed, old enough to breed. (1971, 22)
>> The "bleed" refers to the beginning of menstruation, and the "breed" once again implies sexual intercourse.
> If she smokes, she pokes. (1996, 235)
>> If a girl is old enough to smoke, she can, according to slang, poke, i.e., have sexual intercourse.
> If there's grass on the field, (you can) play ball. (1998, 111)
>> Here are the references cited in our *Dictionary of Modern Proverbs* to show the sick mentality behind the use of this proverb: 1998 Clive Barker, *Galilee* (New York: HarperCollins) 110: "… Mitchell's taste for girls ran to the barely pubescent. 'If there's grass on the field, play ball, that's what he used to say,' the 'classmate' remembered." 1998 Chris Simunek, *Paradise Burning* (New York: St. Martin's Griffin) 80: "'You see the way she looks at you? What are you, some kind of faggot?' 'She's fifteen, man.' 'If there's grass on the field you can play ball.'" 1998 Tobias Wolff, "You Can't Kill the Rooster," *Esquire* 129, no. 6 (Jun.) 94: "The work puts him

in contact with … men who offer dating advice like 'If she's old enough to bleed, she's old enough to breed' and 'If there's grass on the field, I say it's time to play ball.' " "Grass" refers metaphorically to female pubic hair, and "ball" alludes to testicles with "to ball someone" referring to sexual intercourse. (Doyle, Mieder, and Shapiro 2012: 111). My colleague Prof. Dennis Mahoney is certain that he heard this proverb already in the 1980s, showing that oral use is often earlier than written recordings.

As can be seen, there are numerous slang words for the sexual act with yet another one being "to plow someone". That term appears in another male-produced proverb that reduces women to pleasure fields: "What has been plowed once is easier the second time" (1956, 202). After all of this it comes as a sort of relief to mention the proverbial advice of parents to their young daughters going out on a date: "Keep your dress down and your panties up" (1975, 62). Here are a few telling references from the *Dictionary of Modern Proverbs* that reveal the euphemistic use of this modern proverb:

1975 James P. Comer and Alvin F. Poussaint, *Black Child Care* (New York: Simon & Schuster) 315: "In the past, before dates girls were told 'keep your dress down and your pants up.' … Not only was the advice often ignored, it created much discomfort and contributed to unhealthy attitudes about sex." 1976 Alice Walker, *Meridian* (New York: Harcourt Brace Jovanovich) 53: "When Meridian left the house in the evening with her 'boyfriend' … her mother only cautioned her to 'be sweet.' She did not realize this was a euphemism for 'Keep your panties up and your dress down,' an expression she *had* heard and been puzzled by" (italics as shown). 1980 Dindga McCannon, *Wilhemina Jones, Future Star* (New York: Delecorte) 111: " 'I'll get her back on time,' said Joe politely. 'Well, you better! And you, miss, keep your dress down! And your drawers up!' " Currently, the proverb is often used to epitomize and ridicule the kind of instruction about sexuality that previous generations of parents and teachers offered. (Doyle, Mieder, Shapiro 2012: 62–63)

This is harmless, indirect, metaphorical or euphemistic advice, and with the sex education that students receive at school today, parents most likely use it in somewhat of a humorous way. For their college-age children they might also have the relatively new proverbial advice "No glove, no love" (1982, 99) at hand. This proverb with "glove" being a euphemism for "condom" has become very popular during the past three decades due to the AIDS epidemic as well as sexual promiscuity that demand safe sex practices by all (Mieder 1987). Without condoms or the pill, of course, there is always the chance of an unwanted pregnancy. Not surprisingly, two proverbs have become current dealing with this ever-present matter:

> You can't be (There is no such thing as) a little pregnant. (1942, 206)
>> The proverb does not always refer to pregnancy. It can also serve as a humorous response to someone's nonsensical claim of being partially something or the other.
> Better late than pregnant. (1995, 137)
>> "Late" in this case refers to the late onset of a woman's menstrual period. The proverb originated as an anti-proverb based on "Better late than never."

Senior citizens need not worry about getting pregnant, but two proverbs do exist about sexual activities or desires in older age that are quite civil in their word choices. In fact, they are splendid metaphors leaving things to one's imagination:

> Just because there's snow on the roof doesn't mean that the fire is out inside (there's no fire in the furnace / chimney / kitchen). (1943, 236)
>> Looking at this with Freud's eyes, one can well imagine that men and women can employ one of the variants to signal sexual desire.
> Old rats like cheese too. (1977, 214)
>> This refers to an old person's (usually a man's) sexual desire.

If only sexual matters were always this simple and harmless! Unfortunately, there are also modern proverbs that express sexism and racism in sexual terms usually at the expense of women. One of the most painful new proverbs is doubtlessly "It's (They're) all pink on the inside" (1971, 5) that says that all vaginas and thus all women are alike and serve only to satisfy men's sexual needs. The first of the two references from the *Dictionary of Modern Proverbs* contains racial implications while the second statement makes a joke of this despicable proverb, once again showing that context and intent of usage make a big difference:

1971 Breyten Breytenbach, "Vulture Culture," in *Apartheid: A Collection of Writings on South African Racism*, edited by Alex La Guma (New York: International) 138: "Apartheid is the White man's night. ... What one doesn't see doesn't exist. Also, at night one doesn't balk at the skin deep peculiarities of the girl you sleep with. They are all pink on the inside." 1983 David Allen, "Now Since Fear and Goodness Are Different Things, " *Denver Quarterly* 18, no. 2 (Summer) 55–56: "She lead [*sic*] me by the hand to the bedroom, she lay down, she spread her legs. ... I said, 'They ARE all pink on the inside.' And we laughed" (capitalization as shown). The proverb ungallantly asserts—from the male point of view—the sameness of all women for sexual purposes. (Doyle, Mieder, and Shapiro 2012: 5)

Racial issues and prejudices also come to the fore in the following two modern American proverbs that argue against interracial relationships. They are both about fifty or forty years old, and perhaps the American society has become more open about black and white encounters so that their use is hopefully declining:

> You can't think (talk) black and (if you) sleep white. (1969, 256)
>> This African-American proverb suggests that amorously consorting with a white person will compromise one's psychological or ideological "blackness."
> Once you go black, you'll never go back (Once black, never back). (1978, 22)
>> Initially, the proverb was a stereotypical reference to the supposed superiority of black persons (male and female) in sexual performance. Now the proverb can have wider applications.

There are also two related African-American proverbs that originally praised a particularly dark skin color among African-Americans, to wit "The blacker the berry, the sweeter the juice" (1929, 19) and "The blacker the meat, the sweeter the bone (piece)" (1935, 164). In fact, African-American parents might have uttered them to a child who was concerned about being very black (Prahlad 1996: 209–210). However, among adults, the proverbs also can praise blackness usually in regard to sexual desirability. Thus Zora Neale Hurston, the well-known African-American novelist, writes in her *Jonah's Gourd Vine* (1934) in black speech: "Ah could uh married one uh dem French women but shucks, gimme uh brown skin eve'y time. Blacker de berry sweeter de juice." It does, of course, make a big difference whether a black or a white person uses these proverbs in their sexual connotations.

Finally, there are a few modern proverbs that perhaps are not so obviously sexual in their wording but they are more often than not understood in sexual terms. Thus the proverb "If it feels good, do it" (1968, 75) can refer to a multitude of ventures, but its indirection certainly justifies a sexual implication stating that the sexual revolution has brought with it the idea of doing what one enjoys, including sex. The proverb "If you've got it, flaunt it" (1968, 96) permits a similar multifaceted interpretation with one of them most certainly encouraging younger people in particular to display their sexual appeal by way of outside looks and wear. And then there is also the quite new advertisement slogan "What happens in Las Vegas, stays in Las Vegas" (2002, 137) with which the infamous city of Las Vegas continues to lure visitors to its casinos, shows, bars, tattoo parlors and who knows what else. The "else" might well include sexual encounters by married people who would not want their little secret to get back to their partners at home. So while this proverb started as an innocent slogan, it can be interpreted sexually and so can the many variants of it that are based on the structural formula "What happens at ..., stays at ..." (Bock 2014).

Before turning to the second part of this survey about modern proverbs and scatology, it might be refreshing after this preoccupation with sex and sexuality to mention a proverb from this realm that puts a different spin on this obsession. It is not necessarily widespread in its appearance with its sophisticated vocabulary and the reference to the brain instead of more obvious body parts. Even though the medical wonder of Viagra or Cialis has had its considerable influence on modern sexuality, it still remains true that the mind is part of this game. Sexual prowess and bodily fitness alone will not lead to a healthy and meaningful sex life if emotional love is not involved. But here is the proverb together with the references from our *Dictionary of Modern Proverbs* one more time:

> The most important (The most potent, The most) erogenous zone is the brain (mind). The brain is the most important erogenous zone. (1969, 285)

1969 *New York Times* 7 Dec.: "Sometimes [David] Frost simply manages to bring out somebody in a small way, as when he coaxed out of a shy Raquel Welch ... the notion that 'the mind is the most erogenous zone.'" 1974 *Newsweek* 83, no. 11 (18 Mar.) 43: "There cannot be winners in the battle of erectile tissues. Surely the most erogenous zone in both men and women lies not between the legs but behind the eyes." 1977 *Lawrence [KS] Daily Journal* 24 Oct. ("Ann Landers" advice column): "The most erogenous zone in both male and female is located between the eyebrows and the hairline." 1980 Mike Grace and Joyce Grace, *A Joyful Meeting: Sexuality in Marriage* (St. Paul MN: National Marriage Encounter) 26: "If there is com-petition from other things—distractions, other feelings—foreplay may have no erotic effect. This is why we emphasize that the most important erogenous zone is the brain."

The brain, yes, but what has happened with that brain when it comes to another considerable number of modern proverbs that deal with scatol-ogy? In this regard I remember well a Swiss lexicographer claiming some forty years ago that the word "shit" barely appears in American dictionaries due to the puritan language use in the United States. In a relatively short response in 1978 I proved this assertion wrong (Mieder 1978), and by now there are numerous general but also slang and graf-fiti dictionaries that abound with scatological terms and phrases (Green 2010, Hughes 2006, Kunitskaya-Peterson 1981, McDonald 1988, Spears 1990). But speaking of that infamous four-letter word, it is without doubt one of the most frequently used scatological terms in various lan-guages and cultures throughout the world (Dundes 1984). And there is a relatively new two-word proverb that has reached an incredible fre-quency level throughout the English-speaking world, and yes, includ-ing the United States where it appeared in print at first euphemistically as "Stuff happens" and then found its way more directly expressed into a book as "Shit happens" in 1978 (Rees 2005), as has been established in our *Dictionary of Modern Proverbs* by way of the following references and an explanatory comment:

Shit (Stuff) happens. (1944, 228)
1944 Lee Thayer, *Five Bullets* (New York: Dodd, Mead) 232: "Was it just chance? Is there such a thing as pure chance? As 'Vic and Sade' are wont to say, 'Stuff happens.' Yes. Stuff does happen" ("Vic and Sade" was a comic

radio show popular in the 1930s and 1940s). 1969 Jean Hersey and Robert Hersey, *These Rich Years* (New York: Charles Scribner's Sons) 236: "I always like to remember the simple comment of an intelligent friend of ours in the face of a family crisis that came out of the blue. 'Oh, well, stuff happens,' she said with a sigh as she began to plan the next step ahead." 1978 Wesley Brown, *Tragic Magic* (New York: Random House) 98: "Once you know the reason why shit happens, you shouldn't have to ask the question anymore." 1983 Connie Eble, "UNC-CH Campus Slang— Spring 1983" ([Chapel Hill NC: for the author] Ditto-reproduced): "Shit happens" (saying collected from a student). The proverb commonly expresses a sort of stoic resignation at the vagaries and sorrows of life. Even though the citations for "Stuff happens" antedate ones for "Shit happens," it is not unreasonable to suspect, in some instances at least, that *stuff* represents a euphemistic replacement of *shit—stuff* having been more acceptable in print (and in polite oral discourse as well). The "Shit happens" form achieved notoriety in the 1980s when its appearance on bumper stickers occasioned arrests and criminal prosecutions—giving rise to allusive (anti-proverbial) variants that substituted for *shit* the name of some disliked public figure or group.

By now the proverb has been expanded to "Shit happens, and then you die" (1991, 228), with the second part perhaps being a remnant of the modern proverb "Life is a bitch, and then you die" (1982, 141). Considering the popularity of some of these new proverbs, it is not surprising that such blending takes place. Considerably more crass and disgusting are two proverbs that begin with the same "Life is a ..." pattern, but they then conclude it with a disgusting image: "Life is (like) a shit sandwich (without bread) (and every day we take another bite)" (1966, 143) and "Life is a shit sandwich: the more bread [slang: money] you have, the less shit you eat" (1978, 143). Sticking with the revolting idea of eating feces, the proverb "Don't shit where you eat" (1953, 227) comes to mind. And one can also see something positive in yet another two-word modern proverb that simply declares "Everybody shits (poops)" (1968, 227) even though it is a far cry from the proverb "All men are created equal" in the "Declaration of Independence" from 1776 (Mieder 2019). Another "Don't shit ..." admonition brings to mind the much older proverb "A bird does not foul its own nest" (Kunstmann 1939 [1981]) and also expresses the idea that one should not inflict harm on one's own surroundings: "Don't shit on your own doorstep" (1967, 60). Usually such short proverbs like "Shit rubs off" (1997, 229) are clear enough in their disgusting message, but the proverb "Shit flows (runs, rolls) downhill" (1971, 228) might be a bit unclear to the uninitiated. It suggests that onerous tasks or blame for mistakes will get passed from superiors to underlings. The proverb "You can't kill shit (Shit never dies)" (1997, 229) probably does not present a semantic problem, but it might be of interest to state that its origin is actually the medical profession that refers by it to particularly difficult and demanding patients (Winick 2004). Things are, however, clear about what is meant by the very popular modern proverb "Shit (Piss) or get off the pot" (1935, 204) that is frequently heard at universities in utter frustration because administrators don't seem to make necessary decisions.

Other proverbs based on the word "shit" are so disgusting that they really cannot be used in polite society. Yet they certainly are current orally in groups of men (also women at times) to vent frustrations in a colloquial manner with expressive power to be sure:

> You can't put ten pounds of shit in a five-pound bag. (1980, 204)
> If you stir (up) shit, it will stink (you raise a stink). (1982, 227)
> Same shit, different day (Different day, same shit; New day, same old shit). (1998, 228)

Many of these scatological proverbs do exist in euphemistic variants in order to avoid the offensive "shit" word (Allan and Burridge 1991, Ayto 1993, Enright 1985, Holder 1995, Rawson 1995, Spears 1981). This is well illustrated by the following list of modern proverbs that need no special explanation. Depending in what situation one is, the actual proverb or its euphemistic substitute will be employed. It must, however, not be forgotten that most people will know very well what actual scatological original is meant:

> You can't make chicken salad out of chicken shit (chicken feathers). (1949, S1, 91)
> Ninety percent of everything is shit (crap, crud). (1958, 48)
> You (can) find sympathy between shit (sin) and syphilis (in the dictionary). (1961, S1, 117)

If you lie down with pigs, you get covered with shit (get up smelling bad). (1966, 197)
> The proverb parallels to the older "If you lie down with dogs, you get up with fleas."

Shit (Pee, Spit) in one hand and hope (wish) in the other; see which one fills up first. (1971, 115)

If you sift through enough shit (mud, crap, dirt, mud), you may find gold (a diamond, etc.). (1997, 56)

You can't sprinkle sugar on shit (bullshit) and make (call) it candy (dessert, a treat, etc.). (1999, 235)

The last proverb lists "bullshit" as a variant with "bull" as part of that word dating back to the seventeenth-century slang meaning "non-sense". The added word "shit" intensifies the matter, but strange as it might seem, the "bullshit" term is more acceptable than "shit" in normal conversation. It has also found its way into too modern proverbs, to wit "A little bullshit (bull, exaggeration) goes a long way" (1943, 29) and "Bullshit can get you to the top, but it won't keep you there" (1999, 29). Of course, there is also the word "turd" for feces that is perhaps a bit less offensive than "shit". Be that as it may, two modern proverbs contain it as an absurd metaphor. The proverb "You can't polish (gild) a turd" (1976, 266) deals with the impossibility of changing something absolutely worthless into its opposite, and the proverb "Don't kick a (fresh) turd on a hot day" (1980, 265) even has the distinction that President Harry S. Truman, known for his use of expletives and proverbial language, is supposed to have considered it his philosophy of life. The proverb has, however, not been located in his papers and writings and the Truman designation is most likely apocryphal (Mieder and Bryan 1997).

After these modern proverbs about excrement, urination makes up the second largest group of scatological proverbs. Of special interest is the proverb "If it's yellow, let it mellow; if it's brown, flush it down" (1977, 138) from rural America that is not as old as one would expect. Realizing that many country homes have wells that tend to get low or even dry up in summer time, it came into being as a bit of rhyming advice for economizing on the use of water in a flush toilet. It is often heard in Vermont, and I have used this rule myself when our well ran dry! But speaking of advice, the modern proverb "Don't eat yellow snow" (1971, 296) seems a bit absurd, for who would actually do this since yellow snow in winter land marks the site where someone has urinated. But it is conceivable that innocent children might just be attracted to putting such discolored snow into their mouths. Speaking of urine, there is also the solid advice to people to plan ahead for a time and place to relieve themselves: "Never miss an opportunity to relieve yourself (Never pass up a chance to pee)" (1936, 185). The variant includes the colloquial term "pee" here, but such detail is avoided in the following two proverbs that somewhat euphemistically declare that when nature calls something has to be done about it: "When it's time to go, it's time to go" (1936, 260) and "When you've got to go, you've got to go" (1937, 100). It should be noted that these proverbs, due to their general formulation, do not necessarily imply defecation or urination. However, they usually are used as euphemisms for these matters.

Such indirect references to bodily functions obviously also play into the meaning of two further proverbs with their variants. Knowing that a dog is prone to urinate against a fireplug and that a pigeon in a tree might well defecate on a person, these animal metaphors do not only have euphemistic functions but they also express the vicissitudes of modern life:

> Sometimes (Some days) you're the dog, and sometimes (some days) you're the fireplug (Sometimes you're the fireplug, and sometimes you're the dog). (1989, 59)

> Some days (Sometimes) you're the pigeon, and some (other) days you're the statue. (1993, 198)

Yet proverbs can also express matters more directly by employing the word "piss" that is usually not used in polite parlance. This can be seen from such drastic statements as "Never get into a pissing contest (match) with a skunk" (1943, 198) and "It's better to be pissed off than pissed on" (1974, 198) with the latter often being uttered in response to someone being "pissed off" in the sense of angry or acutely annoyed.

With this said, these deliberations have reached the matter of flatulence. Regarding one of the modern proverbs on this topic, our references in the *Dictionary of Modern Proverbs* reach an amazing level of information that even includes W.H. Auden as being fascinated by this topic, as was Wolfgang Amadeus Mozart at the end of the eighteenth century (Dundes 1984: 65–72, Mieder 2003):

> Nobody minds the smell of his own farts (Everyone likes to smell his own farts; Everyone thinks his own farts smell sweet; Only your own farts smell sweet). (1937, 235)
>> 1937 W. H. Auden, *Letters from Iceland* (New York: Random House) 151 (in a list of Icelandic proverbs): "Every man likes the smell of his own farts." 1968 Frederic Prokosch, *Missolonghi Manuscript* (New York: Farrar, Straus & Giroux) 297: "Human vanity reaches its highest, most idiotic pinnacle in the field of flatulence. Our own farts we accept with composure and sometimes even relish." 1976 Patricia E. Raley, *Making Love* (New York: Dial) 78: "Smell is an important and often unsung sense. Think about your body scents. W. H. Auden once said that everyone loves the smell of his own farts." 1981 James Morrow, *Wine of Violence* (New York: Holt, Rinehart & Winston) 156: "Wouldn't you agree that the average person likes the smell of his own farts far more than is commonly supposed?" 1993 Eric Gabriel Lehman, *Quaspeck* (San Francisco: Mercury House) 145: "He never got to know me as a normal person who eats and sleeps and likes the smell of his own farts." Possibly Auden was an agent in the importation of the saying (if not the concept) into English-speaking tradition (although occasionally it has been identified as a Polish or an Inuit proverb); he included it in the collection that he compiled (along with Louis Kronenberger), the *Faber Book of Aphorisms* (London: Faber & Faber, 1962) 37, there identified as an "Icelandic Proverb," under the heading "Self-Love." Cf. the older "Every man's dung is (smells) sweet to him."

A second proverb is heard among good friends and also teasingly among children when farting has resulted in a bad odor with the one commenting on it being accused of having caused it: "The one who smelt it dealt it" (1971, 185). But all scatological humor aside, the proverb is not appropriate for general social interaction.

The same can be said for the proverb "Opinions are like assholes (armpits)—everybody's got one (and they all stink)" (1972, 185). It can occur, elliptically or allusively, with the first clause alone: "Opinions are like assholes" and probably originated as an anti-proverb based on "Everyone has his own opinion." The anal proverb "The toes you step on today may be attached (connected) to the ass you have to kiss tomorrow" (1999, 261) is also rather direct in its message, although the related proverbial expression "to kiss someone's ass" is heard occasionally in good company. Be that as it may, the proverb expresses a solid warning and unfortunately also considerable wisdom. Which leaves the animal proverb "The sun doesn't shine on (up) the same dog's ass every day" (1976, 246) as a final text. Its somewhat opaque meaning is that one cannot have all the luck every day or that sometimes one wins and sometimes one loses. It too should be used cautiously, since it is not appropriate in all social settings, and yet Bruce Springsteen got away with citing the variant "The sun don't shine on a sleepin' dog's ass" in his proverb song "My Best Was Never Good Enough" (1995, Sobieski and Mieder 2005: 215). One might have thought that proverbs as sanctioned wisdom would not stoop so low, but the language of proverbs has always been part of folk speech that is at least in part informed by vocabulary dealing with sexuality and scatology. When, according to the proverb "Love is just a four-letter word", love is meaningless or even obscene as is the case with such four-letter words like "fuck", "piss", and "shit", then these obscene or vulgar modern proverbs deserve to be studied by paremiologists as "monumenta humana" of life.

Bibliography

This chapter was originally published at Tavira, Portugal, as " 'Love Is Just a Four-Letter Word'. Sexuality and Scatology in Modern Anglo-American Proverbs." *Proceedings of the 13th Interdisciplinary Colloquium on Proverbs, 3rd to 10th November 2019, at Tavira, Portugal.* Eds. Rui J.B. Soares and Outi Lauhakangas. Tavira: Tipografia Tavirense, 2020. in press.

Collections and Dictionaries

Allan, Keith, and Kate Burridge. 1991. *Euphemism & Dysphemism: Language Used as Shield and Weapon.* New York: Oxford University Press.

Aman, Reinhold (ed.). 1996. *Opus Maledictorum: A Book of Bad Words*. New York: Marlowe & Company.

Anthropophyteia. Jahrbücher für Folkloristische Erhebungen und Forschungen zur Entwicklung der geschlechtlichen Moral. 1904–1913. Ed. Friedrich S. Krauss. 10 vols. Leipzig: Ethnologischer Verlag.

Ayto, John. 1993. *Euphemisms*. London: Bloomsbury.

Bernstein, Ignaz. 1908. *Jüdische Sprichwörter und Redensarten*. Warschau: Kauffmann; rpt. edited by Hans Peter Althaus. Hildesheim: Georg Olms, 1969; rpt. again Wiesbaden: Fourier, 1988.

Bernstein, Ignaz. 1918. *Proverbia Judaeorum Erotica et Turpia. Jüdische Sprichwörter erotischen und rustikalen Inhalts*. Als Manuskript gedruckt. Wien and Berlin: R. Löwit; rpt. Haifa: "Renaissance" Publishing, 1971.

Broek, Marinus A. van den. 2002. *Erotisch Spreekwoordenboek. Spreekwoorden en zegswijzen*. Antwerpen: L.J. Veen.

Doyle, Charles Clay, and Wolfgang Mieder. 2016. "*The Dictionary of Modern Proverbs*: A Supplement." *Proverbium*, 33: 85–120.

Doyle, Charles Clay, and Wolfgang Mieder. 2018. "*The Dictionary of Modern Proverbs*: Second Supplement." *Proverbium*, 35: 15–44.

Doyle, Charles Clay, and Wolfgang Mieder. 2020. "*The Dictionary of Modern Proverbs*: Third Supplement." *Proverbium*, 37: 53–86.

Doyle, Charles Clay, Wolfgang Mieder, and Fred R. Shapiro. 2012. *The Dictionary of Modern Proverbs*. New Haven, CT: Yale University Press.

Enright, D.J. (ed.). 1985. *Fair of Speech: The Uses of Euphemism*. Oxford: Oxford University Press.

Green, Edwin Miller. 1929. *Proverbs of the Pennsylvania Germans*. Lancaster, PA: The Pennsylvania-German Society; rpt. edited by Wolfgang Mieder. Bern: Peter Lang, 1995. A small supplement of 8 pages with scatological proverbs was published in the same year and is added to this reprint.

Green, Jonathon. 2010. *Dictionary of Slang*. 3 vols. London: Chambers.

Grose, Francis. *A Classical Dictionary of the Vulgar Tongue*. 1785. London: S. Hooper. Reprint with a preface and "A Sketch of the Life & Works of Francis Grose [1731?–1791]" by Eric Partridge. London: Scholartis Press, 1931. Rpt. New York: Barnes & Noble, 1963; rpt. once again New York: Dorset Press, 1992.

Holder, R.W. 1995. *A Dictionary of Euphemisms*. Oxford: Oxford University Press.

Hughes, Geoffrey. 2006. *An Encyclopedia of Swearing. The Social History of Oaths, Profanity, Foul Language, and Ethnic Slurs in the English-Speaking World*. Armonk, NY: M.E. Sharpe.

Keller, H. von. 1910. "Englisches erotisches und skatologisches Idiotikon." *Anthropophyteia. Jahrbücher für Folkloristische Erhebungen und Forschungen zur Entwicklung der geschlechtlichen Moral*. Ed. Friedrich S. Krauss. Leipzig: Ethnologischer Verlag. VII, 36–39.

Kryptadia. Recueil de documents pour server à l'étude des traditions populaires. 1883–1911. No editor given. 12 vols. Heilbronn: Henninger and Paris H. Welter (vols. 5–12); rpt. Darmstadt: J.G. Bläschke, 1970.

Kunitskaya-Peterson, Christina. 1981. *International Dictionary of Obscenities. A Guide to Dirty Words and Indecent Expressions in Spanish, Italian, French, German, Russian.* Oakland, CA: Scythian Books.

Maledicta. International Journal of Verbal Aggression. 1977–2004. Ed. Reinhold Aman. 13 vols. Waukesha, WI, and Santa Rosa, CA: Maledicta Press.

McDonald, James. 1988. *Dictionary of Obscenity and Taboo.* London: Sphere Books, 1988; rpt. Ware, Hertfordshire: Wordsworth Editions, 1996.

McKenzie, Carol. 1992. *Quotable Sex.* New York: St. Martin's Press.

Mieder, Wolfgang. 1986. *Encyclopedia of World Proverbs.* Englewood Cliffs, NJ: Prentice-Hall.

Mieder, Wolfgang, Stewart A. Kingsbury, and Kelsie B. Harder. 1992. *A Dictionary of American Proverbs.* New York: Oxford University Press.

Rawson, Hugh.1995. *Dictionary of Euphemisms and Other Doubletalk.* New York: Crown Publishers.

Richter, Alan. 1993. *Sexual Slang. A Compendium of Offbeat Words and Colorful Phrases from Shakespeare to Today.* New York: Harper Perennial.

Schmidt, J.E. 1967. *Cyclopedic Lexicon of Sex. Exotic Practices, Expressions, Variations of the Libido.* New York: Brussel & Brussel; rpt. as *Lecher's Lexicon. An A-Z Encyclopedia of Erotic Expressions and Naughty Bits.* New York: Bell Publishing Company, 1984.

Speake, Jennifer. 2015. *Oxford Dictionary of Proverbs.* 6th ed. Oxford: Oxford University Press.

Spears, Richard A. 1981. *Slang and Euphemism. A Dictionary of Oaths, Curses, Insults, Sexual Slang and Metaphor, Racial Slurs, Drug Talk, Homosexual Lingo, and Related Matters.* Middle Village, NY: Jonathan David.

Spears, Richard A. 1990. *Forbidden American English. A Serious Compilation of Taboo American English.* Lincolnwood, IL: National Textbook Company.

Secondary Literature

Amali, Idris O.O. 2001. "Linguistic and Semantic Aspects of Obscene Idoma Proverbs." *Proverbium,* 18: 1–14.

Arora, Shirley L. 1993. "A Woman and a Guitar: Variations on a Folk Metaphor." *Proverbium,* 10: 21–36.

Assefa, Endalew. 2015. "Linguistic Violence against Women as Manifested in Sexist Amharic Proverbs." *Ethnorêma,* 11: 67–94.

Bock, Sheila. 2014. "'What Happens Here, Stays Here': Selling the Untellable in a Tourism Advertising Campaign." *Western Folklore,* 73: 216–234.

Doyle, Charles Clay. 1996. "On 'New' Proverbs and the Conservativeness of Proverb Dictionaries." *Proverbium,* 13: 69–84. Also in *Cognition, Comprehension, and*

Communication: A Decade of North American Proverb Studies (1990–2000). Ed. Wolfgang Mieder. Baltmannsweiler: Schneider Verlag Hohengehren, 2003. 85–98.Dundes, Alan. 1966. "Here I Sit—A Study of American Latrinalia." The Kroeber Anthropological Society Papers, no. 34: 91–105. Also in A. Dundes. The Meaning of Folklore. The Analytical Essays of Alan Dundes. Ed. Simon J. Bronner. Logan, UT: Utah State University Press, 2007. 360–374.

Dundes, Alan. 1984. Life is Like a Chicken Coop Ladder. A Portrait of German Culture through Folklore. New York: Columbia University Press. Also in German as Sie mich auch! Das Hinter-Gründige in der deutschen Psyche. Weinheim: Beltz, 1985.

Englisch, Paul. 1928. "Skatologische Sprichwörter." Das skatologische Element in Literatur, Kunst und Volksleben. Ed. P. Englisch. Stuttgart: Julius Büttmann. 129–137.

Ezeh, Peter-Jazzy. 2013. "In Capsule: Saws and Sex Mores Among the Igbo of Nigeria." Proverbium, 30: 1–18.

García de Mesa, Rafael. 1999. "El componente escatológico y sexual en refranes y dichos populares en un ambiente rural." Paremia, 8: 215–218.

Grzybek, Peter. 1999. "South Slavic Erotic Folklore: Remarks on Traditional Erotic Phraseology from Dalmatia." Semiotische Berichte, 23: 131–154.

Krauss, Friedrich S. 1909. "Erotische Sprichwörter bei den russischen Juden." Zeitschrift für Sexualwissenschaft und Sexualpolitik, 5: 452–466.

Kunstmann, John G. 1939. "The Bird that Fouls Its Nest." Southern Folklore Quarterly, 3: 75–91. Also in The Wisdom of Many. Essays on the Proverb. Eds. Wolfgang Mieder and Alan Dundes. New York: Garland Publishing, 1981. 190–210.

Litovkina, Anna T. 2011. "Sexuality in Anglo-American Anti-proverbs." The Pragmatics of Humour across Discourse Domains. Ed. Marta Dynel. Amsterdam: John Benjamins. 191–213.

Mahoney, Dennis F. 2009. "'The Bird and the Fish Can Fall in Love …': Proverbs and Anti-proverbs as Variations on the Theme of Racial and Cultural Intermingling." The Proverbial "Pied Piper". A Festschrift Volume of Essays in Honor of Wolfgang Mieder on the Occasion of His Sixty-Fifth Birthday. Ed. Kevin J. McKenna. New York: Peter Lang. 245–256.

Mieder, Wolfgang. 1978. "Das Wort 'Shit' und seine lexikographische Erfassung." Sprachspiegel, 34: 76–79.

Mieder, Wolfgang. 1982. "Sexual Content of German Wellerisms." Maledicta, 6: 215–223.

Mieder, Wolfgang. 1987. "'Kondom'—ein altes/neues Wort geht um. Eine etymologische Skizze." Sprachspiegel, 43: 99–108.

Mieder, Wolfgang. 2003. "'Now I Sit Like a Rabbit in the Pepper': Proverbial Language in the Letters of Wolfgang Amadeus Mozart." Journal of Folklore Research, 40: 33–70. Also in W. Mieder, "Proverbs Speak Louder Than Words". Folk Wisdom in Art, Culture, Folklore, History, Literature, and Mass Media. New York: Peter Lang, 2008. 313–348.

Mieder, Wolfgang. 2004. Proverbs. A Handbook. Westport, CT: Greenwood Press. Rpt. New York: Peter Lang, 2012.

Mieder, Wolfgang. 2012. "'Think Outside the Box': Origin, Nature, and Meaning of Modern Anglo-American Proverbs." Proverbium, 29: 137–196.

Mieder, Wolfgang. 2014. "'You Have to Kiss a Lot of Frogs (Toads) Before You Meet Your Handsome Prince': From Fairy-Tale Motif to Modern Proverb." *Marvels & Tales: Journal of Fairy-Tale Studies*, 28: 104–126.

Mieder, Wolfgang. 2018. "'Life Is not a Spectator Sport'. Proverbial Emotions about Modern Life." *Emotsional'naia sfera cheloveka v iazyke i kommunikatsii: Sinkhroniia i diakhroniia*. Ed. E.R. Ioanesian. Moscow: Institut Iazykoznaniia RAN. 7–17.

Mieder, Wolfgang. 2019. "'All Men Are Created Equal'. From Democratic Claim to Proverbial Game." *"Right Makes Might". Proverbs and the American Worldview*. Ed. Wolfgang Mieder. Bloomington, IN: Indiana University Press. 287–316.

Mieder, Wolfgang, and George B. Bryan. 1997. *The Proverbial Harry S. Truman. An Index to Proverbs in the Works of Harry S. Truman*. New York: Peter Lang.

Nierenberg, Jess. 1983. "Proverbs in Graffiti: Taunting Traditional Wisdom." *Maledicta*, 7: 41–58. Also in *Wise Words: Essays on the Proverb*. Ed. Wolfgang Mieder. New York: Garland Publishing, 1994. 543–561.

Nwachukwu-Agbada, J.O.J. 1988. "Igbo 'Obscene' Proverbs: Context, Function and Annotation." *International Folklore Review*, 6: 42–52.

Ojoade, J. Olowo. 1983. "African Sexual Proverbs: Some Yoruba Examples." *Folklore* (London), 94: 201–213.

Owomoyela, Oyekan. 1972. "The Sociology of Sex and Crudity in Yoruba Proverbs." *Proverbium*, no. 20: 751–758.

Peek, Philip M. 1995. "The Roles of Sexual Expressions in African Insulting Language and Verbal Arts." *Folklore Interpreted: Essays in Honor of Alan Dundes*. Eds. Regina Bendix and Rosemary Lévy Zumwalt. New York: Garland Publishing. 401–414.

Possa-Mogoera, Rethabile. 2019. "Rape Culture: Are Our Proverbs Perpetuating It?" *Proceedings of the Twelfth Interdisciplinary Colloquium on Proverbs, 4th to 11th November 2018, at Tavira, Portugal*. Eds. Rui J.B. Soares and Outi Lauhakangas. Tavira: Tipografia Tavirense, 2019. 70–83.

Prahlad, Sw. Anand. 1996. *African-American Proverbs in Context*. Jackson, MS: University Press of Mississippi.

Rees, Nigel. 2005. "Shit Happens." *The "Quote … Unquote" Newsletter*, 14: 6.

Reisner, Robert. 1971. *Graffiti. Two Thousand Years of Wall Writing*. New York: Cowles Book Company.

Rudeck, Wilhelm. 1905. "Die Sprichwörter." *Geschichte der öffentlichen Sittlichkeit von Deutschland*. Ed. W. Rudeck. Berlin: H. Barsdorf. 133–138.

Samper, David A. 1997. "Woman as Gallina—Man as Gallo: An Interpretation of a Metaphor in Latin American Proverbs and Proverbial Expressions." *Proverbium*, 14: 347–366.

Scheidlower, Jesse. 1995. *The F Word*. New York: Random House.

Sobieski, Janet, and Wolfgang Mieder (eds.). 2005. *"So Many Heads, So Many Wits". An Anthology of English Proverb Poetry*. Burlington, VT: The University of Vermont.

Tóthné Litovkina, Anna. 1999a. "If You Are Not Interested in Being Healthy, Wealthy and Wise—How About Early to Bed? Sexual Proverb Transformations." *Semiotische Berichte*, 23: 387–412.

Tóthné Litovkina, Anna.1999b. "'Spare the Rod and Spoil the Child': Sexuality in Proverbs, Sayings and Idioms." *Proverbium*, 16: 141–165.

Tóthné Litovkina, Anna, and Szilvia Csábi. 2002. "Metaphors We Love By: The Cognitive Models of Romantic Love in American Proverbs." *Proverbium*, 19: 369–398.

Webster, Sheila K. 1982. "Women, Sex, and Marriage in Moroccan Proverbs." *International Journal of Middle East Studies*, 14: 173–184.

Winick, Stephen D. 2004. "'You Can't Kill Shit': Occupational Proverb and Metaphorical System among Young Medical Professionals." *"What Goes Around Comes Around": The Circulation of Proverbs in Contemporary Life. Essays in Honor of Wolfgang Mieder*. Eds. Kimberly J. Lau, Peter Tokofsky, and Stephen D. Winick. Logan, UT: Utah State University Press. 86–106.

Yusuf, Yisa Kehinde. 1998. "Rape-Related English and Yoruba Proverbs." *Women and Language*, 21: 39–42.

Index

Alan Dundes, *Founding Editor*

Wolfgang Mieder, *General Editor*

This series includes theoretical studies of any genre or aspect of folklore. The series welcomes individually authored and collaboratively authored books, monographs, collections of data, bibliographies, and Festschriften. The emphasis will be on analytic and methodological innovations in the consideration of myth, folktale, legend, superstition, proverb, riddle, folksong, festival, game or any other form of folklore as well as any of the interpretative approaches to folklore topics.

Inquiries or manuscripts in English should be submitted to

Professor Wolfgang Mieder
Department of German and Russian
422 Waterman Building
University of Vermont
Burlington, VT 05405-0160

To order books, please contact our Customer Service Department:

peterlang@presswarehouse.com (within the U.S.)
orders@peterlang.com (outside the U.S.)

Or browse online by series: www.peterlang.com